THE CONFEDERATE PRIVATEERS

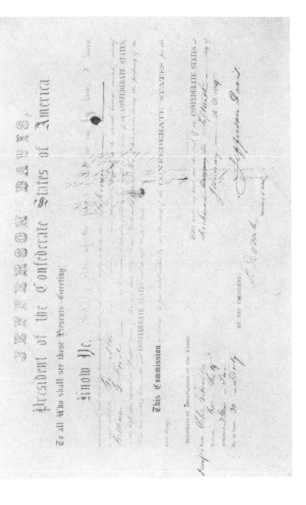

A CONFEDERATE LETTER OF MARQUE

From an original in the Library of Congress.

THE
CONFEDERATE
PRIVATEERS

BY

WILLIAM MORRISON ROBINSON, Jr.

"And the fame of the Dane revive again, ye Vikings of the South!"
"The Sea-Kings of the South," by Edward C. Bruce.
Richmond *Sentinel*, March 30, 1863.

UNIVERSITY OF SOUTH CAROLINA PRESS

Published in Columbia, South Carolina, by the
University of South Carolina Press

Manufactured in the United States of America

Library of Congress Cataloging-in-Publication Data

Robinson, William M. (William Morrison), 1891–
    The Confederate privateers / by William Morrison Robinson, Jr.
        p.   cm. — (Classics in Maritime history)
    Reprint. Originally published: New Haven : Yale University Press,
1928.
    Includes bibliographical references.
    ISBN 0–87249–691–0
    ISBN 0–87249–691–0 (hardback)
    ISBN 1–57003–005–7 (paperback)
    1. Confederate States of America.   Navy—History. 2. United
States—History—Civil War, 1861–1865—Naval operations.
3. Privateering—Confederate States of America—History.   I. Title.
II. Series.
E596.R65   1990
973.7'57—dc20   89–25081
                                                                CIP

TO MY FATHER

William N. Still, Jr., Series Editor

Classics in Maritime History

*What Finer Tradition: The Memoirs of Thomas O. Selfridge, Jr.,
Rear Admiral, U.S.N.*
by Thomas O. Selfridge, Jr.
A Year on a Monitor and the Destruction of Fort Sumter
by Alvah F. Hunter
Confederate Navy Chief: Stephen R. Mallory
by Joseph T. Durkin
*Admiral of the New Empire: The Life and Career
of George Dewey*
by Ronald Spector
Sloops & Shallops
by William A. Baker
The Panama Route, 1848–1869
by John Haskell Kemble
The Confederate Privateers
by William Morrison Robinson, Jr.

Studies in Maritime History

*Stoddert's War: Naval Operations During the Quasi-War with
France, 1798-1801*
by Michael A. Palmer
The British Navy and the American Revolution
by John A. Tilley
Iron Afloat: The Story of the Confederate Armorclads
by William N. Still, Jr.
*A Maritime History of the United States: The Role of America's
Seas and Waterways*
by K. Jack Bauer
Confederate Shipbuilding
by William N. Still, Jr.
Raid on America: The Dutch Naval Campaign of 1672–1674
by Donald G. Shomette and Robert D. Haslach
*Lifeline of the Confederacy: Blockade Running During the
Civil War*
by Stephen R. Wise
Admiral Harold R. Stark: Architect of Victory, 1939–1945
by B. Mitchell Simpson, III
History and the Sea: Essays on Maritime Strategies
by Clark G. Reynolds

CONTENTS

THE CONFEDERATE PRIVATEERS

ILLUSTRATIONS

SERIES EDITOR'S PREFACE

Confederate Privateers was first published in 1928 and was well received by reviewers and the reading public. A reviewer in the *American Historical Review* wrote that "it is not too much to say that this volume by Mr. Robinson takes its place among the indispensable works on the Civil War." The book remains the standard work on the subject.

Colonel Robinson died in 1965. Shortly before his death I had the pleasure of discussing *Confederate Privateers* with him and expressed the hope that the book could be brought back into print. I am most pleased that this new printing is included in the Classics in Maritime History Series.

William N. Still, Jr.

CRITICAL BIBLIOGRAPHY AND
ACKNOWLEDGMENTS

*I*N the larger libraries there may be found many works dealing with the history and status of privateering up to the year 1856. The Declaration of Paris, abolishing this institution among its signatories, which numbered well-nigh the whole civilized world save Spain and the United States, has also been amply covered. Of these references only two need be mentioned.

The Abolition of Privateering and the Declaration of Paris, by Francis R. Stark, LL.B., Ph.D. (Columbia University, New York, 1897), contains an excellent outline of privateering before 1856 and a comprehensive discussion of the right of capture of private property at sea and the Declaration of Paris. *La Guerre de Course*, by Charles La Mache (*Libraire de la Cour d'Appel et de l'Ordre des Avocats*, Paris, 1901), is a delightful treatise on the history of privateering and on the Declaration of Paris and its subsequent working as related to commerce-destroying. However, in both of these works the Confederate privateers are neglected. Stark mentions incidentally President Davis' invitation to apply for letters of marque. La Mache devotes several pages to Confederate commerce-destroying, but concerns himself primarily with the national cruisers, omitting specific reference to any of the private-armed vessels.

This neglect of the deeds of the Confederate privateers is general. Take, for instance, Edgar Stanton Maclay's *History of American Privateers* (D. Appleton and Company, New York, 1899). This volume, one would infer from the reading of the Introduction, was the product of a thorough and complete canvass of American privateering activities. Yet Maclay, after writing over five hundred pages on the letters of marque of the Colonial and Revolutionary wars and the War of 1812, wrote two scant and inaccurate pages on the privateers of the Confederacy and makes no mention of the private-armed vessels of the Republic of Texas in the years 1834 and 1835. Doubtless the principal reason for the failure of historians to recite the narrative of the Southerners has been the lack of ready data.

No text heretofore has been primarily devoted to the history of Confederate privateering. Even John Thomas Scharf's *History of the Confederate States Navy* (Rogers and Sherwood, New York, 1887) allows only one chapter to the privateers. When Scharf wrote this monumental history—which even today remains the sole work on Confederate sea power as a whole—none of the Official Records of the Union and Confederate Navies in the War of the Rebellion (Government Printing Office, Washington, 1894-1927) were available; and he was obliged to rely, as he said, "on contemporary accounts of operations, collected and preserved in newspapers, private letters, and individual papers" and upon the statements of "those officers now living who participated in the scenes and actions described." On the whole, and considering the time of writing, Scharf did a remarkably good job, but there are errors of omission and commission as well as inconsistencies throughout his text.

In his chapter on Privateers, page 89, he said: "The *Lewis Cass* was a clipper-built topsail schooner, of 100 tons burden, and was in the U.S. revenue service when she was seized at Savannah. She was converted into a privateer, armed with one long sixty-eight-pounder taken from the Pensacola navy yard. Her crew numbered forty men and officers." In this chapter on the Alabama Waters, page 535, he gives the history of this vessel differently, and this time correctly, saying: "The only other ship-of-war which was in the possession of Alabama in 1861 was the Federal revenue cutter *Lewis Cass*, which on January 31st was surrendered to the State by her commander, Capt. James J. Morrison, of Georgia, and was regularly enrolled in the Confederate navy by a subsequent transfer from the State to the general government."

Referring again to page 89, we find that the brig *Bonita* "was seized by order of Gov. Brown [of Georgia] and converted into a privateer"; and that, "on the 4th of May [1861], the Georgia privateer *Five Brothers*, Capt. Wm. Barquedo, with a crew of eighteen men, in Cumberland Sound seized the brig *Elisha Doane*, of Boston, loaded with lumber. The *Doane* was detained by a prize-crew for eight days, and then released by order of Gov. Brown." On its face this is an error, for the State of Georgia had, in February, 1861, delegated to the Confederate States the exclusive right to issue letters of marque, and during the brief interregnum between the Union and the Confederacy the State Convention had considered and declined the granting of letters of reprisal. The Confederate President was not empowered to give privateer commissions until after May 6, 1861. Therefore, it was impossible for a privateer, Georgia or Confederate, to have been commissioned or to have made a capture as early as May 4, 1861. Furthermore, no reference to the brig *Bonita* or the schooner *Five Brothers* appears in either the Official Records of the navies or the Confederate Records published by the State of Georgia.

Turning over the page in Scharf's book, we find that the steamer *Wm. H. Webb* was commissioned as a privateer. "She steamed out of New Orleans in May [1861], and on the 24th captured, about ninety miles from the Passes, three Massachusetts whalers, the brig *Panama*, and schooners *John Adams* and *Mermaid*. The prizes reached New Orleans on the 27th, and had on board 215 barrels of whale and sperm oil." The contemporary New Orleans papers as well as the records of the Confederate States District Court in

Admiralty show that these ships were taken by the privateer *Calhoun*. Moreover, though the *Webb* was issued a letter of marque, there is no intimation in the local papers or the Official Records that she actually made a private-armed cruise.

Therefore, it is not surprising that general histories of the War of Secession and works which make occasional reference to it should fall into error. For example, Charles Boardman Hawes in *Whaling* (Doubleday, Page and Company, 1924), on page 226, said that the *Webb* was converted into the privateer *Calhoun*, in which character she took the three whalers before mentioned, burning them at sea, and taking the crews to New Orleans where they were turned loose on their own resources. Again, a reading of the New Orleans newspapers of May to July, 1861, would have shown that these whalers were towed up to the city by their captor, condemned in the Admiralty Court, and sold at auction.

Horace Greely in *The American Conflict* (O. D. Case and Company, Hartford, Conn., Vol. 1, 1865, Vol. 2, 1867) mentions only the captured privateers *Savannah* and *Petrel*, omitting all reference to the successful private-armed cruisers. Prof. James Russell Soley, of the Naval Academy, in *The Blockade and the Cruisers* (Chas. Scribner's Sons, 1883), covered the cruise of the *Jefferson Davis* in a single sentence, and named no other of the Confederate privateers except those captured by the United States naval forces. But one is shocked to find that even Jefferson Davis in *The Rise and Fall of the Confederate Government* (D. Appleton and Company, New York, 1881) does no better; only referring scantily to the *Savannah* and the *Jefferson Davis*, and making the inexcusable blunder of saying (Vol. II, page 11) that "the privateer Jefferson Davis was captured, the captain and crew brought into Philadelphia, and the captain tried and found guilty of piracy and threatened with death."

CRITICAL BIBLIOGRAPHY

Actually, it was one of the prizes of the *Jefferson Davis* which was captured, and the prize master who was convicted of piracy. Herman F. Krafft and Walter B. Norris, Associate Professors at the Naval Academy, in their *Sea Power in American History* (The Century Co., New York, 1920) devoted a paragraph (p. 241) to the Confederate privateers, quite interesting as a generalization but making the mistake of asserting that "all were sailing-craft," overlooking the fact that the *Calhoun, Music, Mariner, Ivy,* and *Gordon* were steamers which successfully waged private-armed warfare on Union commerce.

If the writer has seemed to be only adversely critical, it has been simply to show that there is no real bibliography on those last privateers in the world's history. One must be referred to the newspapers of the sixties, the Official Records, and the unpublished archives of the Navy Department. The writer has made prolonged researches at these sources. Doubtless from time to time, old diaries, correspondence, and even log books may be found in the possession of descendants of Confederate privateersmen, which will supplement, perhaps even revise, some of the tales told in this volume, and very likely add new ones.

The writer wishes to acknowledge the courtesies extended him at the Howard Library, the Louisiana Historical Society, and the Municipal Archives, New Orleans; the offices of the *Mobile Register* and the *Savannah Morning News;* the Georgia Historical Society, Savannah; the State Library and the Carnegie Library, Atlanta; the Charleston Library Society; the State Library and the Confederate Memorial Literary Society, Richmond; the Library of Congress and the Navy Department, Washington; the Maryland Historical Society and the Peabody Institute, Baltimore; the Public Library, the New York Historical Society, and the Naval History Society, New York; and the Biblioteca Nacional, Havana. Especial thanks for assistance in procuring data are due to Miss Carrie Freret, Dr. Y. P. Le Monnier, and the late Mr. William Beer, of New Orleans; Mr. J. Paul Stratton and Mr. Morton Reese, of Augusta, Ga.; Mr. William Mazyck, of Charleston; and Captain Dudley W. Knox, Lieutenant Commander Richard Wainwright, Jr., Miss Nannie D. Barney, and Mr. Carl H. Shaifer, at the Navy Department, Washington.

For their practical sympathy, the writer acknowledges his obligation to M.L.R., S.M.B., M.L.S.E., M.C.C., G.H.G., and S.W.R.

W.M.R., JR.

Augusta, Georgia
30 August 1928.

THE CONFEDERATE PRIVATEERS

★ ★ ★ ★ ★ ★ ★ ★ ★ ★ ★

I.

HOW THE CONFEDERACY LAUNCHED PRIVATEERING UPON THE SEAS

On April 17, 1861, North America was electrified as the telegraph flashed the news from Montgomery that President Davis had issued a proclamation inviting applications for letters of marque and reprisal.

The call for privateers had been for centuries a spark which never failed to fire the souls of the adventurous with dreams of broad, blue waters and fat prizes—and, concomitantly, to fill the hearts of sedentary merchants with fear for the safety of their ships and cargoes. Merchants of the enemy quaked, and denounced the institution of privateering as piracy. The more virile and imaginative shipowners of the power offering the letters of marque accepted them gladly, and joyously armed and sent their ships to sea to make war under their country's flag. When the enemy had a rich merchant marine, foreigners also were oftentimes tempted by the fair prospect of prize-money to equip vessels and cruise under the proffered authority.

For a foreigner to accept a letter of marque has been characterized by at least one writer on maritime law as being little better than piracy. A fine distinction: when an enemy is to be despoiled of his ships and goods is his despoliation any the more tolerable to him that it is committed by a citizen? I think not. The real point is that, whether animated by patriotism and profit or profit

1

alone, the privateersman shall conduct his operations in conformity with the laws of war and act justly and humanely toward his prisoners.

This was not always done, and not infrequently privateering degenerated into piracy. A strong sentiment against the granting of letters of marque began to develop in the eighteenth century, crystallizing, in 1856, in the Declaration of Paris. This document was the product of the European Congress which had met to settle the trouble in Crimea. Its first article read: "Privateering is and remains abolished." This prohibition placed upon the granting of letters of marque applied, of course, only to those powers signing the Declaration. The United States, though invited, did not become a party to it; and, therefore, the Confederate States were not in the remotest way restrained from resorting to privateers. Had the United States been a signatory to the Declaration of Paris, it might have been argued that the new confederation of states—which in 1856 were components of the United States—would have been bound to an observance of the abolition of privateering.

In all past sea wars privateering had been predominately the instrument employed to destroy the enemy's commerce. The operations of the privateers invariably exceeded those of the public cruisers. During the Seven Years' War the French privateers made several thousand prizes. In the year 1761 when the national sea power was so exhausted that King Louis XV had scarcely a ship-of-the-line at sea, the privateers, nevertheless, took more than eight hundred British trading vessels. During the Revolution and the War of 1812 the warfare on British commerce was carried on almost ex-

clusively by the American privateers. With such precedents, the Confederacy's tender of letters of marque
and reprisal to the world at large produced a very pal-
pable flutter throughout maritime circles in America
and in Europe. That the Confederate States were then
without prospect of national cruisers—such as the *Alabama,* the *Florida,* or the *Shenandoah,* which came later
in the war—seemed rather to emphasize than to detract
from the effect of President Davis' proclamation.

In April, 1861, privateering was generally regarded
from the historical viewpoint, and was still believed to
be a powerful weapon. Few subjected it to analysis in
the light of the changes wrought and being wrought, by
the revolutionary economic developments which characterized the epoch. Privateering was a relic of a vanished
civilization. Letters of marque and reprisal connoted a
decentralization of power which was wholly inconsistent
with the new era of rapid communications. They had
their origin in the necessity of a sovereign licensing his
subjects to adjust their grievances for themselves, upon
land as well as sea, where time and distance rendered it
inconvenient for the public authority to act in its own
might. Gradually, as the police power of the state had
increased its reach, letters of marque and reprisal had
become less and less instruments for the rectification of
private injuries and more and more simply a means to
raise an emergency cruising force, supplemental to the
public sea power. It was, therefore, very fitting that the
use of letters of marque and reprisal should be brought
to a close in a war begun by a power without a navy and
hence dependent to an extreme extent upon such private

assistance—and, further, in the exaction of a national reprisal.

In almost all considerations of the War of Secession, the larger issues have been allowed to obscure the precise significance of the opening steps. The Confederate bombardment of Fort Sumter on April 12-13, 1861, was not an act of war, but one of reprisal. The United States troops occupying the forts in Charleston Harbor on December 20, 1860, ceased to be the compatriots of the South Carolinians and became, by the Ordinance of Secession, aliens upon the soil. The refusal of the United States Government to withdraw its troops at the request of the state, and later of the Confederate States, changed their status from simply alien to that of armed invaders. The Confederate Government, after exhausting its diplomatic resources, was obliged to use force to evict the Union garrison from Fort Sumter.

To the Confederates the persistence of the United States troops in Fort Sumter and in Forts Pickens, Taylor, and Jefferson, Florida, constituted an invasion in no less an aggravated light than that in which the Belgians were to see the German invasion in 1914. The attempt of King Albert to repel the German army was not an act of war, but of reprisal. The parallel is even more striking when one recalls that the two invaded countries resisted for about the same length of time, and in the end were alike prostrated.[1]

The genesis of privateering in 1861 is not much concerned with the Florida forts, but is very vitally con-

---

[1] As illustrative of a national reprisal of contrary nature, that is, of territorial aggression instead of territorial defense, the bombardment and occupation of Vera Cruz, Mexico, by the United States naval forces in 1916 may be cited.

nected with the course of events as related to the South Carolina fortress.

When, in November, 1860, it became perfectly clear that the people of South Carolina were determined upon a separation from the Union, President Buchanan and his Cabinet, on the one side, and Governor Gist, on the other, began to consider what policy should be adopted in regard to the public property in Charleston. A gentlemen's agreement was reached between the President and the South Carolina congressmen, in unofficial conference on December 10, that if the Carolinians refrained from attacking or molesting the forts, the existing military status would not be altered, pending "an amicable arrangement of all matters between the State and Federal Government" through the negotiation of accredited representatives.[2] On the twentieth the state seceded. On the night after Christmas Major Robert Anderson, commanding United States troops at Charleston, prejudiced the military status by moving his command from the insecure Fort Moultrie on Sullivan's Island to the well-nigh impregnable Fort Sumter, which stood almost, but not quite, completed upon a shoal in the mouth of the harbor. The state troops at once took possession of the vacated fort and the other un-

[2] Samuel W. Crawford, the surgeon stationed at Fort Sumpter [sic], later Brevet Major General, U.S.A., The History of the Fall of Fort Sumpter [sic], Being an Inside History of the Affairs in South Carolina and Washington, 1860-61, and the Conditions and Events in the South which Brought on the Rebellion; or, the Genesis of the Civil War (New York: 1896), pp. 37-41. The War of the Rebellion: a Compilation of the Official Records of the Union and Confederate Armies. Prepared under the direction of the Secretary of War and published pursuant to Act of Congress approved June 16, 1880 (Washington: Government Printing Office, 1880), Series I, Vol. 1, pp. 116 and 126.

occupied fortifications, Castle Pinckney and Fort Johnson.

On the same day, three commissioners appointed by the Convention of South Carolina, R. W. Barnwell, J. H. Adams, and James L. Orr, arrived in Washington. They were "authorized and empowered to treat with the Government of the United States for the delivery of the forts, magazines, light houses, and other real estate, with their appurtenances, within the limits of South Carolina, and also for an apportionment of the public debt, and for a division of all other property held by the Government of the United States as agent of the confederated States, of which South Carolina was recently a member," and for "a continuance of peace and amity." The President was notified of their arrival, and set one o'clock of the following day as the hour on which he would receive them. But the next morning, when he was informed of Major Anderson's move during the night, he postponed the reception in order that the matter might be discussed in cabinet. When the President met the Commissioners on the twenty-eighth, he informed them that he had not the authority to negotiate with them, but would be glad to lay before Congress any propositions which they cared to make. The interview lasted nearly two hours. The Commissioners repeatedly urged the President to order Major Anderson to return to Fort Moultrie, but Buchanan countered with sundry excuses why he should not.

Barnwell, Chairman of the Commission, was insistent, saying, "But, Mr. President, your personal honor is involved in this arrangement."

"Mr. Barnwell," President Buchanan characteristically replied, "you are pressing me too importunately; you don't give me time to consider; you don't give me time to say my prayers. I always say my prayers when required to act upon any great state affair."

The interview terminated without substantial result. The next day, Saturday, the Commission formally submitted its propositions in writing, and on Monday it received a reply. In his reply the President shifted his position upon many points, showing the influence of his strongly Unionist Secretary of State, Jeremiah Sullivan Black, and, in the end, offered no real encouragement for the Carolinians to continue in their mission. His vacillations so irritated the Commissioners that they addressed the President a very plain-spoken and pointed rejoinder, and immediately left the city.[3]

Coincident with the receipt of the President's unsatisfactory reply, the Convention in Charleston entertained a motion to empower the Governor to issue letters of marque and reprisal, "in case of any attempt on the part of the Federal Government of the United States to coerce the Commonwealth of South Carolina . . . against all vessels belonging to any of the States or citizens of the States lying north of Mason and Dixon's line." The proposed ordinance was not adopted, doubtless in anticipation of the formation of a new confederation of southern states to which the matters of letters of marque would be exclusively delegated.[4]

Similarly, about a month later, Georgia entertained and abandoned the idea of commissioning privateers;

[3] Crawford, *The History of the Fall of Fort Sumpter* [sic], pp. 140-161; *War of Rebellion*, Series I, Vol. 1, pp. 109-111, 115-118, and 120-128.
[4] *Journal of Convention of South Carolina*, December 31, 1860.

but the Georgians had a specific, personal property injury to redress. A lot of muskets consigned to Savannah had been seized on board the steamship *Monticello* in the North River by the New York City police. Governor Brown protested against the seizure to the Governor of New York, and the latter promptly assumed the responsibility. In order to effect restitution and to prevent the repetition of seizure of property owned by Georgia in any northern state, the State Convention, at Milledgeville, considered the issuance of letters of general reprisal "against the commerce going to and coming from the ports of such recusant State under the flag of the United States of America."[5] A few days later the power of the state to grant letters of marque and reprisal was lost to the new Confederate States Government. However, the state instituted very effective reprisals, seizing five New York vessels lying at Savannah wharves. The northern shipowners brought proper pressure to bear, and restitution all around followed.[6]

Meanwhile the Governor of South Carolina had not despaired of a peaceful settlement in Washington, and sent his Attorney-General, Isaac W. Hayne, as a special envoy to President Buchanan. After a few days at the seat of Federal Government, this mission also was terminated, fruitless. Then on March 3 the Confederate Government took over the situation. On this day, Pierre Gustave Toutant Beauregard assumed command of the forces at Charleston as a Brigadier General in the Provisional Army of the Confederate States, and the first

[5] *Journal of Convention of Georgia*, January 29, 1861.

[6] J. Thomas Scharf, *History of the Confederate States Navy* (New York: Rogers & Sherwood, 1887), pp. 623-625.

member of a High Commission (which consisted of Martin J. Crawford, Alfred R. Roman, and John Forsyth) arrived at the Union capital. It was the eve of the new administration, and the Confederate diplomat awaited the first move of the incoming president.

The new head of the State Department, William H. Seward, was very slow in exposing his hand. The Confederates did not unduly press him, for delay was really best suited to their needs. They required time, in which to perfect their military arrangements, before making demands which might call for the support of force. Fearing to receive the Commissioners directly—on account of implying a recognition of the Confederate States Government—Seward held intercourse with them through the personal mediation of Judge John A. Campbell, an Associate Justice of the Supreme Court. Pacific intentions, including an early evacuation of Fort Sumter, were reported to the Commission. The Cabinet only required time in which to conciliate the radical wing of the Republican Party. Similar assurances were received through the Russian Minister. That such was not the case is shown by the secret preparations which were then being made to relieve Fort Sumter.

Seward did not wish to precipitate the crisis until the public view of the issue, in the North, could be changed from one connected with slavery and party to one connected with patriotism and union—this much he plainly stated in a memorandum on policy which he gave to the President. The state of mind of the country was rapidly changing. Rumors became more frequent that a formidable expedition was about to sail from New York: some said that it was to be a Monroe Doctrine demonstration against Spain at Santo Domingo; others that the destination was the Confederacy, but more probably the Gulf Coast than Charleston. On April 7 the Commissioners demanded an explanation of this hostile movement; and were assured, the next day, through the intermediary, that the faith as to Fort Sumter was being fully kept. With this assurance they were not satisfied—and with good cause.

Two days earlier, a messenger had left Washington, secretly, for Charleston to notify Governor Pickens that an attempt would be made to relieve Fort Sumter. On the same day that the Commissioners were being reassured in Washington, the Governor down in South Carolina was being advised to the contrary. The Confederate emissaries now demanded an unequivocal stand on the part of the United States Government. The memorandum received from the State Department was most unsatisfactory, denying that the Confederate States constituted a foreign power to be dealt with diplomatically. Whereupon the Commissioners prepared a reply outlining and denouncing Secretary Seward's conduct of the negotiations, and saying "that the people of the Confederate States have declared their independence with a full knowledge of all the responsibilities of the act, and with as firm a determination to maintain it by all the means with which nature has endowed them as that which sustained their fathers when they threw off the authority of the British Crown . . . the people of the Confederate States will defend their liberties to the last, against this flagrant and open attempt at their subjugation to sectional power. . . ."

Their usefulness in Washington being now brought

to an end, the Commissioners withdrew, April 11, leaving their secretary (John T. Pickett, of whom more hereafter) to prepare, and furnish to the several foreign legations, official copies of the correspondence which had passed between the Commission and the United States Government.

At Charleston the notice from President Lincoln created much excitement. For two days there was a steady exchange of telegrams between General Beauregard and the War Department in Montgomery. The Confederate Cabinet, at length having realized the inutility of words, resolved to use force; and, on the tenth, instructed the general to demand of Major Anderson the immediate evacuation of the fort. Accordingly, at four o'clock in the afternoon of the eleventh, the aides of General Beauregard formally presented the demand for surrender, offering Major Anderson and his command safeguard and all the honors of war if he complied. The demand was refused. But from a remark which Major Anderson made to one of the aides about the shortage of provisions, General Beauregard was led to believe that a second demand might avert the necessity of bombarding the stronghold. Therefore, the aides returned to the fort, at an hour after midnight, and renewed their offer. The major called a council of his officers and after lengthy deliberations returned an answer, stating that he would be obliged by lack of food to evacuate the fort on the fifteenth, unless he was sooner relieved by his Government. As a relieving expedition was known to be then at sea, this reply was considered to be unsatisfactory. The Confederate staff officers then gave the major a note saying that in one hour's time the

11

bombardment would begin. It was now twenty minutes past three, the morning of Friday the twelfth of April.

The sea was calm. There was a bright starlight. At four-thirty, ten minutes after the designated hour, the circle of Confederate batteries opened their rotation of slow but accurate fire. The patrol and dispatch boats in the service of the South Carolina Coast and Harbor Police withdrew to points of safety, and left the fight to the artillerymen. Two of these vessels, incidentally, were destined to privateering careers—the steamer *Gordon* to prosperous cruises, but the schooner *Petrel* to an unhappy end.

By the second day of the siege the trespassers upon the soil of South Carolina had been shelled and starved into submission. Meanwhile the relieving expedition had arrived off the bar—too late. Humorous to relate, this expedition, reversing its intended function, provided the transportation northward for the gallant garrison, whom Beauregard refused to make prisoners of war, but courteously allowed to leave the territory of the Confederacy with colors flying.[7]

While the artillery duel was in progress in Charleston Harbor, the press announced to the people of the Confederacy that President Davis was in cabinet discussing the issuance of letters of marque and general reprisal.[8] However, with the ejection of the Stars and Stripes from the Confederate territory, the new Confederacy would have been quite content to let this reprisal end the matter.

[7] Crawford, *op. cit.; War of Rebellion*, Series I, Vol. 1; *Off. Rec. Union and Confederate Navies*, Series II, Vol. 3; *Messages and Papers of the Confederacy*.

[8] *New Orleans Daily Crescent*, April 13, 1861.

THE LAUNCHING

At once a great war spirit swept the northern states, where there had been much apathy and even open sympathy with the seceded states. The true nature of the assault on Fort Sumter was not appreciated. An angry cry went up that the flag had been fired upon. The northern public ignored the fact that its own Government had goaded the South into just reprisal. Two days after Anderson and his handful of artillerymen had embarked on the ships sent to relieve them, President Lincoln, without awaiting the action of his Congress, issued a *de facto* declaration of war against the Confederate States, calling into service 75,000 militiamen. The border states began to secede. Separation was war.

The gage of battle was promptly picked up. In view of the extraordinary occasion, Davis, ever a rigorous Constitutionalist, had on the twelfth called a special session of Congress to convene in Montgomery on April 29; but he did not wait idly during the intervening days. On the seventeenth, by proclamation, he, and his Secretary of State (Robert Toombs), recognized Lincoln's announced "intention of invading this Confederacy with an armed force for the purpose of capturing its fortresses, and thereby subverting its independence and subjecting the free people thereof to the dominion of foreign power"; and invited "all those who may desire, by service in private-armed vessels on the high seas, to aid this Government in resisting so wanton and wicked an aggression, to make application for commissions or letters of marque and reprisal to be issued under the seal of these Confederate States."[9]

[9] James D. Richardson, *Compilation of the Messages and Papers of the Confederacy*, published by permission of Congress (Nashville: United States Publishing Company, 1906), I, 60-62.

THE CONFEDERATE PRIVATEERS

The moves in the incipient war game were being conducted two days apart. So on the nineteenth it was the play of Lincoln, countersigned by Seward. They made it in this fashion:

Whereas an insurrection against the Government of the United States has broken out in the States of South Carolina, Georgia, Alabama, Florida, Mississippi, Louisiana, and Texas, and the laws of the United States for the collection of the revenue cannot be effactually executed therein, conformably to the provision of the Constitution which requires duties to be uniform throughout the United States; and whereas a combination of persons engaged in such insurrection have threatened to grant letters of marque to authorize the bearers thereof to commit assaults on the lives, vessels, and property of good citizens of the country lawfully engaged in commerce on the high seas and in the waters of the United States . . . now, therefore, I, Abraham Lincoln, President of the United States . . . hereby proclaim and declare that if any person, under the pretended authority of the said States, or under any pretense, shall molest a vessel of the United States, or the persons or cargo on board of her, such person will be held amenable to the laws of the United States for the prevention and punishment of piracy.[10]
(This proclamation also includes the blockade.)

In addition to this gesture calculated to frighten any person from accepting a letter of marque and reprisal, the Lincoln administration made a bid for European discountenancing of the Confederate policy. An offer was made to Great Britain to adhere unconditionally to the Declaration of Paris. The spirit and purpose of the

[10] *Compilation of the Messages and Papers of the Presidents,* prepared under the direction of the Joint Committee of the House and Senate, pursuant to an Act of the Fifty-second Congress of the United States (published by the Bureau of National Literature, 1912), pp. 3215-3216.

offer was too obvious, and the British Secretary of State for Foreign Affairs, Lord John Russell, declined the proposal to sign a convention covering the points of the Declaration of Paris; because, "it might be further argued by the Government of the United States that a European Power signing a convention with the United States, declaring that privateering was and remains abolished, would be bound to treat the privateers of the so-called Confederate States as pirates."[11]

In the meantime, "in response to the proclamation of the President of the Confederate States, the Congress convened in extra session at the Capitol in Montgomery at the hour of noon on the twenty-ninth day of April, A.D. 1861."[12] A little past noon the message was received from the President. The deputies listened as the Secretary of Congress, Johnson J. Hooper, read to them concerning the state of the Confederacy. After reviewing the development of the original Union, the causes which led to secession, and the subsequent acts and attitudes inimical to the new union of the seceded states, the message said:

Deprived of the aid of Congress at the moment, I [Jefferson Davis] was under the necessity of confining my action to a call on the States for volunteers for the common defense, in accordance with the authority you had confided to me before your adjournment. I deemed it proper, further, to issue proclamation inviting application from persons disposed to aid our defense in private-armed vessels on the high seas, to the end that preparations might be made for the im-

[11] Quoted in *The Charleston Mercury*, December 20, 1861, and in *U. S. Senate Document No. 332*, 64th Congress, Session I, serial No. 6952, p. 19.

[12] *Journal of the Congress of the Confederate States of America, 1861-1865* (Washington: Government Printing Office, 1904), I, 159.

mediate issue of letters of marque and reprisal, which you alone, under the Constitution, have power to grant. I entertain no doubt that you will concur with me in the opinion that in the absence of a fleet of public vessels it will be eminently expedient to supply their place by private-armed vessels, so happily styled by the publicists of the United States "the militia of the sea," and so often and justly relied on by them as an efficient and admirable instrument of defensive warfare. I earnestly recommend the immediate passage of a law authorizing me to accept the numerous proposals already received.

I cannot close this review of the acts of the Government of the United States without referring to a proclamation issued by their President, under date of the 19th instant, in which, after declaring that an insurrection has broken out in this Confederacy against the Government of the United States, he announces a blockade of all the ports of these states, and threatens to punish as pirates all persons who shall molest any vessel of the United States under letters of marque issued by this Government. Notwithstanding the apparent authenticity of this proclamation, you will concur with me that it is hard to believe it could have emanated from a President of the United States. Its announcement of a mere paper blockade is so manifestly a violation of the law of nations that it would seem incredible that it could have been issued by authority; but conceding this to be the case so far as the Executive is concerned, it will be difficult to satisfy the people of these [Confederate] States that their late confederates [in the old Union] will sanction its declarations, will determine to ignore the usages of civilized nations, and will inaugurate a war of extermination on both sides by treating as pirates open enemies acting under the authority of commissions issued by an organized government.[13]

[13] *Messages and Papers, Confederacy*, I, 75-76; also *Journal, Cong., C.S.A.*, I, 165-166.

Congress then went into secret session; and, upon motion of Robert Toombs[14] of Georgia, the subject of privateering was referred to the Committee on Foreign Affairs with instructions, if they should think it expedient, to "prepare and report at the earliest convenient time a bill authorizing the granting letters of marque and reprisal against the United States." That was Monday afternoon. Wednesday, the Committee reported a bill to be entitled, "An Act recognizing the existence of war between the United States and the Confederate States; and concerning letters of marque, prizes, and prize goods." It was read a first and second time, and was made the special order of the next day. On Thursday, a substitute was offered for the preamble, and it went over to another day. On Friday, numerous amendments were proposed, but late in the day the bill was passed. On Saturday it was reported as correctly engrossed and enrolled, and went to the President for approval. Then on Monday, the sixth, a message was received by the Congress that the President had signed the act.[15]

The preamble set forth briefly and dispassionately the genesis of the war. It declined, however, to make a present party to the war the slaveholding states and territories still remaining in the Union, saying that "the States of Maryland, North Carolina, Tennessee, Kentucky, Arkansas and Missouri, have refused, and it is believed that the State of Delaware and the inhabitants

---

14 While serving as a member of the Provisional Congress, February 4, 1861, to March 16, 1862, Toombs held the post of Secretary of State, February 21 to July 25, 1861, and also a brigadier generalcy in the Provisional Army from July 19, 1861.

15 *Journal, Cong., C.S.A.,* I, 169, 170, 173, 175, 177-181, and 188.

of the territories of Arizona and New Mexico, and the Indian territory south of Kansas, will refuse to cooperate with the Government of the United States in these acts of hostilities and wanton aggression."[16]

The Act then proceeded to authorize the President "to use the whole land and naval force of the Confederate States to meet the war thus commenced," and to issue letters of marque "against the vessels, goods, and effects of the government of the United States, and of the citizens or inhabitants of the states and territories thereof," except the states and territories before named. The intent of this provision was, patently, to throw nothing in the way of accession to the Confederacy by all the slaveholding states still in the Union. It was only partly successful. Delaware ultimately declined to leave the Union. Maryland's secession was frustrated through wholesale political arrests by the Federal military authorities acting under a suspension of the writ of *habeas corpus*. However, a benevolent attitude was long maintained toward the Marylanders; and the ships of Baltimore generally passed scot-free upon the seas during the first part of the war.

The Act did not differ very materially in its provisions from the privateering law of the United States enacted during the War of 1812, nor from that of the United Colonies during the Revolution. As in 1861, so in 1812, the authority to issue letters of marque and reprisal was contained in the Congressional recognition

---

16 *The Statutes at Large of the Provisional Government of the Confederate States of America* (Richmond: R. M. Smith, Printer to Congress, 1864), Session II, Chapter 3. This act with certain minor differences in punctuation and capitalization may be found in *Messages and Papers, Conf.*, I, 104–110.

of a state of war. But, in 1776, the Continental Congress, anticipating by more than three months the signing of the Declaration of Independence, passed a resolution "that the inhabitants of these colonies be permitted to fit out armed vessels to cruise on the enemies of these United Colonies." Rhode Island, over a year earlier than the epochal July 4, commissioned private-armed vessels.

The first section of the Act recognized the principle that "free ships make free goods;" providing, "that property of the enemy (unless it be contraband of war) laden on board a neutral vessel, shall not be subject to seizure." This rule was acknowledged in 1812; but the Confederates soon extended further immunity to sea trade. By a Congressional resolution of August 13, "touching certain points of Maritime Law and defining the position of the Confederate States in respect thereto," they exempted neutral property on board of an enemy's vessel. This resolution was in affirmation of the Declaration of Paris, with the reservation of "the right of privateering, as it has been long established by the practice and recognized by the law of nations."[17]

The first section of the Act further provided that any private vessels of the enemy then in Confederate ports be given thirty days in which to leave and reach their destination before being liable to capture. This was a very liberal period of grace; for vessels lying in northern ports and owned in whole or in part by Southerners had been at once seized, and the time that had been allowed neutrals in which to depart from the Confederate ports declared to be in blockade was only two weeks.

The second section empowered the President to re-

[17] *Statutes, Prov. Cong.*, Sess. III, Res. 4.

voke at pleasure any letters of marque which he may have granted.

The third and fourth sections told how commissions to private-armed vessels should be issued. Very little red tape was interposed to delay the *bona-fide* privateersmen, but abuses were guarded against. First of all, the applicant must own at the moment of application a specific ship. No commission could be issued in blank, nor would a transfer of flag from one ship to another be tolerated. These two requirements, while placing restriction upon the possible extension of the private-armed service, were wise precautions against adventures which might tend to discredit the national honor. To secure his commission, the prospective privateersman had only to file with the Secretary of State—or, where more convenient, with a collector of customs if within the limits of the Confederacy, or with a duly authorized commissioner if abroad—a complete description of his vessel and her armament, a list of the shipowners, officers, and crew, and a penal bond in the sum of $5,000 or $10,000, according as the ship's complement was under or over 150 men. The securities were the same as required in 1776 and in 1812, but in 1776 the basis of determination was the tonnage of the ship, whether under or over 100 tons burden. The condition of the bond was the faithful observance of the "President's instructions to private-armed vessels," which the President was authorized, by section nine, to prepare.

These regulatory instructions were promptly promulgated by the State Department.[18] They enjoined upon the privateersmen "the strictest regard to the rights of

18 *Messages and Papers, Conf.*, I, 111-113.

neutral powers"; and said, "Towards enemy vessels and their crews, you are to proceed in exercising the rights of war with all the justice and humanity which characterize this Government and its citizens." In order to protect the owners of captured vessels from illegal seizures, "the master and one or more of the principal persons" of each prize were to be sent to an Admiralty Court in the Confederate States "to be examined upon oath touching the interest or property of the captured vessel and her lading"; and at the same time there were to be delivered to the court all of the ship's papers, verified by the affidavit of the commander of the privateer. Contraband was defined as "all arms and implements serving for the purpose of war by land or sea," as "generally whatever may serve directly to the equipment of vessels, unwrought iron and planks only excepted," and as all other articles "that are so declared by the law of nations." "Neutral vessels conveying enemies' dispatches or military persons in the service of the enemy" forfeited their neutral character and were "liable to capture and condemnation." However, this rule did "not apply to neutral vessels bearing dispatches from the public ministers, or ambassadors of the enemy residing in neutral countries." It was the failure of Captain Wilkes, U.S.N., in the famous Trent Affair, to observe the established corollary to this exception that came so near embroiling the United States with Great Britain.

Aside from high patriotism, gain is the incentive which prompts individuals to risk upon the seas their property against the enemy. Sections five, six, seven, thirteen, fourteen, and fifteen, together with the amendments of May 14 and August 30, 1861, saw to it that Confederate privateering might be gainful, and therefore popular. An expeditious procedure in admiralty was provided. Prizes brought into, and condemned in, one judicial district might be sold in the adjoining district if there were a better market. The fee of the marshal of the court in connection with the selling of the prize property was fixed at one per cent on the net proceeds, but in no case was it to exceed $250. Only one-twentieth of the net prize-money was required to be paid into the public Treasury, and that small portion was to be held in trust as a casualty pension fund—no burdensome share being taken by the Government for its own benefit, as had often happened in European history. A further concession permitted all goods brought in on prize vessels to pass the customs at two-thirds the usual duty; but an evasion of the imposts would bring down the penalties and forfeitures of smugglers upon the heads of the privateersmen. Thus practically the whole value of the prizes accrued to the shipowners, officers, and crew, being distributable among them according to proportions determined by contract.

The natural quarry of the privateer was the defenseless merchantman; but, as an incentive to engage with armed ships, a bounty was offered for the destruction of enemy war vessels of equal or superior force. Section ten declared that the Confederate States would pay $20 for each person on board the defeated ship at the commencement of the engagement, and $25 for each prisoner brought into port and delivered into custody of the Government. An amendment of May 21 allowed an additional bounty of twenty per cent of the value of the destroyed vessel, including her armament in the valuation.

From the standpoint of financial benefits to the privateersmen, the Confederate law was sufficiently liberal to have fully reconstituted privateering as an institution of great gain; though it was not, perhaps on the whole, so generous as that under which the Americans had twice thrived upon British commerce. In the War of 1812 fifty per cent of the value of a destroyed man-of-war was allowed to the victorious privateer. The reward for prisoners brought in was fixed at $100, and the deduction for the pension fund was only two per cent. During the Revolution, the American Government exacted no pension fund and the French only required a most nominal fraction of the prize-money to be paid into the king's treasury for the benefit *"des invalides de la marine."* On the other hand, the United Colonies inaugurated no system of bounties.

Lastly, by sections eleven and twelve, the degeneracy of privateering into piracy—as had so frequently happened in American as well as European maritime history—was guarded against, and at the same stroke an instrument of naval intelligence was provided. The commanding officer of every vessel sailing under a letter of marque was required to "keep a regular journal, containing a true and exact account of his daily proceedings and transactions with such vessel and crew thereof; the ports and places he shall put into or cast anchor in; the time of his stay and the cause thereof; the prizes he shall take and the nature and probable value thereof; the times and places when and where taken, and in what manner he shall dispose of the same; the ships or vessels he shall fall in with; the times and places when and where he shall meet them, and his observations and remarks thereon; also, of whatever else shall occur to him or any of his officers or marines, or be discovered by examination or conference with any marines or passengers of or in any other ships or vessels, or by any other means touching the fleets, vessels and forces of the United States, their posts and places of station and destination, strength, numbers, intents and designs." Whenever he should put into a Confederate port, the commanding officer was required to present his commission to the collector of customs and to deliver up to him the cruising journal verified under oath, under the penalty of having his commission revoked and a fine of $1,000 imposed. Before being allowed to sail again, the privateer had to be examined by a customs officer, who must have found her manned and armed as set forth in the letter of marque.

Thus safeguarded and encouraged, the Confederate privateers were launched upon the seas.

II

THE RESPONSE TO THE LURE OF
SEA ROVING

RUMORS that all manner of private-armed ships were taking the sea against United States commerce were rife in the North within a few days after President Davis' proclamation had been issued, and even before the act of Congress had authorized the issuance of letters of marque. Everywhere in the maritime circles of the North there was a panic. Boards of underwriters, ship-owners, and Governors of States were busy addressing communications to the United States Navy Department as to what it ought to do. The New York Board of Underwriters secured an acting master's commission for the captain of their salvaging schooner, for the sake of having combat authority; and boldly sent the *Henry W. Johnson* to sea to defend, "to the last extremity," the United States commerce, but especially those vessels in which "you may have reason to suppose that your employers are interested as insurers." Wild tales came of privateers being fitted out at Liverpool, in Spain, and upon both coasts of South America, and even of prizes being made. Almost every sea captain who came into New York got a write-up in the papers for having seen or outrun a privateer. President Lincoln had declared that any person molesting United States shipping "under the pretended authority" of the seceded states would be treated as a pirate. Veritably the North stood in fear of a revival of buccaneering.[1]

[1] *Official Records of the Union and Confederate Navies in the War of*

THE CONFEDERATE PRIVATEERS

At New Bedford, Massachusetts, a very ludicrous scene was said to have been enacted late in April. Two or three steamers out in Buzzards Bay were mistaken for a concert of privateers about to lay the city under tribute, after the fashion on the Spanish Main, and great excitement followed. Guns were hastily mounted on an old brick fort at Fairhaven across the harbor. Earthworks for a battery were commenced at Clark's Point. A home guard company was improvised, and the New Bedfordians awaited the attack—which the two or three peaceful Yankee steamers never had thought to make.[2]

The hysteria generated by the letter of marque proposals was never dispelled during the continuance of the war. Shortly it was heightened by the proclamation of Queen Victoria, on May 14, through the Palmerston ministry, that the British Empire regarded the Confederate States as a belligerent power: which was to say that Confederate soldiers were not the common brawlers, nor Confederate seamen and privateersmen the pirates, that President Lincoln wished to have them considered. Nor, was the excitement which had been raised among the commercial classes of the Union by this acknowledgement of southern belligerency diminished by the Queen's orders of June 1, forbidding the armed ships of both belligerents to bring their prizes into home or colonial ports or waters of the United Kingdom; nor, by the chief maritime powers following suit.

It would seem that a little clear reasoning applied to

the Rebellion, published by authority of an Act of Congress approved July 31, 1894 (Washington: Government Printing Office, 1894-1922). Series I, Volumes 1 and 4. This work will be hereinafter referred to as *NWR*.

[2] *The True Delta* (New Orleans), May 12, 1861, quoting from "A Boston paper of 28th."

the neutrality orders and proclamations would have shown to the North how severe a blow to southern privateering was the policy of the Great Powers; and should have, therefore, tended to allay its apprehension. For, if one thing was certain, it was that commerce-destroying by private force must be lucrative in order to gain widespread effectiveness. Even though many ships were taken, the private-armed operations would go profitless unless the captures could be sold. Convenient ports into which to carry and dispose of their prizes were most essential to the privateersmen. Prize vessels sent on long voyages back to home ports were subjected to the protracted hazard of recapture, and besides the prize crews were not then easily returned to the mother ship. The manning of prizes was at best a weakening procedure; and it was a well-known fact that many a fine rover had been obliged to suspend a joyous cruise in order to recruit her personnel, depleted by the continuous placing of long absent prize crews. Therefore, at the outset, the Confederate privateers were inhibited from attack on the wider-flung commerce of the Union; and were, economically, restricted to operations within a reasonable radius of the homeland.

Though it was an internationally recognized right of the captor to sell his prize, on the high seas or elsewhere, without the formality of an adjudication, a foreign purchaser would have to accept the risk of recapture by the enemy as long as the war lasted. Consequently, it would be most difficult to find a purchaser abroad in the absence of that formal condemnation which would protect his title against all comers. Had only the hospitalities of neutral ports been accorded to prize vessels, the accomplishment of the legal formalities would have been fairly simple; for the United States judiciary had accorded full recognition to the power residing in domestic courts of admiralty to condemn prizes lying in foreign harbors. With this principle conceded by the enemy, the captured ships might have been duly libeled and condemned in some distant Confederate court; and, when the order of the court was at length delivered to the prize agent in charge, the prizes would be salable with clear titles.[3]

Under international law there was no obligation upon neutrals to shut out prizes; but it was, of course, within their province to do so if they chose, and certainly it would simplify matters for them. Neutrality supposes an impartiality toward the contestants; and, though the interdiction to the ports applied to Unionist and Confederate, and to public and private men-of-war, alike, the effect upon the United States was vastly less injurious than upon the Confederate States. Public cruisers were not subject to the financial necessity of selling their captures as were the privateers; hence, their usefulness as commerce-destroyers was not materially impaired by the neutrality orders. As the whole world knew the relative maritime status of the Confederate States and the United States—that the former had only in prospect an unformed private-armed sea power, and that the latter depended upon an established navy with a plenitude of naval reserves for its augmentation— the policy of the Great Powers amounted, as was even admitted by the British Ministry, to a discrimination in favor of the Union. Against this practical unneutrality,

[3] *NWR*, I, 1, p. 633. *The Charleston Mercury*, June 17, 1861, quoting London *Times*, May 23. *L'Abeille de la Nouvelle-Orléans*, 17 mai 1861.

the Confederacy protested vigorously, and its diplomatic representative in Paris was still holding conversations on the subject with the French Minister of Foreign Affairs in the spring of 1865.[4]

The neutrals not only forbade entry to the prize vessels but also commanded their subjects to refrain, conformably to the spirit of the Declaration of Paris, from fitting out privateers under the flag of either belligerent. It is not likely that this injunction would have restrained adventurous souls from seeking Confederate letters of marque had the economics been favorable. Certainly during the wars for South American independence, many citizens of the United States armed and equipped vessels under commission from the revolutionary states, undeterred by the penalty of death as a pirate, upon which Spain and the United States had agreed by treaty, as the fitting fate of a national of either one who should accept a letter of marque from a third power against the other. Though deprived of the wholesale accessions of private-armed vessels from abroad, which heretofore had invariably flocked to the colors of belligerents having opponents with extensive shipping interests, the response of the Confederate marine was prompt and enthusiastic; and the immediate materialization of privateers on the seas gave substantial ground to the agitation that beclouded the commercial classes of the North.

Applications for letters of marque and reprisal began to come into the Secretary of State's office at Montgomery the day following the President's invitation; but, with Davis' characteristic regard for constitutional

4 *NWR*, II, 3, pp. 12, 54, 57, 59, and 1260.

limitations, he had merely received them until Congress enacted the law "concerning letters of marque, prizes, and prize goods," described in the last chapter. Four days after the passage of the enabling act, the necessary regulations for the government of private-armed vessels were completed and published; and, the same day, May 10, the first commission was given to the *Triton,* of Brunswick, Georgia. This little schooner of 30 tons burden, mounting one 6-pounder swivel gun and carrying a crew of 20 men, was one of the smallest of the privateers. The largest was the *Phenix,* fitted out at Wilmington, Delaware, a couple of weeks later. This was a fine steamer of 1,644 tons, mounting 7 guns, and with a complement of 24 officers and 219 men. By midsummer, application for letters of marque had come in at almost all Confederate ports, but New Orleans and Charleston were preëminently the home ports of Confederate privateering.

In the spring of 1861 privateering was the favorite topic of conversation in all the seaport towns of the Confederacy. Many extravagant predictions were made. A leading Southern journal, the *New Orleans Daily Crescent,* concluded "that, at the lowest estimate, seven hundred and fifty swift-sailing, staunch, substantial vessels, fully equipped, carrying on an average four mighty guns apiece, can be put afloat in four months to wage war upon the Northern commerce, blockade Northern ports, cripple Northern strength and destroy Northern property." This did not seem a fantastic estimate to the Louisiana readers on March 16, 1861; for just exactly a week before the *New York Herald* had, editorially, said that a number of northern shipowners were willing "to furnish vessels, armaments and crews" and to "engage in the destruction of their neighbors' ships and the confiscation of their goods. At first view," continued the *Herald*, "this seems grossly improbable; but when we reflect that for many years slave ships have been fitted out almost exclusively from Northern ports, it is not altogether unlikely that the abolitionists would go a step further, and turn a penny or two by plundering honest traders on the sea."

But all the talk of privateering was not pregnant with hate or distrust. It was sometimes very light and often the theme of jest. *The Charleston Mercury* (June 27) writes up the christening and maiden trip of a yacht, whose "rig is stylish and peculiar," and which was owned by a club of young gentlemen, as "a private-tearing party." The cruise was made up the Ashley River to the plantation of one of the members, where the club at length "arrived after a very delightful passage. The yacht on her way up, captured and took in tow a suspicious looking Yankee built craft, commanded by Captain Smith, who stated that he was in the river fishing, but whose ostensible purpose, from all the circumstances, was something else. The Captain, after a fair and impartial hearing, was sent to town in a spring wagon, and the boat kept until called for. On arriving at the farm the party sat down beneath the huge oaks and partook of a bountiful fish chowder, with *et ceteras,* which had been provided for them by Mr. H., and came away well pleased with themselves and their beautiful yacht."

As in the two Anglo-American wars, every class and kind of ship were among those for which letters of marque were asked. A chronicler of the privateers of

THE CONFEDERATE PRIVATEERS

1812 has said: "At the first sound of war our merchants hastened to repeat their marvelous achievements on the ocean in the struggle for independence. Every available pilot boat, merchant craft, coasting vessel, and fishing smack was quickly overhauled, mounted with a few guns, and sent out with a commission to 'burn, sink, and destroy.' " So it was in 1861 with the Confederate ship-owners, from oysterboatmen to merchant princes.

The little *Sea Hawk,* a boat with crew of nine, having only small arms, was fitted out in Back Creek, Elizabeth City County, Virginia, by one of the former. Her aim was low and was directed at the small craft of the enemy in the Chesapeake. Far from such humble ambitions had the *Isabella,* a splendid steamer, captained by one of her wealthy owners, to whom the glamor of sea warfare appealed. This ten-gun vessel, with 175 New Orleans sailors and 50 marines had high hopes of a rollicking and prosperous life in the Caribbean.

The response of the Confederate merchant marine to the "militia" call was quite comparable to that of the Union in 1812. Then the deadweight capacity of American bottoms was about two million and a quarter tons, and the ratio of privateers was about one to every twenty-five thousand tons. The burden of Confederate shipping at the commencement of the war was, closely, nine hundred thousand deadweight tons, and the ratio of letters of marque issued was one to twenty-seven thousand tons.

In addition, it should be borne in mind that many of the South's best ships were taken in northern ports at the beginning of hostilities. Such were the *James Adger,* the *South Carolina,* and the *Massachusetts,* of the

Charleston line, and the *Bienville* of the New Orleans line; all of these were converted into cruisers by the United States Navy Department. They would have performed splendid service under the Stars and Bars as either public or private-armed vessels. The *Nashville,* a consort of the Charleston losses, was made into a cruiser by the Confederate Navy Department, and later became a transport and then a privateer.

The relation of the shipping of the Union to that of the Confederacy deserves some notice. The tonnage belonging to those states remaining in the Union was eight times as great as that of those which seceded. This disparity, when it is recalled that the length of the Confederate littoral exceeded that of the United States, is astonishing at the first glance.

During the colonial period, the products of southern fields went to market, generally, in English bottoms, and after the winning of independence mostly in New England's, for only about one-sixth of the American tonnage was owned south of the Potomac River, and three-fifths of it east of the Hudson. The Southerner was a planter, in the main, and was not prone to leave his fair lands to roam upon the sea, as the more barren acres of New England had forced his northern brother to do. Then, emancipated by steam from the economy of the southerly trade winds, the trans-Atlantic shipping found the route from Europe to America so much shorter and more convenient by a bee-line to New York, that the foreign trade of the southern ports dwindled and dwindled, till, as we have just seen, in 1861 southern vessels held an appreciably lesser place in America maritime than they had three-quarters of a century previously.

However, while marine transportation as one of the occupations of the Southerner had shrunk in proportions, the South, with her cotton, rice, and tobacco, still furnished more than one-half of the exports in the entire American trade. Thus it was that, though the seafaring class formed but a very small portion of the Confederate population, there was, nevertheless, a large and wealthy class interested in foreign commerce and indirectly in sea affairs. Members of this class at once began to organize stock companies for the purchase and outfitting of private-armed vessels; and high seas captains, coastwise masters, pilots, ambitious but inexperienced gentlemen, native sailors, jolly tars, independent and almost international, and willing landsmen responded to the lure of the roving seas, as had their forebears in other days.

III

PRIVATEERING BEGINS IN NEW ORLEANS

*I*N a city almost wholly French in its traditions, culture, and racial stock, it was natural that there should be found the first privateering expression. The French "had a turn for adventure," had been the witty retort of the Comte de Vergennes, Louis XVI's Minister of Foreign Affairs, to Lord Stormont, when the English Minister had complained, during the early days of the Revolution, that French subjects were giving aid to the American colonists. In New Orleans a glamor of romance hung about the name of La Fitte, the Breton privateersman who had soon tired of ravaging only British and Spanish commerce, had hoisted the black flag, had made the Island of Grande Terre in Barataria Bay headquarters from which to launch the forays that earned him the title of "the Pirate of the Gulf," but who, nevertheless, when the British attacked New Orleans, came to the aid of the Americans and fought so valiantly under General Jackson that President Madison granted him and his men full pardon.

With the gathering of war clouds during the winter of 1861, the thought of many New Orleanians turned to privateering. The subject was always to the fore in the press. It was discussed on the highly decorated horse-cars, just installed in the city; it was the theme of enthusiastic but mysterious conversations between twos and threes who withdrew, during dull moments in the trading on the "flags," to the shady side of Carondelet

Street; it was mulled over excitedly during the forenoon mint juleps and sherry cobblers; then there was the rush for the two o'clock news editions to see what the developments were.

At length, a few days after the promulgation of the letter of marque proclamation, concrete news items began to appear. On April 22, the *Daily Crescent* informed its readers that "there are two large and fast sailing schooners fitting out at this city for the privateering business"; that Walter H. Peters, a notary public at 50 Camp Street, had blank forms of application for letters of marque and reprisal; that there was considerable activity at the dockyards across the river in Algiers, where numerous persons were looking for vessels suitable for privateering, examining them and planning additions, alterations, and repairs. The next day the writer of the "Talk on 'Change" column in the same newspaper said: "There was a deal of side talk about privateering and letters of marque; that there will be several afloat ere long there is not a doubt; but their departure is not to be made known."

During the interim between the invitation to apply for letters of marque and the publication of the regulations under which they might be granted, the popular impatience is reflected in "Talk on 'Change." "The talk," the columnist said on May 9, "is, 'what of the letters of marque and privateers?' Just allow us to hint to the many inquirers, privateering is a private business, and they who embark in it are sufficiently wise and prudent to keep their movements to themselves."

However, the necessary regulations were no sooner published than the *Crescent* was able to announce, on

THE BEGINNING

May 11, "A meeting of those desirous of embarking in the enterprise of fitting out a privateer from this port is called for today at 12 o'clock, M., in the former Circuit Court room over the New Merchant's Exchange. Books of subscription will be kept open until 6 P.M."

Then on the seventeenth the columnist had something electrifying to tell. "Yes, after some days of quietness on the flags, there was something sprung on the street yesterday . . . about meridian the flags were all on the *qui vive* about a dispatch from Pass à L'Outre, announcing the arrival of a vessel, a prize to the private-armed vessel *Calhoun*." Expectations became more extravagant. Everyone wanted to get into the privateering game before United States commerce should be destroyed or the war be brought to an untimely end. Frequent advertisements appeared giving the address where subscription lists might be found. One, very consonant with the popular attitude, describes it as the place, "where the patriotic can yet find an opportunity of investing."

It was rather odd, though fitting, that the first active privateer should happen to bear the name of the great Carolinian leader in the extreme states' rights movement. The *Calhoun* was a towboat of 509 tons burden. She was one of the fleet of the fast, powerful, low-pressure steamers which went regularly to the mouths of the Mississippi River to bring sailing vessels up to the city wharves; for, against the mighty current of the Father of Waters the sails were of little avail. The application for a letter of marque was made on May 13,[1] by

[1] *NWR*, II, 1, p. 349. The names of the owners were W. R. Miles, J. O. Nixon, Geo. W. Gregor, John S. Minor, David Bidwell, Seward Porter, H. Bidwell, John E. McClure, and Thos. R. Smith.

a company of nine gentlemen, and the commission was issued on the fifteenth. It specified an armament of one 18-pounder, two 12-pounders, and two sixes, with a crew of eighty-five under Captain John Wilson—late of the schooner *Minnie Schiffer,* and gallant rescuer of the passengers on the distressed steamship *Connaught.*[2]

On the sixteenth the *Calhoun* put down the river, and that evening off the bar made the first private-armed prize of the war. This was the bark *Ocean Eagle,* 290 tons, Captain Luce, 35 days from Rockland, Maine, with a cargo of 3,144 barrels of Thomaston lime, consigned to Creevy and Farwell in New Orleans.[3] Captain Wilson turned his prize over to a towboat to be carried up to the city and returned to the sea.[4] Two days later the *Calhoun* made a double haul: the fine ship *Milan,* 699 tons, Captain Eustis, 81 days from Liverpool, with 1,500 sacks of salt as part ballast, consigned to Meeker, Know and Company, New Orleans; and the schooner *Ella,* 92 tons, with tropical fruits, from Tampico, Mexico, for Pensacola, Florida. The privateer immediately steamed for New Orleans with her prizes, arriving there on the night of the nineteenth.[5]

After remaining in port but a short time, the *Calhoun* put down the river and into the Gulf again. On the twenty-first she lost a fat prize to the superior speed of a sister privateer; but three days later had the good fortune to fall in with three New England whalers which had been cruising in the Caribbean. The vessels were the

[2] *Mobile Daily Advertiser,* June 25, 1861.

[3] *The Daily Delta* (New Orleans), May 17, 1861. *New Orleans Daily Crescent,* May 18, 1861.

[4] *Daily Delta.* May 28, 1861.

[5] *L'Abeille de la Nouvelle-Orléans,* 20 mai 1861.

*THE FIRST CONFEDERATE PRIVATEER AT SEA, THE CALHOUN
OF NEW ORLEANS*

From an old photograph.

brig *Panama*, 158 tons, and the schooner *Mermaid*, 145 tons, both of Provincetown, Massachusetts, and the schooner *John Adams*, 200 tons, of Boston, with combined crews of some sixty-five men. They had on board 160 barrels of oil.[6] After cruising around in the Gulf for a few more days, the privateersmen made a contact with the U.S.S. *Brooklyn*, and scurried for the Passes, where they gathered up their whalers and proceeded up the river.[7] The big frigate's twenty-two 9-inch Dahlgren smoothbores were most impressive, and lent authority to the blockade of the Mississippi River, which Commander C. H. Poor, U.S.N., declared was set on foot on May 26.[8]

One finds a bit of humor in the Marine Intelligence column of the *Daily Crescent* under date of May 28. The second cruise of the *Calhoun*, is reported thus: "Towboat *Calhoun*, Wilson, from the Passes—went down light—brought up brig *Panama*, schooners *Adams* and *Mermaid*."

The glorious privateering had come to an untimely end. As recently as the twenty-fifth, *The True Delta* exultantly had written:

Scarcely a day passes that dispatches are not received announcing the capture of prizes. The success which has rewarded the activity of the privateers has surpassed the expectations of the owners. Well freighted ships seem to fall into their hands as by the power of fascination. The trim little vessels make a circuit and immediately a fat prize presents itself as if by process of predestination. We rather like the working of "piratical" theology.

[6] *Daily Delta*, May 28, 1861.
[7] *The True Delta* (New Orleans), May 29, 1861.
[8] *NWR*, I, 4, p. 187.

Then on the twenty-ninth (May), the same paper described the end, under the caption "Chasing a Privateer" —without seeming to realize the finality of prize-making from the port of New Orleans:

One of the privateers, the *Calhoun*, it is said, was chased for two hours off the Balize by the lumbering old war steamer *Brooklyn*. The men of the little vessel saw her afar off, and her guns grew awfully large. They looked grim and thunderous, but for all that the privateer fired a defiant gun or so, keeping in mind, that "distance lends enchantment to the view." The little sea-rider was not to be caught by the big one, her heels being as swift as Burns' gray mare Meg, when Tam O'Shanter ran away from the witches.

Captain Wilson promptly entered libels against his prizes in the Confederate States District Court for Louisiana, sitting in New Orleans, and in due course all vessels were condemned for the benefit of the captors. They were severally advertised for sale but after some postponements were all sold at the same auction on July 27. The highest bids, however, averaged only about half the appraised valuations. The *Milan* brought $9,000; the *Mermaid,* $8,300; the *Ocean Eagle,* $6,800; the *Panama,* $1,400; the *John Adams,* $1,150; and the *Ella,* $1,050. The cargo of the *Ella* was found to be English-owned and was restored to the claimant, S. L. Jolly, but the other cargoes were adjudged good and lawful prizes. The salt on the ship *Milan* was sold at $1.50 a sack.[9]

Among the crews of the whaling vessels there were eight negro sailors. What disposition to make of them presented a problem. The Confederate States marshal refused to accept them; but the city recorder accepted

[9] *Daily Delta,* July 2, 12, 14, and 28, 1861; *L'Abeille,* 23 mai 1861.

their custody, locking them up at the Second District police station, and telegraphed to the Attorney-General (Benjamin) in Richmond for instructions. The answer "passed the buck" by saying that the case should be handled in accordance with the laws of Louisiana.[10] However, the Department of Justice, something more than a month later, on July 12, published regulations for the disposal of prisoners of war and other persons captured at sea. United States citizens not in the public service of the enemy captured on board unarmed private vessels were not to be regarded as prisoners of war, but were to be deported as alien enemies, at the expense of the Department.[11] No differentiation was made as to race or color. But in the meantime the *New York Journal of Commerce* was led to wonder whether captured negroes would be regarded as property and "sold like silks and other merchandise for the benefit of the captors."

Operating at the same time as the *Calhoun,* were the private-armed steamers *Music* and *V. H. Ivy.* The *Music* was a fast coastwise packet steamer, 172 feet in length and of 29-foot beam, with a 6-foot hold, displacing 273 tons. The application to put her in the private-armed service was signed, on May 14, by Thomas McLellan, as sole owner and nominal captain. It recited that her armament consisted of two 6-pound cannon and her crew of fifty men. The commission was issued on the next day. The *Ivy* was a towboat, probably the fastest one on the river. She was 191 feet long, had a 28-foot beam and a 9-foot hold, and measured 454 tons.

---

[10] *L'Abeille,* 29 mai and 5 juin, 1861; *Daily Crescent,* May 30, 1861.
[11] *Daily Delta,* July 21, 1861.

The application for her commission was made, on May 16, by W. H. McLellan and Napoleon B. Baker, with the latter as captain and Thomas McLellan as one of the sureties. The vessel was armed with one 15-pounder gun and carried a crew of fifty men. The customhouse officials were becoming most expeditious. They took two days to give the *Calhoun* her letter of marque, and one day for the *Music,* but the *Ivy* got hers, and sailed, on the same day that she applied for it.[12]

The *Music* was as quickly at the prey. When nearing the mouth of the Mississippi known as the Pass à L'Outre she found the ship *John H. Jarvis,* flying the United States flag, lying at anchor opposite the telegraph station, whither the master, one Henry S. Rich, a native of Maine, had gone. The Confederate States naval cutter *Pickens* (formerly United States revenue cutter *McClelland*) was close by; but Captain McLellan and several armed privateersmen at once went aboard, exhibited their letter of marque and took possession of the ship and her cargo of 2,980 sacks of salt, "in the name of Jefferson Davis."[13]

Between eight and nine o'clock the next morning the *Ivy* was seen coming into the Southwest Pass, having in tow the fine ship *Marshall,* Master Elisha T. Sprague.

[12] *NWR,* II, 1, pp. 348-351.

[13] *True Delta,* July 21, 1861, reporting the case of McLellan *et al.* vs. ship *John H. Jarvis.* In each of the *Music's* three prize cases the name of the libellants is given as S. C. McClelland *et al.* on the cost docket, which is the only Confederate court book remaining in the United States District Court in New Orleans. The city directory of 1860 gives a Samuel C. McClelland, broker, with office at 253 Peters Street. The *True Delta,* October 6, 1861, reporting the case of the prize ship *Marshall* gives the libellants as Stephen C. McLellan, Captain of Steamer *Music,* and N. B. Baker, Captain of Steamer *V. H. Ivy,* and the owners. It would appear that the spelling on the record is in error.

The privateersmen had sighted her some fifteen or twenty miles off the bar, had gone alongside and made fast without any show of force as though about their one-time business of towing. When just within the river an armed party from the *Music,* led by Captain McLellan, clambered on board the *Marshall,* and took possession of her as prize. The procedure was most extraordinary, but was the result of a joint arrangement previously entered upon. The prize was owned in Providence, Rhode Island. She was in ballast from Le Havre, *via* Key West, having left France on March 24.[14]

On the same day the *Ivy* was reported to have captured the ship *Enoch Train,* Captain Burwell, from Singapore, with a cargo of 4,425 sacks of salt.[15] This ship had for some time appeared in the marine news as having cleared and sailed for New Orleans on March 4.[16] She was listed in the newspapers of the eighteenth, nineteenth, and twentieth, as "below, coming up"; but is never shown as arriving in port, nor was she ever libeled in court. However, the ship *Abaellino,*[17] listed as having cleared and sailed from Boston for New Orleans on April 4, was reported on the twentieth as "below, coming up," with a cargo of 1,025 tons of very welcome ice,[18] which was worth some $20,000; and two days later ar-

14 *True Delta,* October 6, 1861.

15 *Daily Delta,* May 18, 1861. The *Daily Crescent,* May 18, however, states that the *Enoch Train* sailed from Liverpool on March 14. The *New York Herald,* June 2, after listing the prizes held in New Orleans, including the *Enoch Train,* said: "Of the above vessels some doubt attaches to the seizure of the *Enoch Train* and *Wilbur Fisk,* but the probabilities are that they have been confiscated."

16 *True Delta,* May 7, 1861.

17 Variously spelled in the press Abalino, Abellano, Abellino, and Abedona.

18 *Daily Delta,* May 20, 1861.

rived under the towage of the *Millandon*.[19] The next day S. C. McLellan *et al.* filed a libel against her. That morning the French newspaper[20] had credited her capture to the *Ivy*, but it is probable that the *Music* in some way shared in the prize. The court filed a decree of condemnation on August 28.

With their two other prizes the McLellan privateersmen were not so fortunate. The District Attorney on behalf of the Confederate States intervened and claimed them, on the ground that the captures were made within the territorial jurisdiction and not upon the high seas, where alone the letter of marque had force. As to the *Jarvis* there was no dispute and the privateersmen readily yielded to the Government's claim; but they made contention for the *Marshall*. The court, however, held that when the *Ivy* took the latter in tow, she did not exhibit the *animus capiendi* without which there was no capture; and that when the armed party from the *Music* boarded the *Marshall*, it was then too late, for they were within the river. Both ships were condemned for the benefit of the Confederate States. At the marshal's sale the *Jarvis* brought $14,250,[21] and the *Marshall*, $35,-000.[22] The poor privateersmen were dismissed with empty hands.

The *Music* seems to have ended her private-armed career with the capture of the *Abaellino;* but the *Ivy* continued her cruising. Somewhat of the flavor of *la guerre de course* in those May days of 1861 is preserved in a letter written from the *Ivy* to the New Orleans

[19] *Daily Delta,* May 23, 1861.   [20] *L'Abeille,* 23 mai, 1861.
[21] The *Daily Picayune* (New Orleans), September 8, 1861.
[22] *Daily Delta,* September 27, 1861.

Daily Delta, dated the twenty-first and signed "Repard."[23] Monsieur Repard began:

Last Friday I left New Orleans for this place and boat for a little privateering—to assist in annoying the enemy's commerce; but the enemy's commerce has ceased almost to spread its wings in this latitude. On board the *Ivy* are guns and men enough to accomplish great destruction, were we called on to open with our cannon. Our human fighting material is constituted of good bone, sinew and pluck, and some of the crew having entered the privateer service with only one intent—commendable revenge on the North.

Today we succeeded in sighting a vessel of the largest dimensions, and full rigged, which proved to be the *Sarah E. Pettigrew,* which, to our sorrow, was without a cargo, there being in her hold only two or three thousand sacks of salt, from Liverpool. We soon had a prize crew on her broad decks, greatly to the muddled surprise of her officers and crew. After the formality of taking possession, your correspondent being among the boarders—we do not pay weekly—I overhauled the flag-bag, and soon had bunting in plenty for a pretty Southern Confederacy flag, which was immediately set afloat to flutter defiance to all who don't like us. The *Ivy's* capacity enables her to do her own towing, and after she had cruised around in the Gulf two or three hours to overhaul other sails, she returned to us and we turned our prows toward Pass à L'Outre, near where the *Pettigrew* now lies, awaiting to be towed to your city. The privateer *Calhoun* gave chase for the same vessel, but the *Ivy* was too fast for her.

We lie in or near the river every night, but start out soon after midnight, and keep a sharp lookout for any speck on the horizon, and when the cry of "sail-ho!" is heard the *Ivy's* "tendrils" don revolvers, swords, knives and rifles with great

23 Printed in issue of May 26, 1861.

excitement and good nature. We have exceedingly good times and "duff" but I fear all will be closed with the appearance of the blockading force.

This was speedily the case, and the *Pettigrew* was the *Ivy's* best and last prize—the court condemned her, August 27, except as to the fractional interests of certain southern owners.[24] However, the *Ivy* continued to hang around the Passes, much to the annoyance of the blockaders; and more than one boat expedition was organized to surprise and cut out this privateer, but she was never caught napping.[25] When the C.S.S. *Sumter,* Commander Raphael Semmes, was at the Head of the Passes, during the latter part of June, awaiting an opportunity to escape to sea to begin her famous cruise of destruction among United States merchantmen, the *Ivy* was in constant attendance upon her as a scout, for which duty her very great speed rendered her particularly valuable.[26]

The New Orleanians, however, were loath to give up private-armed cruising; and, on July 1, four of the gentlemen who had fitted out the *Calhoun* joined in applying for a letter of marque (which was granted on the third) for the *J. O. Nixon,*[27] a schooner of 95 tons, armed with an 18-pounder pivot and two 6-pounder carronades.[28] She carried forty men and was commanded by Captain John Wilson, erstwhile of the successful *Calhoun.* For a while she cruised in the Mississippi

[24] *NWR,* I, 16, pp. 571, 572, and 657.
[25] *Daily Picayune,* August 28, 1861.
[26] Log of the *Sumter* in *NWR,* I, 1, pp. 692-693.
[27] J. O. Nixon was editor of the *Daily Crescent* and president of the New Orleans Board of Aldermen.
[28] *NWR,* II, 1, pp. 367-368.

sound;[29] but on August 2, taking advantage of a fair wind, she left Pascagoula

intending to go Yankee hunting on the deep blue sea. When about twelve miles from Horn Island Pass, she discovered a large Federal steamer [the U.S.S. *Huntsville*] ahead, attempting to cut her off. The *Nixon* tacked and stood in again for the Pass, and reached the bar about a mile ahead of the Federalist. The latter then opened fire on her at that distance; the *Nixon* immediately responded, and the exchange of shots was carried on for about twenty minutes.

In the meantime the little lake steamer *Arrow* [a Confederate gunboat] came up, and, when within the range of the Federalist, let slip some of her 32's at the Yankees. At the end of about twenty minutes from the time the firing commenced, the Federalist, with three of the *Nixon's* heavy pills in her hull, got up a big head of steam, and, crowding on every inch of canvas she could use, made regular Manassas time seaward.

Not the slightest injury was received by the *Nixon* or the steamer *Arrow*, whilst it is thought that the additional weight of the three balls which were lent the Federalist by the *Nixon*, may impede her progress to some extent. She has not been seen in that quarter since.[30]

However, with this affair the cruising warfare of the New Orleans privateers came to an end; while over on the Atlantic coast it was just reaching its heyday.

[29] Hansboro (Miss.) *Democrat,* July 30, 1861, quoted in *True Delta,* August 2, 1861.

[30] *L'Abeille,* 6 août, 1861. However, Commander Cicero Price, of the U.S.S. *Huntsville,* in reporting this engagement to the flag officer, August 5, makes no mention of injury to his ship (*NWR,* I, 16, p. 613).

IV

THE BRIEF AND ILL-FATED CRUISE
OF THE SAVANNAH

*I*N the latter part of May, 1861, the small boys who lived on South Battery in Charleston found it vastly more diverting to watch the preparations being made aboard the pilot boat *No. 7* than to go to school. It was well known that this schooner was going to be a privateer, and sail the seas in quest of Yankee ships. She lay close ashore in the Ashley River, and sometimes the boys were allowed to visit her. Many were the wild adventures that bloomed in the boyish fancies. But it was not alone imaginative youth that was fascinated. Twelve grown men of Charleston were captivated by the idea, and had put their money into her; and two of them went out to sea in her as officers.

It was in the minds of these two that the cruise first took form. During the monotonous days when T. Harrison Baker and John Harleston, members of the Vigilant Rifles, were serving in the state volunteer forces on Morris Island—simply onlookers while the United States decided whether it should be comedy or tragedy at Fort Sumter—Baker often looked seaward and was lured into thoughts of life upon the ocean. He talked it over with Harleston, telling him that as soon as their ninety-day enlistment was over he intended to try to get up a party to go privateering, and offered him the berth as first officer. Baker said he had been a sailor and would be the captain. That suited Harleston, who said

THE CONFEDERATE PRIVATEERS

that though he was no sailor, he "had always liked the sea and understood enough of navigation to work out a position and could steer a ship and work the men."[1]

These were camping days and soldier thoughts, and after Sumter and the return to civilian life, Harleston forgot all about their schemes. But Baker did not. Presently, he had formed a syndicate and sent word to his late comrade, who reluctantly joined the enterprise, for the latter's mind was now on entering a company under orders for Virginia.

One cannot help but wonder what thoughts may have coursed through Captain Baker's mind as he entered the Customhouse to file an application, on behalf of himself and the eleven other owners, for a commission to sail under arms, in the service of the Confederate States, their newly acquired schooner *Savannah,* the one-time pilot boat *No. 7.* He knew what he or any other privateersman might expect if captured by the enemy. He knew the stories of how, a century and a half before, the buccaneers, who had at first been welcomed in Charles Town and even at one time had assisted the Charlestonians to defend their city against the Spaniards, had turned pirates, had been captured, imprisoned on the site of this same Customhouse, and hanged. If taken a prisoner he himself might be hanged, should President Lincoln dare to do what he had proclaimed. But undaunted the captain was, and, under the expeditious procedure, the letter of marque and general reprisal was promptly

[1] An article, in the *Sunday News* (Charleston, S. C.) February 9, 1919, on "John Harleston's Life," extensively quoting from his diary, is used throughout the chapter.

issued by Mr. Colcock, the collector. This was the eighteenth day of May.[2]

In two weeks' time the schooner was ready for her cruise. New sails were fitted. A short 18-pounder, model 1812, was mounted on a pivot carriage amidships. The armory was stocked with a stand of flint and steel muskets altered to percussion, pistols, and cutlasses. The last were forged by a local smith. The privateer left her berth in the Ashley River and dropped down the bay to an anchorage under the guns of Fort Sumter. It was Saturday night, June 1, when the men began to come aboard. The next morning, anchor was weighed and the *Savannah,* with some heads that were still a bit thick and groggy, stood down to the outer roads, where with the fresh sea breezes beclouded perceptions began to clear. After dark the privateer put out to sea.

The United States screw frigate *Niagara* had appeared off Charleston on May 10, and, after announcing the blockade and remaining four days, had left the station for the Gulf of Mexico.[3] Then on the twenty-eighth she had been succeeded by the steam frigate *Minnesota,* 47.[4] The sailing brig *Perry,* of seven guns, was also on the coast.[5] Despite the force that was known to be in the offing, the little *Savannah,* who knew that she was a fast sailer, was not afraid. She saw no blockaders as she put out to sea. Over the waves she sped, on the watch for the enemy's merchantmen. Captain Baker planned to

[2] *NWR,* II, 1, pp. 345-346. The letter of marque named the following as shipowners: T. Harrison Baker, James Bancroft, Jr., J. Dawson, F. Dawson, W. W. Leman, Charles D. Farrar, Chas. C. Cohrs, O. J. Burn, D. B. Cloud, James Robb, and J. M. Harleston.

[3] *NWR,* I, 4, pp. 176 and 206.

[4] *NWR,* I, 5, p. 682.

[5] *Ibid.,* pp. 640 and 683.

cross the Gulf Stream and to lie in wait off the Hole-in-the-wall, the Bahamas, to intercept the West Indian trade.

Though the cruise of the *Savannah* was destined to be brief and ill fated, her crew was, nevertheless, to play a rôle in the war out of all proportion to the magnitude of the little schooner.[6] It may be well, therefore, to scrutinize the privateersmen a bit closer. Baker, the captain, a pleasant man of thirty-seven, florid, fine looking, stood six feet in height, and wore his reddish beard *pasha* cut. He was born in Philadelphia. Harleston, the first lieutenant, also endowed with a splendid physique, one time a rancher in Texas, was an educated Charlestonian of twenty-eight. The sailing-master, Henry C. Howard, was a true North Carolinian, also twenty-eight, and just off a Baltimore schooner on which he had been first mate. Charles Sidney Passalaigue, nineteen, full of pluck and longing for adventure, left the staff of the Charleston *Mercury* to become the purser. James Evans, a Charleston bar pilot, tall and straight and with eyes that bespoke fear of no man or thing, was on board as a prize master. Crews are cosmopolitan, and this one was no exception. There were three Irishmen, a couple of Scots, a German, a Filipino steward, and a Chinese cook. In all there were twenty persons within the confines of the schooner's sixty-eight feet of length.

Early Monday morning the lookout at the masthead sang down that there was a sail over the starboard bow.

[6] *Trial of the officers and crew of the privateer* Savannah, *on the charge of piracy, in the United States Circuit Court for the Southern District of New York, Hon. Judges Nelson and Shipman, presiding.* Reported by A. F. Wharton, stenographer, and corrected by the counsel (New York: Baker & Godwin, printers, 1862).

The course was altered so as to cut off the vessel, which was presently made out as a Yankee brig. The chase lasted three or four hours, but when the privateer got within half a gun shot the stranger hove to. The *Savannah* then came alongside.

"Brig, ahoy, where are you from?"

"From Cardenas bound to Philadelphia."

Captain Baker then ordered the skipper of the brig to come aboard with his papers. The skipper was suspicious. Over an hour before, with the aid of his glass, he had made out on the schooner an ominous looking thing amidship. The schooner then was flying the United States flag, now she had a different ensign. So Captain Meyer, before he would leave his own vessel, demanded to know by what authority the order was given.

"By authority of the Confederate States."

A boat was then lowered and Captain Meyer came aboard his captor with the papers of the brig *Joseph.* Baker met him at the bulwarks and courteously assisted him over, telling him that he regretted the necessity of taking his vessel from him but that it was all a matter of reprisals. It is interesting to recall that the first vessel captured in the Gulf hailed from Rockland, Maine, and that now the first vessel taken by a privateer in the Atlantic was likewise of the same port.

The prize thus easily made was found to contain 215 hogsheads and 47 tierces of muscovado sugar.[7] Prizemaster Evans picked his crew and went aboard the captured brig, whose course was now set for the South Carolina coast. In due time the *Joseph,* with her six prisoners on board—Captain Meyer having been retained on the

[7] *The Charleston Mercury,* June 7, 1861.

THE CONFEDERATE PRIVATEERS

Savannah—reached Georgetown. This, the first prize of a Charleston privateer, was joyously announced in the press of that city on the sixth. The estimated value of vessel and cargo was $30,000. The District Court of the Confederate States for South Carolina sitting in Admiralty at Charleston promptly condemned the ship, and adjudged the prize good and legal.[8]

While the elation of the capture was at its height, the lookout reported another vessel. Soon the glasses showed that the cut of her sails was English, and presently the name *Berkshire* of Liverpool was made out on her stern. She being apparently a neutral the privateersmen passed on. Shortly another sail was made. It was now about three o'clock in the afternoon. The *Savannah* and the *Joseph* had been sailing along in company, but now the privateer parted with her prize, and stood to the westward to intercept the newly sighted vessel. The eager eyes of the Confederates discovered her to be a brig, then to be a man-of-war and that she was apparently as anxious to meet the *Savannah* as the *Savannah* had been a moment before to meet her. It was with merchantmen that the privateersmen wished to form acquaintance, not warships; so they tacked and attempted to clear the newcomer. The vessels were only three or four miles apart. The *Savannah* had lost part of her top rigging in a blow the night before, and the war brig gained steadily, getting the weather-gauge of the privateer.

The Stars and Stripes were run up on the stranger, and the privateersmen answered the challenge with their colors. It was rapidly growing dusk. At ten minutes to

[8] *The Charleston Daily Courier*, September 4 and 12, 1861.

eight, the vessels were only half a mile apart. The twilight was now almost night and the ships were barely distinguishable to each other. The stranger opened fire and the privateer replied in kind. In the darkness, the firing on both sides was wild. The engagement had lasted twenty minutes, when the fire from the schooner ceased. The two combatants had sighted each other by the flashes from the guns. Now on the inkiness of the water the brig lost sight of the *Savannah* for a moment. It turned out that the latter had lowered her sails as a token of submission. The man-of-war wore round and passed near her, asking if she surrendered. The answer was not intelligible. Again the brig executed the maneuver without firing, and this time the answer was clear: "We surrender."[9]

Watermen but not naval men, most of the privateersmen, under fire for the first time in their lives, in fear hid themselves; and only the four officers and one man stood bravely at the gun. Though they had but one piece of artillery to the enemy's seven, and could not hope to defeat him, still in the darkness their chances of escape would have been good had all the crew stuck manfully at their stations.[10]

The privateer was now a prize to the United States brig *Perry,* and the privateersmen were transferred to the man-of-war. A prize crew under Midshipman Mc-Cook was placed on the *Savannah,* who took her to New York, where in the course of events she was condemned and sold.

[9] *NWR,* I. 1, pp. 29-30, and 5, pp. 692-693.
[10] Captain Baker's statement in *New York Herald,* June 26, 1861, re-quoted in *Mercury,* July 3, 1861.

Falling in with the *Minnesota* on the morning of the fifth, the prisoners were removed to the frigate, and the *Perry* turned southward to take station off Fernandina. After cruising between Charleston and Savannah for ten days, the *Minnesota,* flagship of the Atlantic blockading squadron, returned to Hampton Roads. The prisoners were there transferred to the United States revenue cutter *Harriet Lane* and in her were taken to New York.

A little over three weeks after the *Savannah's* people had gleefully set out upon their cruise, they wound up as prisoners in New York harbor. The arrival of the "pirates" attracted many visitors to the Navy Yard. A reporter from the *Evening Post* managed to get aboard the cutter before she docked, and secured a story for his paper. He found the captives taking their fate philosophically, and, in speaking of the officers, said: "The general appearances of these four men was favorable. They have nothing of the desperate or even rowdy look that would naturally attach to men in their profession."[11]

Taken ashore, the prisoners were marched in irons to the Tombs. The captain, the executive officer, and the purser were linked together. The others followed in couples. The procession was headed by policemen and flanked by deputy marshals. The press of the day has recorded graphic descriptions of how the people thronged the streets and crowded the windows, how mothers held up their children to see the "pirates" being paraded to felons' cells.[12]

Passing under the eyes of the rabble, insulted with its

[11] Quoted in *Mercury,* July 1, 1861.
[12] *Herald,* June 26, quoted in *Mercury,* July 3, 1861.

taunts, entering the grim old prison, and being thrust into a loathsome cell, did Captain Baker recall the pleasant old plastered brick building at the foot of Broad Street, in that city by the sea where the Gulf Stream sweeps close, almost inshore, to make the land tropical with palm trees? One cannot but believe that there must have been curiously associated in his mind that distant Customhouse,[13] charming, century-old—where the collector of Confederate customs was perhaps even then issuing another letter of marque and reprisal; with its own damp dungeon, on a level with the tides, constructed on the spot where Stede Bonnett and the pirates of 1718 had languished[14]—and this foreboding, chilling place of northern incarceration. How like to the condition of Bonnett and his men was that of Baker and his crew, yet how different in the consciousness of the rightfulness of their acts!

However they might know that international law was altogether on their side, there hung over their heads the noose of public hate. There was loud clamor that the "pirates" should have been hanged at the yardarm when taken. The war press demanded the speedy infliction of the death penalty.

[13] Now used as a museum.

[14] Mrs. St. Julien Ravenel, *Charleston, the Place and the People* (New York: The Macmillan Co., 1922); Shirley Carter Hughson, *The Carolina Pirates and Colonial Commerce, 1670-1740* (Baltimore: The Johns Hopkins Press, 1894); old maps in the possession of the Charleston Library Society.

V

THE JOLLY CRUISE OF THE JEFFERSON DAVIS

*W*HILE the privateersmen of the *Savannah* were sweltering in the Tombs, other Charlestonians were enjoying the sea breezes as they trod the deck of the private-armed brig *Jefferson Davis*.

Here was a ship with a past showing well the mutability of ships—a merchantman, a slave ship, a brig of commerce again, a privateer. Built in Baltimore about 1845, a trader registered as the *Putnam* of the port of New Orleans, she had abandoned respectability and nationality and gone into the prohibited traffic in black people, as the brig *Echo*. But in Charleston the opprobrium had been washed away, and she had regained a decent place among ships.

This came about by reason of a decree in the United States District Court for South Carolina, entered on December 16, 1858. In August, 1858, with a cargo of Africans, the *Echo* had been hovering off the northern coast of Cuba awaiting an opportunity to land her contraband. Her suspicious movements attracted the attention of the United States brig *Dolphin,* which was cruising in the West Indies for the protection of American commerce and for the suppression of the African slave trade. It was on the twenty-first when Lieutenant John Newland Maffitt,[1] commanding the *Dolphin,*[2] saw, and

[1] This officer entered the Confederate Navy, and commanded the famous cruiser *Florida*.

[2] The *Dolphin* was one of the war vessels abandoned to the State of Virginia upon the evacuation of the Norfolk Navy Yard, in April, 1861.

decided to investigate, the stranger. The American man-of-war commenced the chase, and, when nearing the suspect, hoisted the English colors and fired two blank cartridges to signify that she wished that vessel to show her colors. The strange brig took no notice, but upon a shot being fired across her bow, followed by another, she displayed the United States colors. Whereupon the *Dolphin* then hauled down the English flag and hoisted in its place the Stars and Stripes. A third shot was now fired at the main topsail, and the chase brought to. The boarding officer found her a nationless ship with the hold stowed with negroes, almost entirely naked, but separated as to sexes. A prize crew was put on board, and the slaver and slaves were taken to Charleston. From this port the negroes were returned to Africa on board the U.S.S. *Niagara*. This frigate sailed from Charleston on September 12, with 271 blacks, but 72 of them died on the way to the rehabilitation colony in Liberia.

When the case of the United States vs. the brig *Echo* came up for hearing, no defense was made. The brig was declared forfeited and condemned "for a violation of the 1st and 4th Sections of an Act of Congress of the United States, passed the tenth day of May, 1800"; and the marshal was ordered to sell the vessel at public auction. This he did early in January, 1859, and the vessel again became a respectable brig, resuming the name *Putnam*.[3]

Within the week after the publication of President Davis' invitation to apply for letters of marque, the

[3] *Messages and Papers of the Presidents,* pp. 3058-3059; Naval Archives; American Lloyd's, 1862; Emma Martin Maffitt, his Widow, *The Life and Services of John Newland Maffitt* (New York and Washington: The Neale Publ. Co., 1906), pp. 199-202.

owner of the *Putnam,* Robert Hunter, Esq., of Charleston, petitioned His Excellency for the grant of such letter. He proposed to rename the brig the *Rattlesnake,* and proceeded to associate seven other Charlestonians with himself in the venture.[4] The Association grew, and, before the actual sailing of the vessel, it numbered twenty-seven persons, among whom were some of the city's best citizens.[5] Some delay occurred in the issuance of the commission, during which the company asked, and received, the permission of the State Department to re-christen the vessel the *Jefferson Davis,* in honor of the President.[6] At length, on June 18, the commission was delivered,[7] and about a week later the alterations aloft and below were finished, the letter of marque read to the crew, and all preparations were completed for a cruise.[8]

Considerable difficulty, experienced in common by all the Confederate privateers, was had in securing proper armament. The captain, Louis M. Coxetter, also one of the owners, was obliged to content himself with five obsolete guns, old iron pieces made in England in 1801.

[4] David Riker, P. J. Esnard, Zadock Miller, R. Hunter, John F. O'Neill, H. L. P. McCormick, John C. Martin, and Louis M. Coxetter.—*NWR,* II, 1, p. 351.

[5] John C. Martin dropped out, and the following names were added: Maier Triest, Jas. K. Robinson, R. H. Riker, Wm. Matthiessen, Robt. A. Pringle, E. D. Robinson, Hugh E. Vincent, Henry Buist, Thomas E. Ryan, W. P. O'Hara, A. J. Salinas, V. Malga, H. F. Hall, J. F. Breland, H. M. Faust, F. M. Bamberg, J. M. Eason, Thos. D. Eason, E. Lafitte, and A. T. Browning.—*NWR,* II, 1, p. 363.

[6] *NWR,* II, 1, pp. 351-352.

[7] *Ibid.,* pp. 362-363.

[8] Principal authorities for this chapter: *Mercury,* July 23 and August 26, 1861; *NWR,* I, 1; *The Jeff Davis Piracy Case. Full report of trial of William Smith for piracy as one of the crew of Confederate privateer Jeff Davis* (Philadelphia: King and Baird, printers, 1861).

Four of these, two 24-pounders and two short 32-pounders, were mounted in broadside, and a long 18-pounder was pivoted amidships.[9] The armory was well stocked with double-barrelled shotguns, muskets, cutlasses, and revolvers.

It was on Friday evening, the twenty-eighth of June, that the cruise of the *Jefferson Davis* began. The day had been one of general celebration in Charleston, and the crew, who had participated in the festivities, were in high spirits as the brig crossed the bar into the midnight sea. Now at the outset of another war for independence, this June 28 had a meaning for Charlestonians as perhaps no anniversary of that severe punishment inflicted by the Colonials upon the fleet of the British Admiral, Sir Peter Parker, had had since the memorable year of 1776.

The *Davis,* fully equipped for a long sea voyage, was by daylight of the next morning well out at sea, "notwithstanding," to preserve the language of the Charleston *Mercury,* "the very efficient blockade of Abraham I."

The first day out, a quiet one, affords an opportunity to look about at the ship and the captain and his men. The brig looks more like a foreign vessel than an American. The sails are of hemp, instead of the snowy staple of the Southland, and have a deep reach. The clews are cut sharp. There is but little rake to the masts. She has

9 *Mercury,* July 23, 1861. The armament is also reported as being "four light carronades and one old long 32-pounder on a pivot amidships."—Intelligence report of Lieutenant C. R. P. Rogers, U.S.N., Commandant of Midshipmen, Newport, Rhode Island, July 12, 1861, to the Secretary of the Navy, in *NWR,* I, 5, pp. 193-194. Captain Smith, of the prize schooner *Waring,* gave an interview to the *New York Herald,* July 22, in which he stated the armament to be one long 18-pounder amidships and two 18-pounders and two short 12-pounders in the waist.

a square stern and a billet-head; and is black—mastheads, yards, and hull. Her pivot gun is visible above the rail, and on the topgallant forecastle the funnel has a wooden cover which gives to it the semblance of a bow-chaser. The cabin is half under and half above deck. There is a boat on each quarter, and a number of studdingsail booms are lashed across the stern. She wears a rusty but nonchalant air as though having been long at sea upon a secret and satisfying mission: she looks in character. She probably registers a little less than two hundred tons and draws about twelve feet of water.

One seldom sees Captain Coxetter, a very reserved man who keeps to his cabin. He is somewhat stout for his five feet seven inches of height, wears a moustache and goatee, dresses in plain clothes without a sword, and looks the part of a very easy-going gentleman of middle age. He issues orders in a very mild, calm tone. Though he is thought to be of Hollandish origin, his English is excellent with a scarcely perceptible foreign accent.

The executive officer is the busiest officer on shipboard and a far more important personage than the captain. Lieutenant W. Ross Postell, in early life a midshipman in the United States Navy,[10] is in every respect the bold privateersman. With all the characteristics of a lover of adventure and the dash of a hero, and

[10] Postell was warranted as a midshipman in the United States Navy, December 31, 1831; and was passed, June 15, 1837. On June 15, 1839, he resigned to enter the navy of the Republic of Texas with the rank of lieutenant, and was assigned to the command of the schooner-of-war *San Jacinto*. Commodore Edward W. Moore, T.N., referred to him in a report to the Texas Navy Department, dated, Texas Sloop-of-War *Austin*, At Sea, August 28, 1840, in the following terms: "I take this occasion to state to the Department that he is *much* the most efficient officer I have under my command."

with his lightly bearded face, his litheness and activity, and a tendency to be volatile in temper and language, he seems much younger than he really is.

The second lieutenant is a young Carolinian named Stuart and a pilot by profession. The captain of the marines, Frederick Sandvrie, is a Dane of some forty winters. He stands a bit above medium height, has sharp features, and wears a long, sandy beard. The marine lieutenant, who was not selected for any personal beauty or charm, is apparently an Irishman though he calls himself by the peculiar name of Baya. There are two medical officers. Edward M. Seabrook is first surgeon. W. H. Babcock is second surgeon and secretary. The four remaining officers are pilots who are to act as prize masters.

The crew is mostly Anglo-Saxon but has a sprinkling of the Germanic and Latin races. There is no uniform, and the men, in the variety of costume with which the past has endowed them, look somewhat a motley crew.

A Charleston reporter saw in them "as spirited and gallant a crew as ever braved the dangers of fire and water." But a New York paper carried a description not so flattering. The latter said:

No two of the men are dressed alike. Many have on loose "jumpers," or shirts made out of blue denim, similar in texture, quality and color, to the overalls worn by laborers; others wear coarse shirts made of yellow flannel, such as may be seen in the South, while others had nothing on the upper part of their bodies but their undershirts. Their nether garments—the extremities of which are, in many cases, pushed into their boots—are of every imaginable color and quality, rivaling, in diversity of hues, the variegated tints of Joseph's coat. The majority wear ordinary cloth or glazed caps, but some have on black felt hats, with high sugar-loaf crowns, resembling the Spanish sombreros, or the hats of Italian brigands. The men appear to have been shipped without the least regard to seamanship, are generally of small stature, and had been tailors, shoemakers, idlers, loafers, and the like, on shore. They were shipped principally in Charleston and Savannah. Some twelve only are armed with old muskets, and about twenty are armed with cutlasses, extemporized out of long knives used for cutting canes on the Southern sugar plantations. The crew are generally a cut throat set, and would make an army such as Falstaff would have been proud to lead.[11]

So different do the same men appear, according to the point of view! There is no doubt that the New Yorkers were given a caricature to meet the popular conception of pirates. On the other hand, it was an hyperbole of patriotism to describe the crew in such superlative language as was used in the Charleston paper.

In fact, in 1861, there was still a freedom in the matter of dress, even among regular navy men, that now no longer obtains except on certain classes of merchant vessels where one may yet see costuming (save in the matter of sugar-loaf hats) not unsuggestive of the caricature by the New York reporter. The constant watchfulness after the set and trim of sail to meet the fickleness of the wind, bred in many followers of the sea an indifference to the details of dress, which was sometimes swept away in reaction to a dandyism wherein the individual taste broke through regulations with results more or less fantastic.

11 Quoted in *Mercury,* July 23, 1861.

THE CONFEDERATE PRIVATEERS

The Confederate privateersmen were no exception to the seamen of the period. They dressed as they pleased. But the sailors of the *Davis* maneuvered the ship with seamanlike smartness. The marines kept the guns and small arms clean, and maintained the guard well. When a prize was to be made, the gun ports were unlashed, powder and shot served up from the magazine, small arms distributed from the armory, and a prudent readiness to meet any unexpected resistance maintained. If there should be a few bad spirits among the crew—and there were—who, chafing at the restraint placed upon their plundering instincts, planned a mutiny, and were defeated by the officers, it was but an experience most common in all the days of privateering.[12] As we shall see, the cruise of the *Jefferson Davis* may be ranked as the last truly classic cruise in the history of private-armed sea power, worthy to stand with the most notable cruises of our letters of marque of 1776 and 1812.

Some of the officers of the *Jefferson Davis* wore double-breasted, blue flannel coats with brass buttons, whose raised device was the palmetto with the initials *SC*.[13] Around the edge of the buttons there was printed in cameo letters the left part of the duofold motto of the State of South Carolina: *Animis opibusque parati*.[14]

On Sunday, the second day at sea, the masthead lookout reported two sails ahead, but owing to a derangement in the fore-topmast gearing they were allowed to go unpursued. Later the same day a large vessel came

12 See page 99.
13 *New York Herald,* July 22, 1861.
14 Virgil's *Aeneid,* Bk. 2, l. 799: "Ready in soul and resource." The right part of the Carolina motto is *Dum spiro, spero* (While I breathe, I hope).

in sight, but as she appeared to be French no effort was made to overhaul her.

Before light southerly winds, the privateer cruised up the coasts of the Carolinas for nearly a week without speaking a prize. It was now Thursday, the Fourth of July, and another celebration seemed in order. The Confederate flag was run up at the main and the national salute was fired. Then, by the order of Captain Coxetter, all hands "spliced the main brace." After generous libations, life did not seem so discouraging. Luck was certainly going to turn. Then, sure enough, a sail was made on the lee bow. On nearing her, "Long Tom," from his pivot amidships, sent a shot bowling across the water that brought her to. She proved, upon examination of her papers, to be the English brig *Grace Worthington,* and was at once dismissed. In the evening there came a brig from Baltimore, which was also allowed to pass, because, as it may be recalled, the Confederacy did not regard itself as at war with Maryland. The life was less encouraging—albeit the harvest was destined to be rich.

Early Saturday morning, July 6, a brig was descried in the latitude of southern Delaware and about three hundred miles offshore. The privateer was standing to the southward under all sail, and the stranger was steering east by north with studding sails set. Here at last was a prize. Captain Fitfield of the prize brig afterward narrated the incident to a northern reporter:

At 8 : 30 the privateer tacked and stood N.W., at the same time setting a French ensign, and from the fact of her having French-cut hempen sails we supposed she was a French merchant brig. In answer to her colors we set the Stars and Stripes, and thought no more of the stranger. At 9 o'clock, to our surprise, she fired a shot across our bows, when we took in the studding sails and hove the *John Welsh* to. We then supposed her to be a French man-of-war brig; but her ports were closed and the guns covered up, while but few men were to be seen on her decks. She came within musket shot of us, and lowered a boat which was manned by expert seamen and contained Lieutenant Postell, late of the United States Navy. Just before the boat came alongside the French flag was hauled down and the Confederate flag run up. In about two minutes afterwards the armed crew was on our deck. After inquiring after my health, Lieutenant Postell desired me to show him the brig's papers. I invited him into the cabin, and after showing them, I stated the cargo was Spanish property. Said he, "You are our prize, and the Spaniards had no business to ship their cargoes in American bottoms." He then came on deck and ordered four of my men to go in the privateer's boat, and told the remainder of the crew to pack up their things and stand by to do as ordered. They immediately set to work and broke out the ship's stores and took about eight months' provisions on board of the privateer, leaving only enough to take the prize-crew back with the vessel. This occupied about five hours. I was transferred with the remainder of my crew on board of the privateer, and they took my boat and sent theirs on board of the *John Welsh,* as mine was the best. A prize-crew corresponding in appearance and number was then put on board in charge of Prize-Master Stevens, and she was ordered to go South but I was not allowed to know of her destination. I think they will palm themselves off as the genuine crew if they fall in with the Federal cruisers. After the work of transferring the stores had been completed, Capt. Coxetter mustered all hands aft and said to them, "Boys, if you molest the crew of that brig or their things to the value of a rope yarn, I will punish you to the utmost of my power. Do you understand? Now go forward." Turning to his officers he said, "Gentlemen, I desire that you do everything in your power to make the stay of these gentlemen as agreeable as possible." He then invited me to dine with him in his cabin while my mate was taken into the officer's mess.[15]

The *John Welsh* was a Philadelphia brig, in passage from Trinidad to Falmouth, England. She was a good freighting vessel, only three years old, in fine order, and had a very valuable cargo of sugar. It consisted of 273 hogsheads, 54 tierces, and 286 barrels of muscovado sugar, and 436 boxes of clayed sugar.[16] The prize crew brought her safely into Savannah, where she remained until early September; then, having been condemned by the Prize Court which sat in Charleston, she was taken to the latter port to be sold at auction.

The morning had proved quite profitable to the privateersmen, and the afternoon's cruise was to bring them another prize. This was the schooner *Enchantress,* Captain Devereaux, of Newburyport, Massachusetts, bound from Boston to Santiago de Cuba, with provisions, grindstones, glassware, and pine boards. The schooner was placed in charge of Prize Master William Wallace Smith, a Savannah pilot, who was ordered to take her into that port. The subsequent tale of the afternoon's prize (told in the next chapter) does not form as happy a digression as that of the morning's capture; and concerns how the *Enchantress* stood southward, and when off Hatteras was retaken, by the U.S.S. *Albatross.*

The following day being Sunday, the ship's prayers were read. Scarcely was the church flag down before a sail was descried astern. A message from "Long Tom"

15 Quoted in *Mercury,* July 23, 1861.
16 *Mercury,* August 22, 1861.

quickly brought to the schooner *S. J. Waring,* of Brookhaven, Long Island, bound to Montevideo with a valuable cargo. She proved a good prize, and was very shortly sailing for a Confederate port.[17]

Monday went out a blank day, but in the wee hours of Tuesday a sail was discovered. This, however, proved to be a "Blue-nose Yankee," and to the minds of the privateersmen not worth the shot and powder to bring her to. So she passed safely by. With morning, another vessel was reported by the lookout. Chase was made until noon, when the ship *Mary Goodell,* Captain McGilvery was overhauled. Mrs. McGilvery was on board. Partly out of a gallant consideration for the lady, and partly as a means of getting rid of a number of prisoners held on board from the three prizes, the *Mary Goodell* was turned into a cartel and released. But the reason assigned by one of the prisoners, who was thus released, after he had gotten home, was that the ship drew eighteen feet of water and that therefore the privateersmen knew that she could not be gotten over the bar at any convenient southern port. Though Captain Coxetter relieved the *Goodell* of four casks of her fresh water, and burdened her with twelve involuntary passengers, and though two[18] of the *Goodell's* crew deserted

---

[17] Captain Smith, of the *Waring,* confirms the fact of kind treatment accorded to prisoners on the *Davis.* In the *New York Herald,* July 22, 1861, he says: "We expected from the statements made in the New York papers, that we would be stripped of everything and treated with the greatest severity; but our treatment was entirely different from that which we expected. Each officer did all in his power to make us comfortable."

Bartlett Jones, mate of the prize *Santa Clara,* also gave Captain Coxetter an excellent character, speaking of the latter's "gentlemanly conduct" and "humane feeling."—*New York Herald,* August 21; *Courier,* August 28; and *Daily Delta,* August 29, 1861.

[18] *NWR,* II, 1, pp. 364-365. But according to *Mercury,* July 23, this

and joined the privateer, Captain McGilvery was delighted to escape with his ship, and cheerfully promised to continue the voyage to Buenos Ayres. However, once out of sight, McGilvery broke his pledge and ran his ship for Portland, Maine, to spread the alarm that a Confederate letter of marque was ravaging the New England coasts.

While the *Goodell* affair was being brought to a conclusion, the brig *Mary E. Thompson* from Searsport, Maine, with lumber, for Antigua, came running down and was made a temporary prize.[19] But as she did not seem to be valuable enough to warrant a prize crew, Coxetter placed the remaining nine prisoners on board her and released her, also on condition that the voyage be continued to the original destination.

The events of this July 9 indicate the easy-going gentleman that Captain Coxetter was. But humane considerations may be carried too far in war. When, for any reason, a prize cannot be sent into port for condemnation, the captor has the legitimate option of bonding or destroying the ship. He did neither. If he could have cared for the prisoners, even at the expense of their comfort, it would have been far better to have burned both prizes. At any rate, since the first prize was still within recalling distance when the second prize was

number is five, and *Daily Delta,* August 29, four. One of the *Goodell's* turncoats, J. Clark, was made boatswain on the privateer, and went as second in command in the prize crew on the *Alvarado.*

19 The *Merchants Magazine,* December, 1861, in a summary of prizes made by Confederate privateers and cruisers, credits the *Mary E. Thompson* and the *Mary Goodell,* both under date of July 9, 1862, to a privateer called *Echo.* This confusion with the former name of the *Jefferson Davis* and the further mistake of one year in the date have been followed by several subsequent writers.

made, one or the other prize should have been made to take all the prisoners and the remaining one then destroyed. As it was, Coxetter's kindness and forbearance was ill repaid; for the second vessel also hurried back to a northern port, and soon the enemy had nine men-of-war and hastily armed steamers on the track of the lone privateer.

The *Jefferson Davis* continued her cruise as far northward as the Narragansett Shoals, and then put about for the West Indies. After this only foreign vessels were seen until the twenty-first, when an American bark was sighted in the vicinity of latitude 26° north, longitude 50° west. Upon signal the newcomer promptly luffed up into the wind, and a boat from the privateer shot alongside. The boarding officer found a good prize in the bark *Alvarado,* Captain G. C. Whiting (and wife), of and for Boston, 51 days from Cape Town, Africa, with a cargo of 458 bales of wool, 26 bales of buchu leaves, 290 bales of sheepskins, 231 hides, and a quantity of old copper and iron. The top value of the bark was about $10,000 and of her burden about $75,000. The next day the prize was sent on her altered way for the Confederate littoral under Gilbert Hay, who might well have been given the appositive soubriquet, the Unfortunate, for he was destined to be thrice the loser in the privateering game—as it remains to be seen. He took with him a prize crew of nine men. However, their berths on the privateer were partly refilled by the accession of five men from the Yankee crew of the *Alvarado*—for the obligation of flag generally sits very lightly on the sailor.

The *Alvarado,* shaped her course for Fernandina, Florida. The morning of the fourteenth day after parting company with the privateer, the prize was standing along the land with a fair wind toward the entrance of the selected haven. All seemed well with the prize men, until a sloop-of-war, the *Jamestown,* was made out blockading the mouth of the St. Mary's River. Then Hay seems to have lost his head, for, with the enemy four miles to the eastward and very little to leeward and the entrance channel close at hand, he suddenly ran his vessel upon the southeast side of the shoal extending out from the lighthouse on Amelia Island—whether from ignorance of the coast or by intent it does not appear. Hastily the privateersmen lowered and got into their boat, which was already hanging over the side, and pulled for the shore, leaving the bark abandoned with all sail set.

It was necessary for the sloop to tack in order to get to the southward of the shoal. There was no coast pilot on the blockader; and her commander, Charles Green, was afraid to come in closer than three miles, which did not bring his guns within range of the stranded bark. He then concluded to cut her out with a boat expedition. It was three o'clock in the afternoon when the sloop's launch and two of her cutters left the ship's side. In the meantime a section of Confederate field artillery had arrived on the beach from Fort Clinch. The *Alvarado* was about a mile from the shore. The tide was flood, and the bark looked as though she would float. If the boats could be driven off the Confederates might return to her and yet get their prize into port. The two 6-pounders on shore opened a cross fire upon the approaching boats, but the boats' crews seemed to have been too much occupied with struggling against wind and tide to reply with their light 12-pounder howitzer. In spite of the barrage, the boats at length reached the derelict. At this moment the lookout on the *Jamestown* saw the smoke of a steamer coming out of Fernandina. Fearing that his boats might be cut off, Commander Green recalled them. The boarding parties set fire to the *Alvarado* and brought off the ship's papers and the journal of Mrs. Whiting. Incidentally, the Boston skipper and his wife, who had been captive on board of the prize, arrived in Fernandina quite destitute, but their needs were relieved by the philanthropy of the good ladies of the town. The afternoon was far spent when the boats pulled back toward the *Jamestown.* The burning bark, with her cargo of skins, made a spectacle rivaling the sunset. When morning came, nothing but the charred sternpost was in sight.[20]

In the meantime, the *Jefferson Davis* was going on, without knowledge of disaster to her prize. The newspapers, sometimes only a day or so old, found on board of her prizes, kept her pretty well informed as to the major events of the war. The accounts of the Confederate victory at Bull Run, July 21, were read but a few days after the battle.[21]

The next Yankee vessel hailed was a bark bound from St. Thomas for Cork, having on board the cargo of a British vessel which had suffered shipwreck; and was generously allowed to pass. A few days later Captain

[20] *Daily Delta,* August 29, 1861, quoting *Boston Traveler,* August 19; *True Delta,* August 14, 1861; *NWR,* I, 6, pp. 56-59. The men of the *Alvarado* who joined the privateersmen signed themselves as follows: Andrew Jackson, George Page, H. (his x mark) Dutch, W. (his x mark) Powers, Franklin Sears, and John F. McCowen.—*NWR,* II, 1, p. 365.

[21] *Mercury,* September 5, 1861; *True Delta,* September 11, 1861.

Coxetter put into San Juan, Porto Rico, for water and provisions. But the break in the business of destroying United States commerce was very brief, and the privateer was shortly out again on the West Indian seas. Several sails were made and vainly chased, then, on August 5, two prizes came together.

The schooner *Windward,* with salt from Turks Island for Holmes' Hole, first appeared; and, before the boarding party could complete the prize, a more desirable brig showed on the horizon. The schooner was dropped and chase was made immediately for the distant vessel. Soon "Long Tom" had fetched the hermaphrodite brig *Santa Clara* alongside. The *Windward* was now overhauled, and, the prisoners from the *Alvarado* and the *Santa Clara* having been put on her, she was released as a cartel.

The brig seemed a valuable prize, probably worth some $65,000; and though all the available officers had been sent away as prize masters, Captain Coxetter was so loath to lose the *Santa Clara* that he entrusted her to a prize crew, the ranking member of which was only a helmsman. However, the brig was successfully brought into Savannah, where she and her cargo were duly condemned in the District Court for Georgia. The tackle, apparel, furniture, and cargo of the prize were sold at auction on April 24, 1862. The bidding was spirited; 287 hogsheads of Porto Rico and muscovado sugars bringing from $9\frac{1}{2}$ to $14\frac{3}{4}$ cents a pound, and 20 hogsheads of Porto Rico molasses from 85 to $87\frac{1}{2}$ cents a gallon. The sails, rigging, and furniture brought "fair prices."[22] The brig herself was seized by the Confederate

[22] *Mercury,* September 13, 1861; *Savannah Republican,* April 25, 1862.

authorities, and, together with two other prizes then in the hands of the Court, was sunk in the Savannah River, in November, 1861, in order to obstruct the inland waterway against the passage of the enemy's fleet, which had just captured Port Royal, South Carolina. After many delays and interventions the condemnation proceedings were brought to a close, January 15, 1863, the Court ordering the Confederate Government to pay the appraised value of the brig to the privateersmen.[23]

With the sending in of the *Santa Clara,* Captain Coxetter absolutely exhausted his prize-crew possibilities. His provisions and water were also running short. So, perforce, he shaped his course for a return to the Confederacy. Approaching the coast of Florida, the *John Carver,* Captain George W. Edge, was overhauled. This ship, drawing twenty-two feet of water, was too deep to enter any South Atlantic port; but being a chartered transport, conveying coal to the Gulf Squadron, of course, could not be released as Coxetter had often generously done with purely private ships. The crew being taken off, the prize was scuttled and set on fire, forward and after. This was early in the evening. The burning ship illuminated the night, and then disappeared under the water just before the dawn.

The privateersmen just missed having a fight to secure this prize. Before sailing from Philadelphia, Captain Edge and the owners of the *Carver* had applied to the collector of customs for two guns suitable for the protection of the vessel on the chartered voyage. The

[23] *Minute Book, Admiralty Cases,* Confederate States District Court for Georgia. (Now in U.S. District Court for Southern District of Georgia, at Savannah.)

chief of ordnance and hydrography approved the request; but the Navy Department endorsed, "if they are
not willing to take the coal let them put it out."[24] The
captain and owners probably wished they had, and
voided their contract.

Homeward bound were the privateersmen. On Friday evening, August 16, just exactly seven weeks at
sea, the *Jefferson Davis* arrived off the port of St. Augustine; but as the wind was blowing a half-gale, she
did not venture to cross the bar. All of Saturday, Coxetter waited for an abatement of the wind. Fortunately
no enemy cruisers appeared, to add to the discomfiture
of the situation. On Sunday morning, he essayed the
passage and grounded. He tried to relieve the brig by
throwing the starboard guns overboard, but she bilged
and only the stores and small arms were saved.

In the meantime lighters had come out from the port,
and the privateersmen with their effects were conveyed
to the city. There a great ovation was accorded to them.
The bells of the town rang out joyous peals of welcome.
The shipwrecked heroes—for they had gained notoriety
or fame, according to the sympathy, throughout the
world—received such hospitality from the Floridians
that they quickly recovered from the rigors of the cruise
and shipwreck. When Captain Coxetter arrived in
Charleston, a fortnight later, he was met at the railway
station by a crowd of admirers, and presented with a
massive gold watch and fob.[25]

Charleston was delighted with the performance of this
privateer of hers. The daily *Mercury* said: "The name

[24] *NWR*, I, 1, p. 46.
[25] *Mercury*, September 5, 1861.

of the privateer *Jefferson Davis* has become a word of terror to the Yankees. The number of her prizes and the amount of merchandise which she captured have no parallel since the days of the *Saucy Jack*"[26]—which, incidentally, was one of the most successful privateers of the War of 1812, and a Charleston schooner.

[26] *Mercury,* August 26, 1861.

VI

THE MELANCHOLY FATE OF TWO PRIZES

*W*HAT seems to have been Captain Coxetter's aversion for the negro race gave rise to the two melancholy tales to be told: the loss of good prizes, the butchery of one prize crew, and the jeopardy of the hangman for another.

As we saw in the last chapter, the Yankee schooner *Enchantress,* Devereux, fell prize to the Confederate private-armed brig *Jefferson Davis* on July 6, 1861. The details, which give quite an intimate picture of the privateering method, are fully developed in the transcript of a famous trial, known as the United States vs. William Smith, which began on October 22, 1861, in the Circuit Court of the United States for the Eastern District of Pennsylvania.

The schooner's mate, one Charles W. Page, was first called. It is the duty of the first officer to see and know all, and he was worthy to be heard.[1]

On that day things went on as usual on board up to about two o'clock in the afternoon, when we descried a sail to windward. We could just make out that she was a square-rigged vessel. We kept on our course. We gradually gained upon her, and we found that she was a square-rigged brig. She was standing so as to cross our bow. When within about a mile I should judge, she hoisted the French flag. We hoisted the Stars and Stripes. We still kept on our way, thinking

[1] *The* Jeff Davis *Piracy Case. Full report of trial of William Smith for piracy as one of crew of Confederate privateer* Jeff Davis (Philadelphia: King and Baird, printers, 1861).

she might be a French vessel that wanted to get news from the United States. When within about half a mile, she altered her course and ran towards us. The vessel was hauled to the wind, her studding sails lowered, and we were ordered to heave to. . . .

Captain Devereux told him that he could not heave to in the position he was. He said, "I will cross your bow and run to windward and heave to." We did so, went to windward of him and hove to. He immediately lowered a boat. The boat came alongside of us with an officer and some six men. [The *Enchantress* was distant from the privateer] perhaps some seven or eight times her length; I could not state the exact distance. It was within hailing distance. The officer, when he came over the gangway said to one of his own men, "Haul down that flag in the main rigging. . . ." [The United States ensign fluttered down.] The men went all over the vessel, anywhere they chose. The officer went aft to the captain.

He asked him where he was from, and where bound, and what was his cargo. The captain told him. He then said, "I will thank you for your papers, captain, you are a prize of the Confederate brig *Jefferson Davis;* get ready to go on board of her." The officer asked if I was mate of the vessel. I told him I was. Said he, "Show me where your stores are." I showed him. He took two of his men down into the cabin, and they took out whatever stores they wanted and put them into their boat. The lieutenant and three men remained on board the schooner. . . . Three men rowed back to the privateer. . . . Some half-hour's time elapsed, and they came back to our vessel with the prize crew, five men. The lieutenant then gave Captain Devereux, his son, and myself orders to get ready to go in the boat. We put our things in the boat and got in ourselves, and they rowed us to the brig, and we went on board.

The mate then, in answer to sundry questions, testified that though it was about seven-thirty, and getting dark, that he could plainly see some twelve or fifteen men on the deck of the privateer when the latter ordered the schooner to heave to and that, as the *Enchantress* went across the bow of the *Jefferson Davis* to go to windward, the big pivot gun was swiveled around to follow the movements of the merchantman—on which the armament was only one musket. The position at noon had been taken in latitude 38° 52′ north, longitude 69° 15′ west.

What the mate knew and testified about established in the mind of the District Attorney the guilt of the man on trial, William Smith, formerly a branch pilot of Savannah, now captured prize master from the retaken schooner *Enchantress*. He was a man of thirty-seven, small in stature, with a dark complexion, and long heavy whiskers.

Where the story of the mate ends, William Smith[2] and prize crew are blithely parting company with the brig in high hopes of taking the schooner into Charleston through the glistening waters of Bull's Bay.

The frustrator of well-laid plans was one Jacob Garrick, the schooner's cook, black, suave, composed, resourceful. He told his story to the court.

On the 6th of July, about two or three o'clock, we made a sail. I heard them sing out "Sail ho." I looked and saw the sail myself. We were going on our course with a pretty fair breeze of wind, this sail still coming on to us. It came on pretty late. I had supper about half past five o'clock. When

[2] Charleston *Mercury*, August 27, 1861; Savannah *Morning News*, October 30, 1887.

we came on deck after supper, we saw the sail, having the French flag flying. Some of the men said it was a French vessel. It kept coming along and got pretty near us. I was washing my dishes, and I heard one of the men sing out forwards "That's a privateer." I looked over my galley, and I saw they had the French flag set and were ramming home a cartridge. I saw the big gun amidships. She came around, hailed us, and told us to heave to. The captain sung out something to her, and she kept on and came round on the stern. Then I heard them sing out for us to lower away our fore-sail and haul down our jib. The captain did so, and hove our vessel to, and then I saw a boat come to us. Previous to that, when they got on the starboard side of us, they hauled down the French flag, and hauled up the Confederate flag, then they lowered the boat. The boat came alongside of us, and some of the men got off and spoke to the captain. I took notice of a man with a glazed cap on and a white coat.

The Confederate boarders said to the sailors on the *Enchantress:* " 'Men, get ready to go on board the *Jeff. Davis;* take all the things belonging to you!' " Garrick and his bag piled into the boat with the rest of the crew; but when it came alongside the *Davis* he heard someone say: " 'Take that colored individual back; you need not pass up his things.' " And the colored individual went back to his schooner, and was faithful cook to his new masters for fifteen days. Upon the sixteenth day, the twenty-second of July, the worm turned!

Soon after dinner I took my dishes to the galley and washed them. In going back to the cabin with the dishes, I saw Smith have a spy glass. I looked under the lee of the mainsail and I saw a vessel coming that I thought was a steamer. I took another look, and I saw it was a steamer. The steamer was coming right in our direction. Smith said to the men to take the flying jib off to bend; but they sang out to Smith, "You had better not bend that jib now, because if they see us making sail they will think something and come at us." He said, "Go ahead and bend it." Then they started out to bend it, and he said, "Never mind, you can let it lie." Then I heard him say, "One of you men go up and sheer over that topsail sheet." A man went up to do it and was there a considerable while. Then Lane[3] said to me, "You can go in the forecastle, steward; and if they should come and overhaul us, and your name is called, you can answer." I said I would rather stay in the galley. I went in the galley and watched the steamer coming. When the steamer saw us back ship, she hauled right up for us. I kept looking through from one galley door to the other, according as we would go about. We went about three or four times. The schooner was going pretty fast. I still kept looking to see how near the steamer was getting to us. I heard one of the men say, "She has hoisted her flag," and they went out and hoisted our flag. The steamer hoisted the American flag; and we hoisted our American flag. The steamer kept coming on. I heard them say, "It is a man-of-war." When the steamer got pretty close to us, I heard a hail, "What schooner is that?" The reply was, "The *Enchantress.*" "Where bound to?" "St. Jago de Cuba."[4] As soon as that was said, I jumped out of my galley and jumped overboard, singing out that it was "a captured vessel of the privateer *Jeff. Davis*, and they are taking her into Charleston." I sang it out so that they could hear me on board the steamer.

The steamer's boat picked me up . . . when the boat picked me up they took me on board the schooner, and then

---

[3] This man claimed secret loyalty to the United States in "The Trial of the 'Pirates,'" Chapter XII.

[4] Same as Santiago de Cuba.

they took the prize crew off the schooner and took me on board the steamer along with them.

When the steamer, the U.S.S. *Albatross,* was coming down on the schooner, the prize crew

were arranging themselves to take the names of the *Enchantress'* crew. One was to act in place of the captain with his name; another in the place of the mate with his name; and so on through the crew. . . . They were short one. . . . I heard that they were to say that man was washed overboard.

The boarding lieutenant compelled the prize crew to row him back to the cruiser,

leaving his boat's crew to take charge of the *Enchantress.* . . . A prize crew was put on board from the steamer, with me along as cook. Then we made sail in her and steered to Hampton Roads.

Thus Jacob Garrick, menial, by being retained upon his vessel through the vicissitudes of three crews, proved that civilized man cannot live without cooks, but at the same time, that the stomach, quite often, gets him into trouble. Prize Master Smith and his men were now in plenty of trouble; for, when the *Albatross* docked at the Philadelphia Navy Yard wharf, a deputy marshal came aboard, read them a warrant charging piracy, and took them, handcuffed and ankle-chained, to Mayamensing Prison.

Whether from a disinclination on the part of Captain Coxetter to bring colored individuals upon his brig or from a desire to provide his prize crew with well-cooked food, it matters not. But the tragedy of the prize

schooner *S. J. Waring* came at the hands of another retained steward.

This man, a Rhode Island negro named Tillman, un-
suspected of bad intent, cooked the meals of Prize
Master Montague Amiel (a Charleston pilot), Seamen
George Stephens and Malcolm Liddy, who acted as
mates, and two other privateersmen, one named Milnor
and the other Smith, as well as of two captured sailors[5]
and a passenger,[6] who had been left on board to assist
in the navigation of the prize. No restrictions were
placed upon the negro or the captured white men,
whether on watch or below. In fact, the watches were
most indifferently kept, and the prize officers were singularly unsailorlike and careless.

On the tenth night of the prize voyage, when only a
hundred miles off Charleston, came the tragic hour. The
prize master and the first mate were sleeping in their
cabins, the second mate was asleep on the poop-deck,
and the two Confederate seamen were lounging in the
forecastle—a criminally negligent state of affairs, and
one which could cost their lives. It did. The big, burly
Tillman, seizing the opportunity, stole silently into the
master's cabin. A dull thud followed. Swiftly and noiselessly, the negro ran into the first mate's room, and
pounded this poor man several times on the head with
a heavy axe. Then he dashed to the poop, where the second mate had just been wakened by the gurgling out-
cries of his superiors, and dealt this officer a mortal blow
at the base of his skull. Tillman did not hesitate a moment, but picked up the wounded man and threw him

[5] William Stedding and Donald McLeod.
[6] Bryce Mackinnon.

85

overboard. The murdered mate rose on a wave, uttered a last hoarse cry, and sank forever. Returning to the captain, who despite a horrible hole in the head, was not yet dead, the black giant administered a second blow, a *coup de grâce,* before tossing the body overboard. The first mate seemed hard to kill. More blows were rained upon his unhappy head. Still faintly articulate, half dragged, half walking, his head a pulpy mass lying over upon his shoulders, he was carried up the companionway. A third splash, and there ended a deed as cruel and brutal as any committed by the veritable pirates of the black flag. Tillman, having overawed all others aboard ship, sailed the schooner into New York.

The negro steward knew nothing of navigation, but succeeded in making the land, and, holding close to the shore, sailed up the coast with all sail set. A kindly Providence spared him the hazards of the sea and brought him safely to the pilot ground at New York. The recaptured schooner anchored off the Battery in the Hudson River at four o'clock on Sunday afternoon, July 21. The New York papers the next morning carried glowing accounts of Tillman's "heroism."[7]

The two captive privateersmen were arrested on a warrant charging piracy, and imprisoned in the Tombs. The one who had signed, with his mark, the shipping articles of the *Jefferson Davis* as T. Smith now called himself James Dorsett,[8] of New Jersey, and claimed

[7] *Rebel Pirates' Fatal Prize; or, the bloody tragedy of the prize schooner* Waring *enacted as the Rebels were attempting to run her into Charleston, S. C., July 7, 1861. By a passenger of the* Waring *and eye witness to the bloody scenes* (Philadelphia: Reechner & Co., 1862).

[8] Spelled Dorsett in the *New York World,* July 23, and in *Harper's Weekly,* August 3, 1861; but Dawsett in the *New York Herald,* July 22, 1861.

to have been impressed. He is described in the press as one "who appears to be an innocent sort of person."

Tillman was taken to the House of Detention and held pending the investigation of the grand jury.[9] After he was released, he was engaged by the great showman Phineas T. Barnum to appear in the latter's museum of "real and pretended wonders"—which was the publicity equivalent in 1861 to our present-day scheme of going into the motion pictures. The negro—a splendid physical specimen, five feet eleven inches tall—took with him his bloody hatchet, and the prize flag, which was the Stars and Stripes recut into the Stars and Bars; and continued for some time to relate his adventures for the delectation of the curious public.

But a salary and notoriety were not the only profits that Tillman got from his adventure. The recaptured schooner was promptly libeled in the District Court for the Southern District of New York; and, on February 6, 1862, a decree was filed ordering the owners of the schooner *S. J. Waring* and her cargo to pay $17,000 as salvage money to the negro and his assistants. Tillman's share was fixed at $7,000. William Stedding, his principal assistant, was awarded $6,000, and Bryce Mackinnon, the passenger, $3,000. Donald McLeod, the remaining member of the original ship's company, seems to have taken but little part in the matter, yet he was allowed $1,000. The salvage money was assessed against the several owners of the vessel and cargo, placing the value of the *Waring* at $9,000 and the aggregate worth of her cargo at $50,052. The owners appealed the case,

9 Records of U. S. District Court for Southern District of New York (New York City).

filing bond, on March 25; but, on the eighth of August following, they consented to the execution of the decree —which is to say that about a year after the suit was begun the black butcher of sleeping men and salvor of a captured schooner was paid $7,000 for his exploit— less, of course, what his proctors took for their services.

VII

THE JAUNTY LITTLE DIXIE

A WISP of another Charleston privateer, called the *Dixie,* left her anchorage under the guns of Castle Pinckney on July 19, 1861. Fine weather and a kindly moon took her to sea, and she had a right jolly cruise.[1]

The *Dixie* was a schooner of 110 tons, built at Baltimore, in 1856, as the *H. & J. Neild.* In 1860 she had been sold to Captain Thomas J. Moore, who employed her in the West Indian trade until the commencement of the war. Then changing her name to the *Dixie,* Moore, a Virginian, and a bold and enterprising man, ran her through the blockade into Charleston. There he organized a stock company and sold the schooner to it for $5,500[2]. The company applied for and received a letter of marque on June 26. The application stated that the armament would consist of three guns, and the ship's company of thirty-five persons, with Captain Moore commanding.[3]

The gay little privateer had only been four days at sea when she took her first prize. Pursuing a southeasterly course, early on the morning of the twenty-third, she came upon a sail off the lee quarter. Tacking ship, Captain Moore soon overhauled the stranger, which lay to in ready response to a signal from "Long Tom."

The master of the vessel was ordered to come aboard the *Dixie,* and bring his papers with him. This he did

[1] General authority for this chapter is *Mercury,* August 28, 1861.

[2] *Baltimore American,* October 17, and *Courier,* November 4, 1861.

[3] *NWR,* II, 1, pp. 365-367.

promptly, and the privateersmen had the gratification to find that their prize was the bark *Glen,* Captain L. Holmes, of Portland, Maine, loaded with 391 tons of anthracite coal belonging to the enemy, and bound to Fort Jefferson on the Tortugas.[4]

The prize crew took her into Moorhead City, North Carolina. The admiralty court duly condemned her; and she brought at auction $3,700, with the coal selling at the "enormous price" of $18.50 a ton, netting over $10,-000 prize money to the owners and crew of the *Dixie.*[5]

A day of idleness passed and then came the schooner *Mary Alice,* in latitude 29° north, longitude 77° 10' west, with a cargo of West Indian sugar intended to sweeten the tea of New Yorkers, though now to sweeten the life of the privateersmen. However, it is ever a question of he who laughs last, for the *Mary Alice* was recaptured from the prize crew by the U.S. Frigate *Wabash.* Some privateersmen then went along with the sugar to taste the bitter opprobrium of piracy.[6]

After parting with the prize, without a thought of losing her, the privateer went blithely on her way. Again there was a day on which the privateersmen saw nothing but the broad expanse of water. Then, on Saturday, the twenty-seventh, two sails were in sight for a short time. A heavy squall came up suddenly. A waterspout developed just ahead. When the weather was clear again the quarry was gone. On Monday two sails were descried but they outran the *Dixie.* The next day the her-

---

[4] *Mercury,* August 6, 1861.   [5] *Ibid.,* September 17, 1861.

[6] *NWR,* I, 6, pp. 62, 68, and 88; *Mercury,* August 14, 1861. This prize was erroneously credited in the *Merchants Magazine,* December, 1865, to the C.S.S. *Winslow.*

maphrodite brig *Robert R. Kirkland,* of and for Baltimore, was spoken and asked to receive a few of the prisoners. This the Marylander consented to do.

On Wednesday afternoon, the thirty-first, no less than nine sails were in view. About sundown one was selected to be pursued. The chase soon appeared to be an armed bark. The privateersmen then stood to their guns prepared to do battle, but the signal from "Long Tom," instead of drawing a fire, brought to the merchant bark *Rowena,* of and for Philadelphia. The prize was from La Guayra, Venezuela, and had on board a thousand bags of coffee. Her crew numbered thirteen and besides there were four passengers, so that these with the other prisoners outnumbered the privateersmen. Captain Moore, unwilling to risk an uprising, decided to go on board the bark himself as prize master, taking the majority of the crew and prisoners with him and leaving the junior lieutenant L. D. Benton, "a very smart and determined man,"[7] on the *Dixie* with the remainder.

The vessels were about three hundred miles off the Georgia-Florida line. Together they turned their heads westward and sailed for the Confederate coast. The *Dixie* with only five privateersmen on board was no longer able to function as a letter of marque and sought rather to avoid than to find a sail. On Friday she managed to elude a strange steamer, and again on Sunday she was obliged twice to forego her natural wont to chase and to flee instead. Slowly the two, privateer and prize, beat up the coast, always dodging any sail that showed, lest unwarily they fall prize to some enemy blockader.

[7] *NWR,* I, 12, p. 426.

At length after four weeks the *Dixie,* closely chased, made Charleston by the way of Bull's Bay; and, on August 27, she was again anchored under the guns of Castle Pinckney.[8]

Destined to a showy but brief cruise, the jaunty little 3-gun schooner was now laid up and her career as a privateer was ended. The venture yielded handsome profit to the stockholders. The *Rowena* was promptly condemned and advertised for sale.[9] On September 12 Captain Moore held a public reception on board her.[10] The sale, which was held a few days later, was well attended, and the bidding was spirited. The bark, a 330-tonner, built in Gloucester, New Jersey, in 1857, in excellent condition, brought $12,000.[11]

The stock company decided now to bag the profits, as they had done the *Rowena's* coffee, and closed out. The *Dixie* was sold, on October 15, to Messrs. A. J. White and Son at a depreciation of only six hundred dollars.[12]

[8] *Courier,* August 28, 1861.
[9] *Ibid.,* August 29, 1861.
[10] *Ibid.,* September 13, 1861.
[11] *Mercury,* September 17, 1861.
[12] *Ibid.,* October 16, 1861.

VIII

IN THE COURT OF ADMIRALTY OF THE CONFEDERATE STATES OF AMERICA FOR SOUTH CAROLINA DISTRICT

*I*N the case of all captured vessels, goods, and effects which shall be brought within the jurisdiction of the Confederate States, the district courts of the Confederate States shall have exclusive, original cognizance thereof as in civil causes of admiralty and maritime jurisdiction.[1]

So it had been with the United States District Courts. Thus it chanced that the Federal Court which sat in Charleston during the summer of 1861 had had experience in prize cases, for the same judge was on the bench as at the trial of the *Echo* in 1858.[2] Judge A. B. Magrath was continued by the Confederate Government in the office he had held under the Union. At the end of the fall term of 1860, he had dramatically thrown off his robes as a sign that this was undoubtedly the last time a Federal Court would sit in Charleston, but with the spring he resumed his rôle as a federal judge under the new federation.

The first prize case to come before the Court was that of the *A. B. Thompson,* a ship captured by the Confederate States gunboat *Lady Davis.* It is notable that in this case, as in the first prize cases brought before the United States Courts for violation of blockade, the defendants set up the claim that a public war did not exist;

[1] *Statutes, Provisional Congress,* Sess. II, Chap. 3, Sec. 7.
[2] See pp. 59-60.

but Judge Magrath, as likewise his northern brethren, disallowed the claim.[3]

The case of the *Joseph* was the first one brought into court by the privateers. The litigation was long drawn out by reason of the interposition of certain Spanish claimants for the cargo, but involved no special points.[4]

The capture of the bark *Rowena* by the privateer *Dixie* brought before the Court the question of disposition of persons captured on board enemy vessels. There were several neutral passengers who petitioned the Court, alleging that by reason of the "capture of the bark and the consequent deviation from her course and termination of her voyage," they should be reimbursed from the proceeds of the prize in the amount of the expenses which they had incurred and in addition should be allowed such amount as would enable them to reach Philadelphia, the port of their original destination.

Counsel for the captors replied that the claim was without precedent or authority in the history of prize adjudication, and observed that

he who, in time of war, takes passage in an enemy's vessel, takes the risk of her capture or any deviation in her voyage resulting therefrom. . . . So, when one of his own accord chooses an enemy's vessel for passage, and she is captured, he may be entitled to be set at liberty, upon proof of neutral character, but can have no claim against the captors, by reason of his having been brought in with the vessel, alleged as property of the enemy.

In this view the Court concurred.[5]

[3] *Courier,* June 6, 1861; *True Delta,* June 30, 1861; *Mercury,* July 18, 1861.

[4] *Courier,* September 4 and 12, 1861.

[5] *Ibid.,* August 30, 1861.

IN AN ADMIRALTY COURT

In connection with this case the Court declared that colored seamen taken on board a prize and brought within the jurisdiction of South Carolina ought not to be prosecuted under the state law of 1835 forbidding the introduction of free negroes, in that they were here without fault of their own. The judge suggested that the state prosecuting officer should not bring a case against them, but that the Confederate marshal should deport them, as in the ordinary course of events with white persons so taken.[6]

The decision, August 26, in the case of "L. M. Coxetter, master, and the owners and crew of the *Jefferson Davis* vs. the brig *John Welch* and her cargo," is interesting.[7]

After discussing English jurisprudence, the Court said:

In this case the papers of the captured vessel clearly establish her national character. Her register bearing date the 28th May, 1861, sets forth that she was built in Philadelphia, in the State of Pennsylvania, and was owned by certain persons, all of the city of Philadelphia, in the State of Pennsylvania. No testimony, which can be produced, can affect the conclusive character of that which the register affords. The vessel, as the property of the enemy, must, therefore, be considered as lawful prize.

But the question of proprietary interest in the cargo requires a more extended investigation. [The judge then discussed pertinent public law, and whether the treaty of 1795 between Spain and the United States were binding upon the Confederate States. He held that it was not.] The bill of lading [he continued] merely establishes the facts that Salvator Zulueta shipped on board of an enemy's vessel a cer-

6 *Courier*, August 29, 1861.   7 *Mercury*, August 27, 1861.

tain cargo, consigned to A. E. Campbell and Company, of London, the vessel bound for Falmouth and a market, and the freight to be paid by the consigners or their assigns at the port of discharge. This paper does not in any manner set forth, at whose risk or for whose account the shipment has been made. Connected with this is the declaration before the British Consul, that the shipper is the sole owner of the cargo. And on the same day is the official certificate of the administrator of the customs at Trinidad, that the cargo was shipped by Salvator Zulueta on account and risk of whom it may concern. [In view of this conflict,] no effect can be produced by these declarations or certificates. The question then, in the case and in regard to the cargo, is narrowed down to this point; in an enemy's ship, is the bill of lading alone, setting forth a shipment by a neutral sufficient to rebut the presumption resulting from its being on board the vessel of an enemy that the cargo is also the property of an enemy?

Such a principle of law, it is believed, has never found its sanction in a Prize Court. The neutral who ships his property on board of the vessel of the enemy, is presumed to know the inconveniences to which he may be exposed; the risks which, under certain circumstances, he will run. From these he may protect himself, at least so far as the loss of his property is concerned, by placing on board of the vessel which carries the property he claims, the evidence which will either prove it to be the property of a neutral, or, at least, induce a Court to order further proof in support of that neutral character. . . . If the mere bill of lading as in this case, is not that evidence, which alone will either sustain a decree for restitution or an order for further proof; condemnation will follow. Because that which on board of the vessel of an enemy is not proved to be the property of a neutral, is treated as the property of the enemy.

The Court then cited the cases of *Flying Fish* (2 Gall R 373) and *London Packet* (Mason R 14).

The decisions in these cases, which are consistent with the cases upon the same point in the Prize Courts of Great Britain, are sufficient to show that a bill of lading, unsupported by other evidence, is not, even when it sets forth upon whose account and risk the cargo is shipped, evidence upon which restitution will be ordered. . . .

It has been said that the omission of the captors to produce the officers and crew of the captured vessel, entitle the claimant to an order for further proof. But the suppression or omission of the owner of the cargo, whether neutral or hostile, to put on board any documentary evidence of title, completely forfeits all title to relief.

Under those circumstances, the cargo will be condemned. But the irregularity in the conduct of the captors, already referred to, will render it necessary to consider the explanation which may be given of it, in order that it may be determined whether the benefit of the capture shall be given to the captors, or transferred to the Government of the Confederate States.

The irregularity on the part of the captors consisted in the failure of Captain Coxetter to bring or send in "the master and one or more of the principal persons belonging to the captured vessel," as witnesses. In this connection Judge Magrath had said:

The defective manner in which the proof has been produced in this case, renders it necessary to bring to the notice of those who have an interest in these cases, the consequences to which, from such causes, they become exposed. It is not a matter of choice, but of positive obligation that the master and mate at least of the captured vessel should be brought into port, and their testimony submitted to the Court upon the standing interrogatories. That testimony, and the papers which may be found in the captured vessel, and all of which must be produced, is the only evidence upon which, in the first instance, the Court proceeds to consider the question of condemnation or restitution. The obligation to produce these witnesses is not only imposed by rule of public law in such cases everywhere recognized and enforced, but it is, moreover, made the subject of one of the special instructions which the President of the Confederate States has issued to those who obtained from him letters of marque; and a refusal or neglect to comply with this instruction may, with other consequences which it involves, cause him to recall the letters he has thus issued.

Captain Coxetter filed an affidavit, reciting that he had found it equally impractical to send any of the crew of the *John Welch* into port with that vessel or to retain such on board the *Jefferson Davis,* alleging that in the one case it would have imperiled the lives of the prize crew and the safety of the prize and in the other it would have jeopardized the privateer herself.

The reasons given for this situation were the sentiments of extreme hatred expressed by the captured crews and a defection which had developed among his own men. In support of his course in this instance, he recalled the unhappy fate of the prize schooner *S. J. Waring,* on board of which he had left part of the original ship's company, and how three out of five of that prize crew had been murdered and the schooner retaken. Coxetter concluded with the assertion that his course, under the circumstances in which he was placed, was actuated simply by necessity and a prudent care for himself and his men.[8]

[8] *Mercury,* September 12, 1861.

Counsel for the privateersmen argued that bad faith must have been exhibited in order to warrant a forfeiture of the prize, consequent upon irregularities in procedure; but the district attorney replied that it is a first principle that captures inure to the Government and that the right of captors lies merely in the sanction of the Government. The judge, pursuant to his general policy, gave the benefit to the captors.[9]

A decree of sale was entered on August 28, and the marshal sold the *John Welch* on September 16 to a Captain Ferguson for the sum of $9,400.[10] The cargo was not put up for sale until October 31.[11]

In regard to the defection among the privateersmen, an item in a Charleston paper said that certain northern papers had reported that a bottle was picked up at sea containing a note which purported to give the location of the privateer and information as to how she might be taken easily. The alleged writer of the note, one Henry Wilson, claimed to have been impressed into service; but it is interesting to observe that the name Henry Wilson does not show among those who signed the shipping articles of the *Davis*. At any rate, on the affidavit of one of the crew, four of the privateersmen were arrested in Charleston on a charge of conspiracy to kill the officers and take the ship into New York. A true bill was found by the Federal Grand Jury against only one of them.[12] When the case came to trial on October 17, the witnesses had gone beyond the jurisdiction of the court, and the accused, in the absence of accusers, was released "on his recognizance" until the next term

9 *Courier,* September 12, 1861.   10 *Mercury,* September 17, 1861.
11 *Courier,* October 30, 1861.   12 *Mercury,* October 11, 1861.

of court. The *Charleston Courier,* in commenting on the affair, said that this man had faithfully served his country for twenty years, and merited the congratulations of his friends on the virtual quashing of the case.[13]

On November 11, the first term, prolonged and busy, of the Confederate States District Court for South Carolina closed. Acting District Attorney C. R. Miles and Deputy Marshal Irving buckled on their swords and joined their respective regiments.[14]

[13] *Mercury* and *Courier,* October 18, 1861.
[14] *Courier,* November 12, 1861.

IX

THE RENDEZVOUS AT HATTERAS

*T*HE advantage of geographical nearness to an enemy, or to the object of attack, [said Admiral Mahan in discussing the elements of sea power,] is nowhere more apparent than in that form of warfare which has lately received the name of commerce-destroying, which the French call *guerre de course*. This operation of war, being directed against peaceful merchant vessels which are usually defenseless, calls for ships of small military force. Such ships, having little power to defend themselves, need a refuge or point of support near at hand; which will be found either in certain ports of the sea controlled by the fighting ships of their country, or in friendly harbors. The latter give the strongest support, because they are always in the same place, and the approaches to them are more familiar to the commerce-destroyer than to his enemy.[1]

The value of this geographical advantage is well illustrated by the Confederate use of Hatteras Inlet. This inlet offered the safest and most reliable escape from the terrible seas off the North Carolina capes into the peaceful waters of the sounds. Hatteras is at the point of maximum outward swing on the great bow that the North Carolina coast presents to the surging Atlantic Ocean. The American coasting ships and the West Indian trade passed within its lights, and the lookouts in the lighthouses exercised surveillance over the transit-trade.

[1] A. T. Mahan, *The Influence of Sea Power on History, 1660-1783* (Boston: Little, Brown, & Co., 1896), pp. 30-31.

"A sail to the northwards," "several sail in sight," and so forth were the signals for the Confederate sea-dogs to dash forth.[2]

The first armed vessels to utilize the natural advantages of Hatteras were the gunboats of the North Carolina navy. Immediately, following her secession, and prior to her admission into the Union of the Confederate States, the Old North State had organized an army and navy. The latter consisted of the *Winslow,*[3] a side-wheel steamer, mounting two guns, and the two canal towboats, the *Raleigh* and the *Beaufort,* carrying one gun each. The *Winslow,* Lieutenant Commanding Thomas M. Crossan, N.C.N., being the fastest of the squadron, usually got the pickings.

The first prize came to the North Carolinians in May, and was the brig *Lydia Frances,* of Bridgeport, Connecticut, bound from Cuba to New York, with a cargo of sugar. A little later the bark *Linwood,* while returning to her home port, New York, with coffee from Rio de Janeiro, fell into their hands; as also did another bark, carrying flour, lard, and white pine, and the schooner *Willet S. Robbins.* In the latter part of June the *Winslow* captured the chartered transport *Transit,* Master Knowles, of New London, Connecticut, returning northward after having carried provisions and munitions to the United States forces at Key West. The *Transit,* a schooner of 193 tons, costing about $13,000, was safely taken into New Berne by H. Seawell, prize master. A few days later, on July 3, the *Winslow* took

---

[2] General reference: *NWR,* I, vols. 1 and 6, and II, vol. 1.

[3] Sometimes called *Warren Winslow;* before being taken for war purposes this steamer was known as the *J. E. Coffee* of Norfolk.

the schooner *Herbert Manton,*[4] of Barnstable, Massachussetts, coming up from Tunas de Zaza, Cuba, with 175 hogsheads and 45 tierces of sugar and 70 hogsheads of molasses on board, and valued at $30,000.[5]

On June 25, while cruising in the Gulf Stream some thirty miles southeast of Cape Hatteras, the energetic *Winslow* recaptured the hermaphrodite brig *Hannah Balch* from the enemy's prize crew. This brig had been captured by the U.S.S. *Flag* five days before, while attempting to run the blockade into Savannah: but it seemed predestined that she should deliver her cargo of molasses to a Confederate port.[6]

A fortnight later the little North Carolina cruiser again assisted Confederate commerce. Seeing a sail off Ocracoke bar, she gave chase; and, at length, opened fire upon the fleeing vessel. Thereupon the schooner *Charles Roberts* surrendered. However, the apprehension on the one side and the pleasant expectation on the other were soon ended. The boarding officer found the prize to be a Confederate vessel with a cargo of West Indian molasses for Wilmington. The *Winslow* then made amends by convoying the schooner to her destination.[7]

Shortly afterward, the North Carolinians made another prizeless capture. The schooner *Priscilla* was taken into New Berne; but, her Maryland ownership becoming established, she was released and allowed to

---

[4] This schooner's name is given in the *New York Herald,* August 3, 1861, as *Herbert Marston.*

[5] *Mercury,* June 10 and July 3 and 12, 1861; *Raleigh Register,* June 29, 1861; *True Delta,* July 7, 1861; *NWR,* II, 2, pp. 161-163.

[6] *NWR,* I, 5, p. 744; *Mercury,* July 3, 1861.

[7] *Ibid.,* July 15, 1861.

complete her voyage to Baltimore. By her the Confederate Government sent home a number of the seamen brought in on the captured merchantmen.

About the last of July the North Carolina naval forces were transferred to the Confederate States navy.[8] It was also at this time that the privateers began to rendezvous at Hatteras.

The first of them was the saucy-looking *York,* formerly the pilot boat *Florida* of Norfolk. This little schooner was of only 68 tons burden, mounted one 8-pounder rifle, and carried about thirty men. She fitted out in her home port, under Captain John Geoffrey, and came down into the North Carolina sounds by way of the Albemarle Canal. The *York* was singularly unfortunate. On July 23, she captured the brig *B. T. Martin,* three days out from Philadelphia, bound for Havana, and laden with staves and a complete sugar mill. The capture was effected about 110 miles eastward of Hatteras. A prize crew was put on the brig and the brig's people taken on board the privateer.

The next day, the prize crew, on what seems to have been a scare, beached the brig some twenty or thirty miles north of the cape. The privateersmen, assisted by the natives, began to strip the prize of her sails and rigging and to land the cargo. The work of unloading and dismantling the *Martin* was about completed when the U.S.S. *Union* put in an appearance and began to shell the wreckers, who fled precipitately into the woods. The cruiser then landed five or six boat parties, which burned the brig and the salvage piled near by.

The *York's* career ended in disaster on August 9.

[8] *Daily Delta,* July 28, 1861.

She was now under the command of Captain T. L. Skinner. On Thursday, the day before, she had recaptured the Texan schooner *George G. Baker,* at a point about seventy-five miles northeast of the rendezvous. This schooner was, at the moment of recapture, in charge of a prize crew from the U.S.S. *South Carolina,* which had taken her in the Gulf of Mexico for violation of the blockade and was sending her to New York for adjudication. Captain Skinner had put four men on board and ordered them to take the prize into Hatteras. Early on Friday morning, with the lighthouse on the Cape in sight, the privateer and her prize discovered that they were being chased. The *York* attempted to run into an inlet but her enemy, the U.S.S. *Union,* intervened, and she then tacked and stood directly in for the land. After running the vessel ashore, the privateersmen set fire to her in several places and made their escape, carrying away with them the captured prize crew. The *Union* remained by the little letter of marque until she burned to the water's edge, and then gave chase to the *Baker,* which in the meantime was beating seaward. About 3.30 in the afternoon the enemy again took possession of the schooner. The Confederate prize crew[9] was thrown into double irons, and a second United States prize crew continued the interrupted voyage to New York.

Closely following the *York* came the *Mariner* to the rendezvous at Hatteras. This privateer was a small screw-steamer, single masted, fitted out at Wilmington under the command of Captain B. W. Berry. She mounted one 6-pounder rifle and two 12-pounder smooth

[9] Composed of Patrick McCarthy, Arch. Wilson, John Williams, and James Riley.—*NWR,* I, 1, p. 61.

bores, and carried about thirty men. On July 25, she captured and brought in her only prize, the schooner *Nathaniel Chase*. It was the same day that the *Gordon* arrived with her first prize in tow.

This new letter of marque was of Charleston outfitting. She had been a packet running on the Charleston-Fernandina line, and was a fast side-wheel steamer of 519 tons. She carried fifty men and mounted three very fair pieces of ordnance. Her commander, Captain Thomas J. Lockwood, at the commencement of the war the master of a sister ship, the *Carolina,* likewise belonging to the Florida Steam Packet Company, had been handed his commission on July 15.[10]

On the morning of the seventeenth, the *Gordon* left Charleston and stood up the coast of the Carolinas. She met with no interference from blockading vessels except in the vicinity of Cape Romain. There she encountered one, which she eluded by putting into a North Carolina port. After eluding the enemy, Captain Lockwood again put to sea. At seven A.M., on the twenty-fifth, while some forty miles off Hatteras, he fell in with the brig *William McGilvery,* of Bangor, Maine, freighting Cuban molasses to Boston. To advise the Yankee skipper that his presence was desired on board the steamer, a shot was fired in his direction. It fell short, and the brig paid it no heed. But a second shot passed disconcertingly between the head stays and the foresail, and Master Hiram Carlisle hove to. The privateer steamed alongside, and ordered the obstinate skipper to come on board with his papers. This he declined to do until

[10] Lockwood's account of his cruise may be found in *Mercury,* August 31, 1861.

Captain Lockwood threatened to sink his brig under him. All hard-headedness then disappeared, and Carlisle discreetly complied without further ado. The papers showing the *McGilvery* to be a lawful prize, the *Gordon* carried her into Hatteras Inlet to join the goodly company of prizes assembled there.

The *Gordon* was on the wing again without loss of time; and soon fell in with the schooner *Protector,* of and for Philadelphia, with luscious fruit from the beautiful Cuban port of Matanzas. This prize hove to promptly when a shot went hurtling across her bow. Making fast to her with a towline, the privateer returned to the rendezvous.

On the thirtieth, while cruising off Cape Lookout, the *Gordon* was seen by a United States man-of-war, which gave chase; but the privateer showed a clean pair of heels and made into Beaufort, North Carolina. Here she remained three days and then returned to Hatteras.

The privateer *Gordon* and the C.S.S. *Winslow* were the leading vessels on the station, and got the prizes. The smaller public- and private-armed ships, however, did not fail to carry on. The routine on these lesser war vessels may be exemplified from the log of the *Beaufort* —a little gunboat which later played a gallant part in all the fleet actions in the James River from the memorable March 8, 1862, to the fall of Richmond in April, 1865. The terse phrases of the watch officer etch for us a picture of the life on the rendezvous:[11]

August 1. The lookout at the light-house signalized a man-of-war steamer to the southward. At 12 M. cleared ship for action and got the ship ready for slipping cable. Enemy

[11] *NWR,* I, 6, pp. 794-795.

stood down for the entrance and laid to for some time, then stood back close inshore, reconnoitering the harbor, and finally steamed away to the northward. At 3.25 called all hands to quarters and prepared the ship for action, bringing our gun to bear on the steamer standing in for the entrance and which afterwards was ascertained to be the *Mariner*. At 4.25 the *Mariner* came to anchor in the Old Swash. At 5 P.M. [C.S.S.] *Edwards* signalized, bearing to the southward. At 5.30 the *Edwards* came to anchor in Wallace's Channel.

August 2. At 7.30 A.M. the *Mariner* put to sea, returning and anchoring in Wallace's Channel. At 10.15 the [C.S. army steamer] *Post Boy* came to anchor off Beacon Island. At 2.40 steamer signalized from the light-house, which was soon discovered to be the privateer *Gordon*, bound to the northward.

August 3. At 5.10 A.M. a fore-and-after reported off the bar. Got up steam immediately and at 5.30 stood out in chase of schooner, the [C.S.S.] *Teaser* also getting up steam. At 6.15 crossed the bar, the steamer *Teaser* standing out after us. Stood up N.E. by E. for the chase, and when near enough to see her, a squall of rain being between us and the schooner, saw a steamer near her, which we took to be the *Gordon*, and being satisfied that we had lost the prize stood back again for our anchorage. The *Teaser* stood on for the schooner. The *Gordon* finally left the schooner and stood in for Hatteras. The *Teaser* went alongside of the schooner and afterwards left her and stood out to sea. The schooner must have been one of our own vessels or under British colors and clearance. Took up our usual anchorage. Sent a boat with pilot and second master to erect a proper mast for signals. At 10.45 a sail reported in sight to the southward. At 11.20 the steamer *Colonel Hill* hove in sight. At 12.30 got underway and stood out for a three masted schooner, and, on nearing her, discovered the *Gordon* near by and that the schooner was sailing under British colors and bound for one of our ports——New Berne, I think; returned to our anchorage.

August 4. At daylight signal made from the lookout at Ocracoke light-house, "Man-of-war to the northward." The *Mariner* and *Gordon* went to sea. The *Gordon* stood to the northward and eastward, the *Mariner* to the southward and eastward. Signals made from the light-house, "Several sail in sight." Waiting the appearance of the man-of-war [which had been signaled]. At 11, not seeing any man-of-war, concluded to go out to sea, and got underway, crossed the bar, and stood out to sea S. E. by E. and ran out about 10 miles. Saw the smoke of a steamer to the northward and eastward. A thick black squall of rain setting in ahead of us and shutting off our view to seaward, and not considering it proper to go out further, a signal made from the light-house which we read to be, "A man-of-war to the northward," stood in for the bar and steamed up to our anchorage. Sent to the light-house; signal was wrong, and that no man-of-war was in sight. Also learned that the *Winslow* had towed one brig into Hatteras and the *Gordon* two schooners. The man at the lookout said had we stood on, which we should have done if the signal had been made right, twenty minutes longer we would have come up with a schooner, the thick rain squall preventing us from seeing her. At 4.30 the C.S.S. *Ellis* came in and anchored near Portsmouth, Captain Muse commanding. At 5.20 the [C.S.S.] *Junaluska* came in and anchored near Portsmouth, having on board Commodore Barron and suite, on a tour of inspection to the different stations. Captain Cooke, of the *Edwards*, reported his ship as being entirely worthless, the boilers worn out and the timbers of his vessel rotten.

August 5. At 9.15 A.M. sent a boat to the light-house to

give instruction relative to signals and to attach halyards for the purpose of more distinctly displaying the signals to us. Signal made from the light-house on Ocracoke, "A small sail to the northward and eastward," which proved to be the privateer *York*, which stood off to the southward and eastward. At 7 the *Gordon* came in and anchored inshore of us. No chance for the *Beaufort* as long as these fast steamers are here.

The first schooner taken on the fourth by the *Gordon* was the *Henry Nutt,* from Key West for Philadelphia, having on board a quantity of logwood and mahogany. After placing a prize crew on board, the *Gordon* towed her into Hatteras, and then returned to the hunting ground. There the guns of the privateer soon persuaded the schooner *Sea Witch,* of and for New York, from Baracoa, Cuba, to bring her cargo of tropical fruit into the inlet—for the delectation of the North Carolinians.

The activities of the Hatteras gentlemen had become a thorn in the side of the United States commercial interests. On August 9, six marine insurance companies addressed a joint petition to the Hon. Gideon Welles, Secretary of the United States Navy, reciting that their loss "is and has been very heavy," and concluding: "Any project by which this nest of pirates could be broken up would be hailed with gratitude by all interested in commerce."[12]

How the impunity with which the Confederate gunboats and privateers operated out of Hatteras against Union shipping humiliated officers of the United States navy is attested by a letter to Secretary Welles, dated

[12] *NWR,* I, 1, p. 60.

August 10, and written by a lieutenant on board the sloop-of-war *Cumberland*. He[13] wrote:

> I trust in bringing this communication to the notice of the Department, that I may not lay to myself the charge of officiousness; but if I err in so doing, it will be considered in the light of an excess of zeal for the public service.
>
> It seems that the coast of Carolina is infested with a nest of privateers that have thus far escaped capture, and, in the ingenious method of their cruising, are probably likely to avoid the clutches of our cruisers.
>
> Hatteras Inlet, a little south of Cape Hatteras light, seems their principal rendezvous. Here they have a fortification that protects them from assault. A lookout at the light-house proclaims the coast clear, and a merchantman in sight; they dash out and are back again in a day with their prize. So long as these remain it will be impossible to entirely prevent their depredations, for they do not venture out when men-of-war are in sight; and, in the bad weather of the coming season, cruisers cannot always keep their stations off these inlets without great risk of going ashore.
>
> Let eight or ten tugboats be chartered, of not more than 7 feet draft—some less—armed with a 32-pounder and carrying in tow a man-of-war launch with its gun and crew. A steamer of the *Iroquois* or *Seminole* class, with a smaller gunboat, can silence the battery from the outside. Let the fleet of steamers enter the inlet, and cruising in couplets, explore Albemarle and Pamlico sounds. In three weeks there will not be a vessel left that can be productive of harm.
>
> These tugboats should be paddle-wheel, not propellers, as the latter draw too much water, carry 20 men, and may be equipped sufficiently for the service in forty-eight hours. Let them be officered temporarily by the officers of the At-

---

[13] Thos. O. Selfridge.—*NWR*, I, 6, p. 72-73.

lantic fleet, and in three weeks nothing more will be heard of Carolina privateers.

But the United States Navy Department had its own novel plans under way for the closing of the North Carolina inlets. The intention was to seal the entrances to the sounds by sinking in them old vessels loaded with stone. To cover these operations a joint army and navy force was being organized in Hampton Roads. By the middle of August the expedition was ready, but the prevalence of high winds and rough seas delayed the sailing until near the end of the month.

In the meantime, the Confederates, unaware that their day was drawing to a close, continued their forays. But United States flags—due to transfers of registry or to lack of cargoes—were rapidly becoming scarce, and most of the ships overhauled were flying British colors. After her two captures on the fourth, although remaining almost continuously at sea, the *Gordon* saw only two enemy merchantmen and they were under convoy of men-of-war. Then on the twenty-seventh, when putting out from the rendezvous, the privateer made ten ships in the offing, which were supposed to be United States vessels. Seven of them appeared to be steamers and three sailing vessels. Captain Lockwood thought it best to give such an assemblage a wide berth, and stood for a southward cruise. That night, Tuesday, he put into Wilmington, where he remained two days. Early Friday morning, he left the Cape Fear and steamed for home. Passing Bull's Bay he saw a large man-of-war and upon arriving off the Charleston bar he found two more. But they were "not keeping up the blockade—at least, they were unable to keep out the *Gordon,*" said her captain to a news reporter shortly after coming to an anchorage in Charleston harbor, on the afternoon of that same Friday, August 30.

On the morning of the twentieth, the *Winslow* brought in the last of the Hatteras prizes, the steamer *Itasca.* Exactly a week later the Fortress Monroe expedition, which the *Gordon* had sighted, appeared within sight of Cape Hatteras Light, and, during the afternoon, anchored to the southward of the cape. Surf boats were hoisted out and preparations were made for landing troops on the next morning.

Col. William F. Martin, commanding Forts Clark and Hatteras, which guarded the inlet, was an interested spectator of these proceedings. With the aid of his glass he made out the formidable proportions of the expedition, which consisted of the screw frigates *Minnesota,* 47, flagship to Commodore Stringham, and *Wabash,* 46, the sailing sloop *Cumberland,* 24, the screw sloops, *Susquehannah,* 15, and *Pawnee,* 9, the gunboats *Harriet Lane,* 5, and *Monticello,* 3, the steam transports *Adelaide* and *George Peabody,* and the army tug *Fanny.* There were two regiments of infantry volunteers and a company of artillery regulars on board the transports, under command of Brigadier General Benjamin F. Butler. In addition there was the flotilla of stone ships.

It so happened that none of the public- or private-armed vessels of the Confederacy were that day on the station. Colonel Martin, whose garrison consisted of about 350 men, at once sent a courier by small boat to the camp on Portsmouth Island at Ocracoke Inlet for reinforcements.

113

With daylight the next morning the enemy landed troops at a point up the beach, well screened from the forts. A little before nine the squadron stood in and opened fire at long range upon Fort Clark, the smaller and nearer of the two Confederate works. The Confederates returned the fire, but were outranged. By noon all the artillery ammunition in Fort Clark having been expended, the garrison spiked its guns and withdrew to the larger stronghold. Upon Fort Hatteras the bombardment was continued until nightfall.

During the afternoon Commodore Samuel Barron, C.S.N., commanding the naval defenses of North Carolina and Virginia, arrived in the *Winslow*, accompanied by the *Ellis*. That night a great gun was landed from the little flagship and was mounted in the fort on a navy carriage, doing splendid work during the next morning's battle. Colonel Martin, an infantryman, was completely exhausted, and persuaded Commodore Barron to accept the sole command. Thus did the old naval officer, in singleness of patriotism, essay the rôle of coast artilleryman.

The enemy's landing party had been busy during the night, and with the morning the defenders of the fort found themselves fired upon not only from the sea, but also from a battery of naval howitzers planted on the land side. All the morning the enemy's squadrons, from a position just beyond the reach of the greatest elevation of the Confederate guns, poured a flood of shells into the fort. A regiment arrived from Portsmouth, but too late to be of any assistance. Toward noon Barron called a council of war, which "unanimously agreed that holding out longer could only result in a greater loss of life, without the ability to damage our adversaries." A white flag was then displayed, and the garrison surrendered unconditionally.

The *Winslow* and the *Ellis* escaped into the inland waters; but Hatteras, an incomparable sally port upon the extensive navigation which must pass that way, was permanently lost to the Confederate commerce-destroyers.

X

THE SUCCESSFUL CAREER OF THE SALLIE

" 'Privateer! Privateer!! Privateer!!!'

A FIRST class vessel, 170 tons, drawing 6 feet water when loaded for a cruise of four months, will be fitted out for a Privateer as soon as the shares are taken. Those wishing to invest will apply at this office." So ran a notice in the Charleston *Courier,* on Thursday, June 20, 1861, and on a number of days following.

Already there were several private-armed ventures under way in the Carolinian port—as has been seen—and the shares of the *Sallie* seem to have been taken slowly. In any event, it was a little over three months before the company was made up and a letter of marque was secured.[1]

The schooner *Sallie* was a smart clipper, built on Long Island, as the *Virginia,* in 1856. She was armed with one gun and manned by a crew of some forty-odd men. The skipper was Captain Henry S. Lebby, formerly in command of the ship *Gondar,* which plied between Charleston and Liverpool.

On Wednesday evening, October 9, at six o'clock, the privateer crossed North Edisto bar, and stood out to sea. No blockaders were at first in sight, but shortly a cruiser bore down upon the trim little letter of marque,

---

[1] The name of this privateer is spelled *Sallie* in the letter of marque, but in the press it generally appears as *Sally.* The principal data for this chapter may be found in *NWR,* I, 1, and II, 1, and Capt. Lebby's account of his cruise in *Courier,* November 12, 1861.

which, however, soon showed her big antagonist that pursuit was folly.

The next day nothing was seen, but on Friday, a little past noon, a large ship was sighted and the whole afternoon was spent in chase. With night a heavy squall came up, and the tempting prize was lost.

At eight, the next evening, a sail was made on the weather bow, and a chase was promptly begun. Toward midnight the privateersmen got within range of the chase and fired a shot in token that they desired that the stranger should lay to. But to this notice the stranger paid no heed. Steadily but slowly gaining on her and firing an occasional shot, the *Sallie,* at length, about three o'clock, the next morning, came up with the *Prince Alfred,* a British schooner, with live stock, going from New York to Nassau—a lot of wasted energy and ammunition.

It was now Sunday and the day passed quietly, as it should. With the bells announcing the advent of Monday, and the position about latitude 33° north, longitude 71° west, a sail was reported, again on the weather bow. Chase was made, and in an hour's time the privateersmen were consoled for their hard luck of the night before. A single shot across the bow of the stranger brought to the brig *Granada,* 255 tons. The master was ordered on board with his papers, which showed the prize to be of Portland, Maine, with a cargo of sugar, honey, molasses, mahogany, and cedar, from Nuevitas, Cuba, for New York. The Yankees being removed to the privateer, with the exception of the first officer, Russell Butterfield, who was left on board, the brig was put in charge of Lieutenant Edwin Bryant with a prize

118

crew of six men. Before the privateer parted company with the prize, the Confederate flag was displayed to the British steamer *Active,* in passage from New York to Nassau. At half past eight, breakfast over, the *Granada* was on the wing for the Confederacy, and the *Sallie* stood eastward to intercept coffee ships from Brazil.

On Tuesday forenoon the fine feeling of the privateersmen was clouded by an accident. Toby Prig, sailor and unlucky, fell overboard and was drowned, despite every effort to save him. His berth, it may be said, was scarcely allowed to become cool; for later in the day, two Yankee seamen, named Robert Andrews and James McDonald, captured on the *Granada,* decided that they liked the *Sallie* and her prospects. They went before the captain and told him their desire to join his people; and upon their signing the shipping articles they were admitted to the Confederate service.

Late in the afternoon of Wednesday, October 16, a sail was descried on the starboard bow, which on being overhauled was found to be an English schooner, the *Greyhound,* from St. Domingo for New York. The Englishman kindly consented to receive as passengers the captives from the *Granada,* provided that they brought with themselves their bread and bacon. These Captain Lebby cheerfully furnished.

The next day, half an hour after noon, a sail was sighted on the port beam, and the *Sallie* was put about for her. Then the wind died down, but the privateersmen lowered a boat and two of the junior officers, Lieutenants Stuart and Seabrook, with a file of marines, pulled off for her. After they had rowed a considerable way, the wind freshened and took the prize out of their reach.

No sooner was the boat hoisted on deck than a more desirable vessel was sighted and all sail was crowded on for pursuit. But it was now nearly night, and with the coming of dark the quarry made her escape. During the wee hours of the following morning another sail was made on the port bow, and kept in sight until daylight. The new victim was a good sailer, and it was well into the forenoon before she was overhauled. The second shot across her bow brought to the hermaphrodite brig *Betsey Ames*. She proved to be of Wells, Maine, bound from New York for Cardenas, with six passengers and a cargo, which, as was afterward recited in the Prize Court proceedings, consisted "of machinery, boilers, flues, apples, onions, cabbages, corn meal, animal carbon, and other articles." Lieutenant Tolle went on board as prize master, with several seamen and marines, and some ten days later arrived with the prize in Charleston harbor.

Again the lure of privateering tempted the enemy's seamen to join the Confederate colors, and, on the day following her capture, two of the brig's company enlisted.

Now followed a very quiet week, at the end of which the *Sallie* anchored in the roads on the north side of Abaco Island, among the Bahamas. Several days were spent in replenishing the water casks.

On the first day under canvas again, Tuesday, the twenty-ninth, a number of sails were seen, and the schooner *B. G. Harris* and the brig *Tempest,* were overhauled.[2] By an irony, both proved to be so worthless as to vessel and cargo that the privateersmen did not waste time even to destroy them. During that night the *Sallie* passed, undetected, within range of the guns of an enemy's cruiser. On the next day, luck changed and the staunch new brig *Elsinore,* of Bangor, Maine, on voyage to Cuba with hoops, sugar boxes, and lumber, was taken. Lieutenant Stuart and five seamen took her in charge and stood for home.

Early the following morning another sail was made, which, shortly afterward, "Old Jake"—as the privateersmen had affectionately named their great gun—bade heave to. The peremptory command was obeyed without delay. Captain Lebby found his prize to be the brigantine *B. K. Eaton,* of Searsport, Maine, chartered by the United States Government and sailing from New York with a cargo of lime and cement. The crew having been removed, this transport was scuttled and set on fire.

During the afternoon of the same day a sail was sighted, but she proved to be the prize brig *Elsinore* making her way to a Confederate court in admiralty. In due course the *Elsinore* arrived in Savannah and was libeled and condemned, ship and cargo, in the District Court for Georgia.[3]

The *Sallie* had been now a little over three weeks at

2 *Mercury,* November 4, 1861.

3 *Minute Book, Admiralty Cases,* C. S. Dist. Ct. for Ga. (now in U. S. Dist. Ct., Savannah, Ga.). The decree was entered on December 31, 1861. The brig's tackle, apparel, and furniture, and the cargo were sold, and the proceeds were paid into the Registry of the Court and ordered to be distributed in accordance with law. The *Elsinore* was sunk, in November, 1861, in the Savannah River as an obstruction to the advance of the enemy's fleet.

sea, and had not been seriously menaced by the enemy, but her exemption was drawing to a close. It was Hallowe'en when trouble began. "The night was pitchy black," the skipper afterward related, "the wind was high, the schooner was bounding over the troubled waters at her utmost speed, when a large light was descried on her starboard bow." But it was no phantom, for "in a few minutes, she passed so near a Lincoln steam frigate that the striking of seven bells, and the 'All's well' of the sentinel were distinctly heard." It was a bad quarter of an hour on the *Sallie;* but presently it was found that ships that pass in the night do not always speak each other, and the privateer evaded the enemy, unobserved.

The next morning at dawn, there was in sight a United States cruiser, which soon made things quite hot for Miss *Sallie*. Being now in the vicinity of Charleston, Captain Lebby concluded to run for that port. At length Light House Inlet was made, with the enemy in close pursuit. It seemed veritably a case of the devil or the deep blue sea; for ahead was a perilous passage, through white caps and over numerous sand bars. But better, thought the privateersmen, to run the risk of drowning than to fall into the hands of an enemy who wished to hang them. Again and again the schooner thumped the bars, till every plank and spar creaked and groaned. The breakers rolled over the gunwales. But not despairing, the intrepid crew held her straight, and the last bar was safely crossed, leaving the man-of-war outside. The *Sallie* again dropped anchor in the broad, safe harbor of Charleston.

A successful and profitable cruise it had been for the

people and owners of the *Sallie*. The *Granada* and the *Betsey Ames* were sold at public auction upon order of the Prize Court, on November 19, John Fraser and Company purchasing the vessels at $7,000 each. This firm was the Charleston branch of the Liverpool house of Fraser, Trenholm and Company, the Confederate States depository in England. The successful bids for the several items in the cargoes indicate a beginning in the rising cost of commodities due to the war. Sugar quotations in the spring had stood at $4\frac{1}{2}$ to 5 cents, but the sugar in hogsheads on the *Granada* brought $6\frac{5}{8}$ to $7\frac{3}{4}$ cents. Other prices that prevailed at the auction were $42\frac{1}{2}$ to 47 cents a gallon for molasses, $2\frac{1}{8}$ to $2\frac{1}{4}$ cents a pound for melada, 70 cents a gallon for honey, $11.62 to $12.50 for opium, $52\frac{1}{2}$ to 80 cents a cubic foot for cedar, and $1.00 a cubic foot for mahogany.[4]

The owners decided to pocket the profits and advertised for sale the "privateer schooner Sallie, with her sails, rigging, anchors and chains, also gun carriage and cutlasses, barrels beef, pork, flour, bread, mackrel, beans, molasses, sugar; boxes soap, tea, raisins, vermicelli, &c.; large lot of water casks; large lot of mattresses, 1 extra sized cooking stove complete, suitable for a hotel, 1 chronometer, 1 barometer, 1 clock, 2 harness casks, lot tin ware, 2 coffee mills, lot water buckets, 5 lanterns, lot of crockery, lot of hardware, medicine chest, grape shot and balls." The sale took place on December 5, and the schooner was knocked down for $3,200.[5]

[4] *Mercury,* November 19 and 20, 1861.
[5] *Courier,* December 6, 1861.

XI

THE PETREL, THE BEAUREGARD, AND THE RATTLESNAKE, PRIVATEERS WHICH UNLUCKILY MEASURED ARMS WITH MEN-OF-WAR

*I*T was nearly two months after the engagement of the *Savannah* with the United States brig *Perry* already described, before another Confederate privateer was so indiscreet as to flirt with a regular man-of-war. This one was the letter of marque schooner *Petrel,* 2, Captain William Perry.

The *Petrel* before the war had been the revenue cutter *Aiken,* stationed at Charleston. Upon the secession of South Carolina, the state authorities seized her and employed her, for a time, in the Coast and Harbor Police. Then she was lent to the Marine School of Charleston, and was used as the schoolship—superseding an old, unseaworthy brig, named *Lodebar.*[1] Toward the end of May, the state, in line with the policy of all members of the new Confederacy, turned over to the Confederate Government its naval and military property. However, the Navy Department only accepted from South Carolina the *Lady Davis* and the *Fire Fly,* the other vessels not being thought suitable for naval purposes. So it came about that the *Aiken,* already renamed the *Petrel,* was offered for sale with other rejected vessels, "all of which are of the most approved models," as

---

suitable for privateering.[2] A group of Charleston gentlemen bought the old revenue cutter and fitted her up as a privateer, under a commission dated July 10.[3]

Her engagement with a man-of-war happened on the first morning of her cruise, July 28, 1861. She had run out of Charleston during the dark, wee hours. Not long after daylight the privateer and an enemy man-of-war made each other out. Captain Perry ran; and after him went Captain Purviance in the United States frigate *St. Lawrence,* 52. The chase lasted until ten o'clock. The *Petrel* being overhauled, Perry ran up the Confederate flag and went into action. The frigate likewise beat to quarters and commenced firing. A shot from the little 2-gun privateer passed through the enemy's mainsail and took a splinter out of the yard. The big 52-gun frigate from her forecastle battery then delivered a crushing eight-inch shell on the bow of the schooner. Perceiving that his vessel was sinking rapidly, Captain Perry at once struck his colors. The boats of the *St. Lawrence* were lowered and sent to rescue the sinking privateersmen, four of whom drowned. At ten-thirty the waters closed over the *Petrel,* and manacles were fastened on the thirty-six prisoners taken from her.[4]

The crew of the sunken letter of marque was later transferred to the U.S.S. *Flag,* and taken to Philadelphia to stand trial for piracy and treason.[5]

A tale was told in the Northern newspapers, and has

[2] *Courier,* May 25, 1861.

[3] Henry Buist, Maier Triest, Wm. Whaley, Geo. A. Locke, Thos. J. Legare, A. J. Salinas, Wm. M. Martin, Geo. W. King, Daniel Haas, and Q. B. Oakes.—*NWR,* II, 1, pp. 370-371.

[4] *NWR,* I, 1, p. 51; *Mercury,* August 25, 1861; *Courier,* August 30, 1861.

[5] *NWR,* I, 6, p. 69.

been repeated between book covers, that the *St. Lawrence* disguised herself as a merchantman, and decoyed the *Petrel* to her fate. Captain Perry positively denied this story and said that he was aware of the character of his adversary from the beginning of the chase.[6]

The third privateer which was destined to a short and useless life at sea was the *Beauregard*. This vessel had been the *Priscilla C. Ferguson,* of Charleston, and was a schooner of 101 tons burden. In August an advertisement ran in the Charleston *Mercury* inviting subscriptions to fit her out as a privateer. All the shares were taken in Charleston with the exception of one subscription from upstate.[7] The commission was issued on October 14; and on November 5, mounting one 24-pounder pivot rifle, and carrying a crew of 27, she put to sea.

This long, low, rakish-looking privateer was said veritably to resemble the pirates that in the years before had infested the same waters.

When daylight came on the seventh day of her cruise, the *Beauregard,* now in the Bahama Channel, sighted a bark and gave chase. The letter of marque bore down on the stranger expecting a good prize, but upon getting within four miles of the bark, she discovered her mistake. The bark was no merchantman, but a man-of-war. The *Beauregard,* which had been running before the wind, now suddenly hauled by the wind and at-

---

[6] *True Delta,* August 17, 1861, quoting *Philadelphia Press; Mercury,* August 17, 1861, quoting *New York Tribune,* August 9.

[7] James G. Gibbes, of Columbia, the others being: A. F. W. Abrams, Jeffords Cie., Reeder and DeSaussure, John F. O'Neill, Geo. Brown, Jas. Chapman, Bernard O'Neill, E. B. Stoddard & Co., Archd. McLeirt, C. Wellborn, Snyder & Cordray, John G. Crane & Saml. J. Corrie, H. B. & A. L. Olney, W. J. Miller, Peter Tetzenburg, George L. Buist, Johnston & Miller, John Burke, H. Burwinkle, and Gilbert Hay.—*NWR,* II, 1, p. 391.

tempted to escape. The man-of-war immediately made all sail in chase and in two hours brought her under his lee. Gilbert Hay, the privateer captain—who will be remembered as prize master on board the ill-fated bark *Alvarado,* captured by the *Jefferson Davis*—had learned somewhat of Union warships. He did not need to be taught the immense disadvantage inherent in seven guns against his one. Consequently, when called on to bring his papers on board the *Anderson,* he obeyed without hesitation. Since the vessels were only three days' sail from Key West, the captive privateer was taken to that port; and the four officers and twenty-three men composing her crew were there imprisoned as pirates.[8]

The time had passed, however, when the Lincoln Cabinet might really have expected to hang Confederate seamen on the charge of piracy, and the continuance of their imprisonment as felons was purely a matter of spleen or pride, as we shall see in the next chapter.

Incidentally, the *Beauregard* was condemned by the enemy Prize Court at Key West, and sold to the United States Navy, February 24, 1862, for the sum of $1,810. She was put in commission as a cruiser in the East Gulf Blockading Squadron in the spring, armed with one 30-pounder Parrott rifle and two heavy 12-pounder howitzers. She performed good service, and during the three remaining years of the war shared in the capture of six schooners and seven sloops. When the Navy Department began to reduce its forces in the summer of 1865, the one-time merchantman, privateer, and cruiser was sold at auction in Key West for $8,000. So the capture

[8] *NWR,* I, 1, pp. 206, 207, 211; *Courier,* December 7, 1861.

on November 12 proved a profitable one to the United States.⁹

About a year later, Captain T. Harrison Baker, who had commanded the unlucky *Savannah,* and was now released from prison, wished to try his hand a second time against Yankee commerce. He purchased the transport *Thomas L. Wragg,* which, after bringing into Savannah a cargo of arms in July, 1862, had been too closely blockaded to go again to sea.¹⁰

It seems that this vessel had been foreordained to be a privateer. A letter of marque for her had been applied for by C. H. Stevens, of Charleston, on May 4, 1861, when she was the steam packet *Nashville,* lately of the New York-Charleston line; but the Navy Department had stepped in and bought her, commissioning her as the cruiser *Nashville,* and later changing her into a cargo transport. Baker renamed his vessel the *Rattlesnake,* mounted six guns, signed up 130 men, and secured a letter of marque and reprisal, as of November 5, 1862. Thoroughly refitted and painted battleship gray the *Rattlesnake,* 1220 tons, presented a very fine appearance.¹¹

But ill luck pursued Captain Baker, and no reasonable opportunity offered for getting to sea. The blockaders were persistently waiting for him to come out from his place of equipment in the Ogeechee River, just above Fort McAllister.¹² His predicament was somewhat similar to the plight of that other privateer of the same

---

⁹ *NWR,* I, vol. 17, and II, vol. 1; *Annual Report of Secretary of the Navy,* 1865.

¹⁰ *NWR,* I, 13, pp. 193, 349, 417.

¹¹ *Ibid.,* II, 1, pp. 334, 412-415.

¹² *Ibid.,* I, 13, pp. 507, 523, 543.

name in American history, the *Rattlesnake* of Philadelphia, which was caught and eventually lost in the blockade of La Rochelle by the English during the spring of 1814. Late in January, 1863, the blockaders tired of waiting and decided to go up the river and get him.

On the twenty-fourth, the monitor *Montauk,* the wooden gunboats *Seneca, Dawn,* and *Wissahickon,* and the mortar schooner *C. P. Williams* stood in from Ossabaw Bar, but on account of a dense fog made little progress. The weather cleared up on the afternoon of the twenty-sixth, and the squadron proceeded to an anchorage three miles below the fort. Early the next morning, the monitor advanced to within 1,500 yards from the Confederate position, but the wooden vessels stopped about a mile farther downstream. At 7.35 in the morning the fifteen- and eleven-inch Dahlgrens of the Union squadron opened fire, and the Confederates replied with their lighter guns, the heaviest of which was only an eight-inch Columbiad. The first Confederate shot registered on the ironclad. A spirited engagement followed and lasted until noon. Commander John L. Worden, U.S.N., senior officer of the squadron, reported:

At 11.55 A.M., our supply of shells being expended, finding that our cored shot did not affect the enemy, or at least we could not observe their effect with certainty, I ordered the firing to cease, tripped our anchor, and stood down the river, and ordered the gunboats to discontinue the action.

At 1.05 P.M. I anchored, and upon examination I found that this vessel [*Montauk*] was hit fourteen times, to wit, four times on turret, three times on side armor, four times on deck armor, once on smokestack, once in second cutter, and once on a spar lashed athwart our stern as a stern moor-

CONFEDERATE STATES PRIVATEER STEAMER RATTLESNAKE

From an aquarelle in the possession of the United States Naval Library and Records.

ing for our boats. There were no casualties on any of the vessels.

Having received a fresh supply of ammunition, the attackers returned up stream on February 1, and went into action as before, except that the monitor moved up to about 600 yards from the fort. This time the firing began at 7.45 and ended at 11.53 A.M. "with no signs of doing the enemy's guns any damage," as Commander Worden was again obliged to report. But the Confederates, who, as before, had concentrated their fire on the *Montauk,* placed 48 projectiles on the ironclad, fracturing the armor in many places and shooting away practically everything on deck, such as smokestacks, flagstaffs, small boats, and anchors.

The severe trouncing administered to the enemy by the combined armaments of the fort and the *Rattlesnake* —two of whose guns had been landed and emplaced on Richmond Bluff in the rear of Fort McAllister—elicited the thanks of Congress and a departmental general order authorizing "Fort McAllister" to be inscribed on the flags of the defenders.

On the last day of February, the unrelenting enemy came up to try again, and went into action very much as on the other occasions. But this time the engagement had only been in progress a short time, when a shell exploded on the *Rattlesnake,* which had gotten aground, and set her on fire. The flames soon got beyond control. The big pivot rifle abaft the foremast burst from the heat, and half an hour later the magazine exploded with terrific violence, leaving her a shattered, smoking ruin. The *Montauk* was struck five times but had received

131

no appreciable damage when, the mission accomplished, the squadron began its withdrawal. The enemy's flagship, however, was not to go scot free; on the way back down the river, she struck a submarine mine, which warped and tore the bottom so that she had to be beached for repairs.[13]

[13] *NWR,* I, 13, pp. 626-639, 696-709.

XII

THE TRIAL OF THE "PIRATES"

*A*S soon as President Davis learned that the United States Government was proceeding to execute its threat to treat privateersmen as pirates and that the crew of the unlucky *Savannah* had been taken to New York and confined at the Tombs in cells set apart for felons, he dispatched a protest on July 6 to President Lincoln, at the hands of an officer of his personal staff. The letter ran:

It is the desire of this Government so to conduct the war now existing as to mitigate its horrors as far as may be possible; and, with this intent, its treatment of the prisoners captured by its forces has been marked by the greatest humanity and leniency consistent with public obligations; some have been permitted to return home on parole, others to remain at large under similar conditions within this Confederacy, and all have been furnished with rations for their subsistence, such as are allowed to our own troops. It is only since the news has been received of the treatment of the prisoners taken on the *Savannah* that I have been compelled to withdraw these indulgencies, and to hold the prisoners taken by us in strict confinement.

A just regard to humanity and to the honor of this Government now requires me to state explicitly that, painful as will be the necessity, this Government will deal out to the prisoners held by it the same treatment and the same fate as shall be experienced by those captured on the *Savannah,* and if driven to the terrible necessity of retaliation by your execution of any of the officers or the crew of the *Savannah,*

133

that retaliation will be extended so far as shall be requisite to secure the abandonment of a practice unknown to the warfare of civilized man, and so barbarous as to disgrace the nation which shall be guilty of inaugurating it.[1]

Lincoln declined to receive Davis' aide, but the communication was accepted through Winfield Scott, General-in-Chief at Washington, who promised a reply. None was made—though, undoubtedly, its contents were seriously pondered.[2]

[1] *Messages and Papers of the Confederacy*, I, 115-116; *NWR*, II, 3, p. 104.

[2] From a Richmond dispatch of July 12 to the *Memphis Appeal* (quoted in New Orleans *True Delta*, July 18, 1861), we learn that the bearer of the letter was Col. Thomas H. Taylor, and that he went by rail as far as Manassas Junction. At Fairfax he was given an escort of a platoon of cavalry under Lieutenant Breckinridge, and proceeded under a flag of truce toward Arlington. About seven miles from the Potomac bridgehead the Confederates met an outpost detachment of dragoons under Col. Andrew Porter, U.S.A. After the formalities usual to such meetings, characterized by civility and military honor on both sides, Colonel Porter inquired after the health of *Colonel* Lee, who had been his comrade-in-arms in other days; but Colonel Taylor did not know the officer. Thereupon Colonel Porter corrected himself and inquired as to the state of health of *General* Lee, and was informed. The colonel-courier was then taken to the headquarters of Major General McDowell, commanding the army of the Potomac, to whom he bore an unsealed letter. The general being absent, word was sent to Washington of the arrival of the emissary from Richmond. Old "Fuss and Feathers," Lieutenant General Scott, Virginian, Commander-in-Chief of the Armies of the United States, at once sent a carriage with his senior aide-de-camp, Colonel Van Rensselaer, to convey Colonel Taylor to Washington. It was about ten in the evening when he arrived at the quarters of the lieutenant general, who received him, in full dress uniform, surrounded by his entire staff, "in all the pride, pomp, and circumstance of glorious war."

General Scott heard the object of the mission, received the letter to President Lincoln, read it, and dispatched a messenger to convey it to the President and to return with the reply.

"During the absence of the messenger General Scott ordered in wine, introduced Colonel Taylor to his staff, and invited the party to join him in a glass of champagne, a request to which those present responded with an alacrity altogether characteristic of the profession. After the lapse of half an hour, spent in conversation and the interchange of civilities, the messenger returned and reported that the president had retired and could

TRIAL OF THE "PIRATES"

The matter evoked a storm of criticism abroad. The position of the Lincoln administration was adversely commented upon in the British House of Lords. "If one thing was clearer than another," so the remarks of the Earl of Derby were reported, "it was that privateering was not piracy, and that no law could make that piracy, as regarded the subjects of one nation which was not by the law of nations. Consequently, the United States must not be allowed to entertain this doctrine, and to call upon her Majesty's Government not to interfere." The Lord Chancellor gave the opinion that those who treated a privateersman "as a pirate would be guilty of murder."[3]

After three weeks in jail, the *Savannah* privateersmen were again paraded through the streets. It was Wednesday, July 17; the indictment had been returned the day before. A large crowd of excited people followed them to the United States Circuit Court, in City Hall Park, and crowded the court room. The prisoners were placed within the bar, nor were their manacles removed.

not therefore be seen that night. General Scott, promising that a reply should be returned at an early hour, if not on the morrow, and that he would take care it should be entrusted to an officer who would deliver it to this [Confederate] government in person, dismissed Colonel Taylor, recommending him to the hospitalities of General McDowell, with whom he returned to Arlington. There he spent the remainder of the night and on Thursday morning after partaking breakfast at the quarters of General McDowell and being kindly supplied with files of Eastern papers, he bade adieu to his courteous host."

Colonel Taylor's arrival in Washington became generally known but the nature of his mission was withheld from the public. Even Russell, the foreign correspondent of the London *Times,* who was in Washington at the time, and was received in government circles, was unable to learn the subject of communication.—William Howard Russell, *My Diary North and South* (Boston: T. O. H. P. Burnham, 1863), pp. 396-397.

[3] Quoted in *The Rise and Fall of the Confederate States Government,* by Jefferson Davis (New York: D. Appleton & Co., 1881), II, 12.

"They regarded the crowd, and listened to the remarks of counsel with apparently great interest, but none of them seemed much alarmed at their position," wrote the *Herald's* reporter. They were soon to be called upon to plead to the charges.[4]

"I would now renew my motion," said the District Attorney, "that the prisoners at the bar be arraigned under the indictment presented yesterday."[5]

Counsel for the defendants objected that time had not been allowed them in which to examine the voluminous document; and the judge remanded the prisoners until the following Tuesday morning.

To defend the privateersmen, the Confederate Government employed Algernon Sidney Sullivan, a native of Ohio, "a tall, thin, distinguished looking man, a fine lawyer and an eloquent speaker."[6] But as he did not arrive in New York until a short time before the trial, the southern sympathizers in the city had already clubbed together to retain eminent counsel. There were Larocque, of the firm of Bowdoin, Larocque and Barlow, who was spoken of as "an aggressive but magnetic advocate of almost unexampled persistence and persuasive eloquence, as well as accurate professional learning," and Daniel Lord, "who by the amount of gray

[4] *New York Herald,* July 18, 1861.

[5] *Trial of the Officers and Crew of the Privateer* Savannah, *on the Charge of Piracy, in the United States Circuit Court for the Southern District of New York. Hon. Judges Nelson and Shipman, Presiding. Reported by A. F. Wharton, Stenographer, and corrected by the Counsel.* (New York: Baker & Godwin, printers, 1862), p. xiv. The District Attorney, E. Delafield Smith, was assisted by William M. Evarts, Samuel Blatchford, and Ethan Allen.

[6] *Memoirs of John Harleston,* quoted in an article on "John Harleston's Life," in *The Sunday News* (Charleston, S. C.), February 9, 1919. Harleston died on February 7, 1919.

matter in his brain compensated for his almost comic brevity of stature." They represented particularly Lieutenant Harleston. Lord had been a classmate of Harleston's father at Yale. James T. Brady, "of infinite resources in the perplexities of criminal jurisprudence," appeared for Captain Baker. James Ridgway and Maurice Mayer represented certain of the sailors. Joseph H. Dukes and Isaac Davega, former Charlestonians but practicing law in New York at the commencement of the war, volunteered their services.

When Tuesday came, the prisoners pleaded "not guilty" to the wordy document, accusing them on ten counts, which were mostly variations and repetitions of the gravamen:

That [to preserve the quaint language of the law] Thomas Harrison Baker, late of the City and County of New York, in the District and Circuit aforesaid, mariner; and John Harleston, late of the same place, mariner; Charles Sidney Passalaigue, late of the same place, mariner; Henry Cashman Howard, late of the same place, mariner; Joseph Cruz del Carno, late of the same place, mariner; Henry Oman, late of the same place, mariner; Patrick Daly, late of the same place, mariner; William Charles Clark, late of the same place, mariner; Albert Gallatin Ferris, late of the same place, mariner; Richard Palmer, late of the same place, mariner; John Murphy, late of the same place, mariner; Alexander Carter Coid, late of the same place, mariner; and Martin Galvin, late of the same place, mariner, on the 3d day of June, in the year of our Lord, 1861, upon the high seas, out of the jurisdiction of any particular State and within the admiralty and maritime jurisdiction of the said United States of America, and within the jurisdiction of this Court, each then and there being a citizen of the

THE CONFEDERATE PRIVATEERS

THE CONFEDERATE PRIVATEERS

United States of America, did, on pretense of authority from a person, to wit, one Jefferson Davis, with force and arms, piratically, feloniously, and violently, set upon, board, break, and enter a certain vessel, to wit, a brig, called the Joseph, then and there being owned by certain persons, citizens of the United States of America, to wit, George H. Cables, John Cables, and Stephen Hatch, of Rockland, in the State of Maine, and in and upon certain divers persons whose names are to the Jurors aforesaid unknown, the said last-mentioned persons each being then and there a mariner, and of the ship's company of the said brig called the Joseph, and then and there being in and on board of the said brig, the Joseph, did, on pretense of authority from a person, to wit, one Jefferson Davis, then and there piratically, feloniously, and violently, make an assault, and then did, on pretense of authority from one person, to wit, one Jefferson Davis, then and there, piratically, feloniously, and violently, put in bodily fear, and the said brig, the Joseph, of the value of $3,000, and the apparel, tackle, and furniture thereof, of the value of $500, of the goods, chattels, and personal property of the said George H. Cables, John Cables, and Stephen Hatch, and 250 hogsheads of sugar, of the value of $100 each hogshead, of the goods, chattels, and personal property of one Thies N. Meyer, from the said divers persons, mariners as aforesaid, whose names are to the Jurors aforesaid unknown, in their presence, then and there, and against their will, did, on pretense of authority from a person, to wit, one Jefferson Davis, then and there, piratically, feloniously, and violently, seize, rob, steal, take and carry away, against the form of the statute of the said United States of America in such case made and provided, and against the peace of the said United States and their dignity.[7]

[7] *Report of Trial,* pp. xi and xii.

TRIAL OF THE "PIRATES"

Mused the *New York Herald,* and was itself amusing:

Such is the form of the indictment in the case of the privateersmen now in this city awaiting their trial for piracy. In the olden time, the indictment ran—"moved by the instigation of the Devil." Now it is "on pretence of authority from one Jefferson Davis"; and most certainly he is a good substitute for Satan; for no other individual has ever done so great an amount of mischief in the world. According to the authority of Milton, before the creation of Adam and Eve the arch fiend had organized a rebellion in Heaven; and being cast down to Pandemonium with his angels, he sent out his privateers on a voyage of discovery over space, and subsequently landed himself in the Garden of Eden in the form of a serpent, and by his wiles blasted the happiness of the newly created first pair in Paradise, "introducing death into the world and all our woe." In the same way Jefferson Davis found the people happy and contented, under the best form of government in the world, and he resolved to destroy it, and set up a black dominion of his own, preferring, like the arch rebel of old, to "reign in Hell rather than serve in Heaven."[8]

In the absence of a full bench the defense objected to proceeding with the trial. A case tried in a circuit court could only be reviewed if there were a division of opinion between the two Justices who composed the Court; and the privateersmen did not wish to be deprived of a chance of such division. Only "the priestly-appearing Judge Shipman" was present, "the leonine Justice Samuel Nelson" being confined to his home from the effects of a fall from his carriage. The district attorney protested against any material delay on the

[8] Quoted in the *Savannah Daily News,* July 29, 1861.

139

ground that "if the prisoners ought justly to be convicted, such conviction should be speedy, in order to deter their confederates from expeditions partaking of the character of both treason and piracy." The Court, however, held to "the presumption of innocence which the law always interposes"; and continued the case until the fall term.

The principal statute under which the privateersmen stood accused as "pirates" was an Act of Congress of 1790, which provided:

That if any citizen shall commit any piracy or robbery aforesaid, or any act of hostility against the United States, or any citizen thereof, upon the high seas, under color of any commission from any foreign prince or State, or on pretence of authority from any person, such offender shall, notwithstanding the pretence of any such authority, be deemed, adjudged and taken to be a pirate, felon and robber, and on being thereof convicted, shall suffer death.

It is interesting to observe that a statute of similar language existed on the English law books during the War of the Revolution, yet the British had not found it practicable to enforce it against the American colonials who were indisputably rebels.

"The fact that this is the first case of its kind," commented the *New York World,* "and that it is likely not only to establish precedents but to bring to a decision one of the most important questions which have arisen in the rebellion, gives to the approaching trial a peculiar interest." The editor said that the evidence would probably indicate piracy, that the Court would so charge and the jury so convict. President Lincoln must then decide whether or not to show such clemency as would "prevent reprisals and avoid giving to the contest a more sanguinary character than it already has." But, "in this he will doubtlessly be guided by the voice of the people, which now at least demands unmistakably that if these pirates are convicted they shall be hanged."[9]

Three months elapsed and again the privateersmen, the "pirates," were in court. It was Wednesday morning, October 23. The court room was crowded to overflowing. Twelve men were on trial before twelve men.[10] The thirteenth prisoner, Ferris, had turned state's evidence.

The prosecuting attorney in his opening address to the jury after reciting and explaining the statutory law under which the prisoners were charged, said that a pirate "as generally and popularly understood . . . is deemed by the law of nations, and has always been regarded, as the enemy of the human race—as a man who depredates generally and indiscriminately on the commerce of all nations." The fact that the privateersmen only operated against the sea trade of the United States was, of course, so well known that the attorney felt obliged to seek protection for himself and his Government from the criticism of the intelligent world by adding: "whether or not the crime alleged here is piracy under the law of nations, is not material to the issue. . . . Congress is unquestionably empowered to pass laws for the protection of our national commerce and for the punishment of those who prey upon it. Congress

[9] July 18, 1861.

[10] The jury consisted of Edward Werner, Wm. H. Marshall, Wm. Powell, Jas. Cassidy, John Fife, Thos. Costello, Tuganhold Kron, Matthew P. Bogart, Geo. Moeller, Robt. Taylor, Dan. Bixby, and Geo. H. Hansell.— *Report of Trial*, pp. 1-14.

has done so in the statutes to which I have referred. . . .
Although the guilt and mischief of both piracy and
treason may be embraced in the crime and its consequences, the charge is not one of treason, nor necessarily
of piracy, as commonly understood, but the simple one
of violating the statutes." The letter of marque, signed
by Jefferson Davis, could have "no effect, in our courts
of law," because we have "never recognized the so-called
Confederate States as one of the family of nations."[11]

The first witness called was the renegade prisoner
who had turned State's evidence. The examination developed that he was born in Barnstable, Massachusetts,
in 1811, but had resided in Charleston with his family
since 1837. He was a seafaring man by trade and had
been in command of a schooner plying inland waters
when South Carolina seceded. His relation of the organization of the privateering venture and the subsequent cruise was simple and straightforward. The next
three witnesses testified as to the ownership of the prize
brig *Joseph,* after which the master and mate were
called. The second day of the trial Commodore Stringham and several other naval officers told what they
knew. There was no contest in the evidence. The facts
were simple and freely admitted by the defense, who
introduced no witnesses, only offering such documentary
evidence as to show the orderly processes whereby the
Confederate States Government had been formed and
the prize brig *Joseph* condemned in the Admiralty
Court at Charleston. It was altogether a question of
interpretation, of whether the acts amounted to piracy.

With the material facts developed, Mr. Larocque

[11] *Report,* pp. 16, 18, and 19.

opened the case for the defense. The court room was packed and tense. "Baker, the privateer captain, took a seat at the table occupied by his counsel, and on having been presented with a copy of the *Charleston Mercury,* perused it for some time, apparently"—observed the *New York Post's* reporter[12]—"with the deepest interest. His features wore a more stoical expression than during the proceedings yesterday. Young Passalaigue, an object of almost equal interest, exhibited his usual buoyancy of spirits, but occasionally assumed an appearance of much gravity. Harleston, who, when arraigned for indictment, appeared very uneasy, is now quite self-possessed. At times he is apparently altogether unconcerned."

We have now reached that stage in this interesting trial, [began Mr. Larocque, addressing the jury,] where the duty has been assigned to me, by my associates in this defense, of presenting to you the state of facts and the rules of law on which we expect to ask from you an acquittal of these prisoners.

He showed that the prisoners were not "of the City and County of New York . . . each being a citizen of the United States of America," as charged, but that they were all residents of South Carolina, though only two were natives of that state. One was a native of North Carolina, another of Pennsylvania and the remaining eight were of foreign birth and unnaturalized. He argued that the open and orderly manner in which the *Savannah* had been fitted out, manned, and had made the capture of the *Joseph* destroyed all presumption of that intent, *animo furandi,* which was the essential ele-

12 October 24, 1861.

ment in the proof of robbery or piracy. He contended that the prisoners believed that they had the right to embark upon the enterprise for which they were now being tried. If they had been deceived and deluded therein,

there was the strongest excuse for that deception and delusion among those of them who had read the Constitution of their Government, who had read its Declaration of Independence, who had read the contemporaneous exposition of its Constitution, put forward by the wisest of the men who framed it, and on the honeyed accents of whose lips the plain citizens of the States reposed when they adopted the Constitution. If it had been their good fortune to be familiar with the decisions of its Courts, they had learned what the Supreme Court had said with reference to the sovereign rights of the States, and with reference to the strict limit and measure of power which they had conceded to the General Government, and there was, at least, a very strong excuse for their following those doctrines, however unpopular they may have become in a later day of the Republic.

The counsel showed that the commission signed by Jefferson Davis was not merely " 'a pretence of authority from one Jefferson Davis' " but a "document bearing the seal of ten States." Since the United States Government had declined to recognize the separation from the Union by the states of the Confederacy, it followed then that these states were not foreign states, and that there was, in consequence, no violation of the statute on the score of "under color of any commission from any foreign prince or state, or on pretence of authority from any person."

After stating how the United States had derived its

144

power from the several states, which had reserved to themselves "the residuary power beyond the express, limited power granted to the Federal Government," Mr. Larocque said that a state had the right to judge for herself when there was a trespass and further "a right to redress herself with force against the General Government."

The learned counsel for the defendants illustrated his points with many examples from American and English history. He particularly showed how the Americans during the War for Independence had been less entitled to a belligerent status than the Confederates. He raised the question whether humanity—if not the remembrance of those Revolutionary patriots who also claimed for themselves "the right to exercise that privilege of electing their own government"—does not forbid treatment of Confederate privateersmen "as pirates and robbers, as enemies of the human race?" Supposing that the Confederate States were not a government either *de jure* or *de facto,* he must contend, nevertheless, that

there was a state of war existing in the country, and that the attack on the brig *Joseph* was a belligerent act and not a piratical one.

You will certainly reflect, gentlemen, that it was not for a case of this kind that any statute punishing the crime of piracy was ever intended to be enacted. You will reflect, [he continued to address the jury,] after you have received instruction from the Court, that however by technical construction our ingenius friends on the other side may endeavor to force on your minds the conviction that this was a case intended to be provided for by statutes passed in the year 1790, and by statutes passed in the year 1820, it is a monstrous stretch of the provisions of those statutes to ask for a conviction in a case of this kind.

One of the misfortunes of a time of popular excitement like this is that it pervades not only the minds of the community, but reaches the public halls of legislation, and the executive and administrative departments of the Government. And it is no disrespect, even to the Chief Magistrate of the country, to say that he might, in a time like this, put forward proclamations and announce a determination to do what his more sober judgment would tell him it was imprudent to announce his intention of doing. . . . Such an announcement once made it is difficult to depart from. And, therefore, I do most sincerely hope that the administration in Washington, as my heart tells me must be the case, are looking at these trials in progress here and in Philadelphia, with an earnest desire that the voice of the Juries shall be the voice of acquittal—thus disembarrassing the Government of the trammels of a proclamation which it were better, perhaps, had never been issued.

When Larocque finished his long and learned address, it was a little after four in the afternoon; and the Court adjourned until eleven the next morning. Friday and Saturday were spent by the counsel on both sides in arguments on points of law and in citing pertinent decisions by courts of many countries. On Monday and Tuesday the counsel summed up their cases, and on Wednesday, the seventh day of the trial, Judge Nelson charged the jury.

Widespread attention had been attracted to the arguments on the national polity and policy and on the intricate principles of international law. The handling of the case had been creditable to the attorneys on both sides, who displayed great ability and research. The charge was listened to with keen interest. This was the first vital judicial pronouncement on the legal relations of the contending peoples. Washington awaited it. Richmond awaited it. Europe awaited it. The jury, remarkable for its high level of intelligence, retired at twenty minutes past three. Their deliberation extended over exactly twenty hours. On Thursday morning at 11.20, the jurymen were brought back into the court room, where the bench inquired if there was any probability of an agreement being reached. There were several responses of "No." Four stood for acquittal, and the remainder believed guilt to have been established on one or more of the charges. The district attorney asked for a new trial to commence on Monday week; but the Court decline to disturb the order of cases, and the case of the United States vs. Baker *et al.* went over to the next term.

The case that was being tried, at the same time, in Philadelphia was that of the *Jefferson Davis'* prize crew taken on board of the recaptured schooner *Enchantress.* Three separate trials were made of the matter. The indictment of William Smith, prize master, was taken up first, on October 22; and after lengthy evidence, brief arguments, and a short jury session—the opposite in these respects to the *Savannah* trial—a verdict of guilty was brought in on the fourth day. On the twenty-eighth a motion for a new trial was made, and the same day Thomas Quigley, Edward Rochford, and Daniel Mullins were arraigned and plead not guilty. Their trial lasted until six o'clock the next evening, when a verdict of guilty was returned. The third trial was a *pro forma* operation to clear one Eben Lane, who claimed to be a

New Englander, and to have been out of sympathy with the enterprise. He stated that each night he had put the prize's helm northward, and that it was thus due to his skill as a navigator and to his secret loyalty to the United States that the passage to the Confederacy had been retarded and the *Enchantress* retaken. The prosecution submitted no evidence and the self-confessed traitor was acquitted.[13]

No sooner was the result of the trial of William Smith and the privateersmen in New York known in Richmond than the Confederate States Government showed that the word retaliation in the Confederate vocabulary meant action. President Davis' threat of retaliation had been based upon his general military powers, but by an act of August 30 the Confederate Congress had specifically authorized him to proceed to the most extreme limits, "as may seem to him just and proper." On November 9, Brigadier General Winder, C.S.A., in command of the military department in which was located the Confederate capital, received an order from the War office

to choose by lot from among the prisoners of war of highest rank, one who is to be confined in a cell appropriated to convicted felons, and who is to be treated in all respects as if such convict, and to be held for execution in the same manner as may be adopted by the enemy for the execution of the prisoner of war Smith, recently condemned to death in Philadelphia.[14]

---

[13] *The Jeff Davis Piracy Case. Full report of trial of William Smith for Piracy as one of crew of Confederate privateer Jeff Davis* (Philadelphia: King & Baird, printers, 1861).

[14] Apparently the information received through the lines by the Confederate authorities was not complete, in as much as the thirteenth of the

You will also select thirteen other prisoners of war, the highest in rank of those captured by our forces, to be confined in the cells reserved for prisoners accused of infamous crimes, and will treat them as such so long as the enemy shall continue so to treat the like number of prisoners of war captured by them at sea, and now held for trial in New York as pirates.

As these measures are intended to repress the infamous attempt now made by the enemy to commit judicial murder on prisoners of war, you will execute them strictly, as the mode best calculated to prevent the commission of so heinous a crime.

The selection of the hostages was made, the next day, in the Provost Marshal's office in Richmond. The names of the six colonels held in Confederate war prisons were placed in a can, and the drawings were made in the presence of several northern officers and, singularly, a member of Congress from New York.[15] The first name taken out proved to be that of Colonel Corcoran, of the 69th Regiment of New York State Militia. He then stood for the condemned Smith. There were only eleven field

New York prisoners was not on trial, and in that no retaliation was instituted for the three convictions at the second Philadelphia trial.

[15] The Hon. Mr. Ely, Republican, had been captured at Manassas, in July, whither he had gone to witness the dispersion of the rebels—who themselves did the dispersing. He had offered, if released, to go to Washington, and by his intercession secure the release of the indicted privateersmen; but his freedom was not to be so quickly obtained.—*True Delta,* August 1, and *The Daily Picayune* (New Orleans), September 17, 1861. But on October 29, 1861, Lieutenant Albert Kautz, U.S.N., was released from prison in Richmond on a fifty-day parole in order to go North and urge upon the Government at Washington an exchange of prisoners. Kautz had been captured, June 25, while acting as prize master on the brigantine *Hannah Balch,* and had, two months later, been confined to a cell as hostage for Midshipman Albert G. Hudgins, C.S.N., who had been taken while acting as prize master on board of the brigantine *Cuba* (a prize to the C.S.S. *Sumter*), and who had been incarcerated in the Tombs, New York, on charge of piracy.—*NWR,* I, 1, p. 621, and 5, p. 744.

officers prisoners to the Confederacy, and it was necessary to select three captains to complete the required number of hostages. The list reported to the Secretary of War was as follows: Colonels Lee, Cogswell, Wilcox, Woodruff, and Wood, Lieutenant-Colonels Bowman and Neff, Majors Potter, Revere, and Vogdes, and Captains Ricketts, McQuade, and Rockwood. Captains McQuade and Ricketts being wounded, the Department ordered two other captains to be selected in their place, and the names of H. Bowman and T. Keffer were drawn.[16]

The hostages, each officer standing for a specified privateersman, were promptly imprisoned as ordered, to await such fate as might be in store for the individuals whom they severally represented. The United States Government was slow to go any farther, for very practical considerations were now inescapable; and the following February the Administration at Washington backed down, removed the privateersmen from the common jails to military prisons, and accorded to them the status of prisoners of war.[17]

In the meantime, at the preliminary hearing the crew of the *Petrel* had been committed on two charges: first, attacking the United States frigate *St. Lawrence* with intent to plunder, an offense subject to trial in the District Court; and second, treason, a distinct case to be tried before the Circuit Court. Though the Grand Jury brought in a true bill against the men of the *Petrel,* they

[16] *Mercury,* November 18, 1861.

[17] Horace Greeley, *The American Conflict* (Hartford: O. D. Case & Co., 1865), I, 599; J. Thomas Scharf, *History of the Confederate States Navy* (New York: Rogers & Sherwood, 1887), p. 78.

were never brought to trial; and there were no more piracy trials.[18]

In due course of the exchange of prisoners, the privateersmen, during the following summer, were sent south. Many of them were destitute and with only the simplest rags for clothing. A public subscription was opened in Charleston for their relief.[19]

Though the trials had proved that Confederate privateersmen were not pirates, the Union officials and public never quite got over their fondness for applying the epithets "pirate" and "piratical" to everything naval in the South, and the newspapers and state documents of the United States were filled with such expressions as long as the conflict lasted.

[18] *Mercury,* August 25, and November 18, 1861; *Courier,* October 14, 1861.

[19] *Mercury,* August 23, 1861; of the *Savannah* privateersmen, one, Richard Palmer, died of tuberculosis in the Tombs and another, A. C. Coid, died on the enemy's transport at City Point, Virginia, while awaiting exchange.—*The Sunday News* (Charleston), February 9, 1919.

XIII

AT THE HEAD OF THE PASSES

*E*ARLY in October, 1861, the vessels of the Gulf blockading squadron stationed off the mouths of the several passes of the Mississippi River moved up to the Head of the Passes. At this point the vast waters from half of the two contending American republics ran in one channel, emptying by four major passes into the Gulf of Mexico. The Head of the Passes offered a roadstead deep and wide enough for fleet maneuvers, and it was strange that the Confederates had done nothing to defend so important a body of water. The enemy at once made preparations to hold the roads by constructing a battery on the point of firm land between the South and the Southwest Passes near the lighthouse. But scarcely had the fortifications been traced on the ground and some construction material landed than the Confederates began an active interference.

In ejecting the intruders from Louisiana soil, the private-armed ships played the larger share. The *Ivy* opened the action. This privateer had been purchased by the Navy Department and was now, properly speaking, a public vessel. On the afternoon of October 9, the little cockerel stood down the river, and opened upon the enemy a fire which the latter describes, in an official report, as having made his position "untenable." The Confederate gunboat mounted only two guns. But one of them vastly outranged any of the enemy's guns: nineteen on board of the sailing ship *Vincennes,* sixteen on

153

the steamer *Richmond,* ten on the sailing ship *Preble,* and three on the steamer *Water Witch.* Furthermore, the Confederate gunboat was faster than any of the vessels opposed to her, and they could not close with her. The result of the afternoon's gunnery exercise was quite disconcerting to the complacency of Flag-Officer William W. McKean, U.S.N., who at once notified Washington that, "unless this squadron is supplied with rifled guns of heavy caliber, the blockading ships are liable at any moment to be driven from their anchorage by a steamer mounting a single rifled gun."[1]

Three days later, vessels prepared for war by the private enterprise of the South administered another and severe blow to the United States navy. On the night of the eleventh, Commodore George N. Hollins, C.S.N., was at the forts, situated in the bend of the river, some twenty-odd miles above the Head of the Passes. His flag was carried on the privateer *Calhoun,* Lieutenant Commanding J. H. Carter, now under charter to the naval service. The other war vessels on the anchorage were the sometime privateers *Ivy,* 1, Lieutenant Commanding Fry, and *Jackson,* 2, Lieutenant Commanding Gwathmey, the converted cruiser *McRae,* 6, Lieutenant Commanding Huger, the gunboat *Tuscarora,* 2, Lieutenant Commanding Kennon, the revenue cutter *Pickens,* 5, the towboat *Watson,* Acting Lieutenant Averett, with fire rafts, and the privateer ironclad ram *Manassas,* 1, Captain Stevenson.

The last-named vessel was an original craft and, as the world's first fighting ironclad steamer, deserves some

[1] *NWR,* I, 16, p. 700; *The Daily Picayune,* September 20, October 1, 4, 5, and 9, 1861.

extended mention. She was rebuilt upon the frame of the tug *Enoch Train,* and was the achievement of John A. Stevenson, Secretary of the New Orleans Pilots Benevolent Association. It is said that Stevenson raised $100,000 by subscription to undertake the construction of this naval neophyte, after having discussed the design with the authorities in Montgomery and having received their encouragement.[2] The work was done with a fair degree of secrecy, for no mention of the ship was made in the local press until after she was completed and had made her trial trip on September 9.[3] Two days later *The True Delta* carried a small item, reading as follows:

Something very like a whale was seen yesterday morning up and down the river below the city, and thousands of people went out to see what they could see. We shall probably see and hear "more anon."

Despite efforts at secrecy, news of the *Manassas* leaked out. The enemy's naval force off the mouth of the Mississippi heard of her, but their information was not accurate. An altogether fanciful account of an ironclad privateer was painted in the *New York Commercial Advertiser* in August. She was called a "monster mosquito" which would "affix its sting" by nosing into its victim and boring a hole in the ship's side with an "augur or lancet" carried in the prow, in the meanwhile being absolutely protected from the enemy's point blank fire by means of her heavy iron covering. Foolish as such an idea may seem, just as freakish a conception in naval architecture had been advanced by a naval architect in

[2] John Smith Kendall, *History of New Orleans,* I, 246.
[3] *Daily Picayune,* September 19, 1861.

New Orleans in April.[4] The metamorphosis of the seagoing tug into the ironclad ram was accomplished in the
dockyard of J. Hughes at Algiers. The *Enoch Train,*
single-decked, two-masted, 128 feet long, of 28-foot
beam, 12½-foot depth, and 385 tons burden, had been
constructed at Medford, Massachusetts, 1855, by James
O. Curtis, as an ice-breaker.[5] Being therefore strongly
built and having very powerful engines, she was well
adapted for the purpose in hand. She had been brought
to New Orleans some two years earlier to serve as a
towboat. This steamer should not be confused, though
she has been, with the ship *Enoch Train,* a cargo carrier,
which arrived at the Passes of the Mississippi in the latter half of May, 1861.[6]

First, the upper works of the tug were cut away; and
upon the razeed frame a convex deck was constructed
of oak, twelve inches thick, and sheathed with one and
a half inches of iron plate. The bow was filled in solidly
with timbers so as to form a massive cleaver twenty feet
long. Relying upon the collisional force of the solid bow
to smash and sink the enemy, the builder of the *Manassas* mounted on her only one piece of heavy ordnance.
This was a nine-inch Dahlgren smoothbore,[7] fired
through a bow porthole so small as to allow of no lateral
training. With no stern-chaser it is obvious that this
privateer, like the traditional Roman soldier, was not
equipped for retreat. An iron shutter automatically

4 *Mobile Daily Register,* April 28, 1861.

5 Letter from Collector of Customs, Boston, Mass., to Commodore O. V.
Badger, U.S.N., Navy Yard, Charlestown, Massachusetts, March 29, 1883,
now on file in U.S. Naval Library and Records.

6 See page 43.

7 This gun was obtained from the Navy Department through political
influence. *NWR,* II, 1, p. 792.

CONFEDERATE STATES PRIVATEER RAM MANASSAS

From an aquarelle in the possession of the United States Naval Library and Records.

closed the port when the gun was run in. Two hatches, one forward and one abaft of the smokestacks, were the only other openings into the vessel. To repel boarders an arrangement was installed to eject a shower of scalding water and a cloud of blinding and suffocating steam over the curved iron deck, making it slippery and untenable. When the work was completed the new *Manassas* was fifteen feet longer than the old *Enoch Train,* five feet wider, and of four and a half feet greater draft; and, save for the two smoke funnels, looked like a huge cigar floating in the water.[8]

As soon as the *Manassas* had demonstrated her navigability, Stevenson applied for a letter of marque, naming himself as captain, and fixing the crew at 36 men. The commission was issued on September 12.[9]

The *Manassas* was easily the most formidable vessel that rode at anchor between Forts St. Philip and Jackson, on the evening of October 11, 1861; and Commodore Hollins was unwilling to have her act independently of his command. Therefore, at the last moment before the squadron started down the river to attack the blockading squadron, he determined to seize her for the navy and put her under his own officers. Accordingly he detached Lieutenant Alexander F. Warley, from the *McRae,* and sent him on board of the *Manassas* to take possession and command in the name of the Confederate States Government.[10] Captain Stevenson went ashore

[8] *True Delta,* October 13, 1861.

[9] *NWR,* II, 1, pp. 259 and 382-385. While Stevenson appears in the application as the sole owner, there is every reason to believe that he was acting for a stock company, of which he was probably president.—*NWR,* II, 1, p. 725.

[10] When testifying before a Congressional investigating committee, Sep-

with tears in his eyes. The new commander assembled all hands and read to them his authority, also explaining that their prize-money agreement would be no longer in force and that under the Navy Regulations all war vessels in sight at the time of a capture were entitled to share in the prize-money. This summary turn of events created much dissatisfaction and fourteen privateersmen took their bags and went ashore. Their places were quickly filled by volunteers from the fleet.

It was a pitch black night, and for a surprise attack none could have been better. The order of battle placed the *Manassas* in the lead. Her instructions were to attack only by ramming, withholding fire (there were but a dozen shells in her magazine). The iron vanship glided noiselessly downstream. The porthole and the after hatch were closed down. The forward hatch was opened about four inches to permit the captain and the helmsman a view ahead. Little it was that they could see in the inkiness of the outside, save the slightly luminous play of water that sprayed and veiled over the conically shaped bow. The eerie stillness which greeted the two Confederates who peered anxiously into the night was a little relieved by the faint musical rippling of the parting water. At length their practiced eyes discerned several darker spots, arranged in inverted-V formation.

"Let her out, Hardy, let her out," was shouted down to the chief engineer. Instantly the tar, tallow, and sulphur that had been held in reserve for this moment were thrown into the furnace. Around whirled the hand of the steam gauge. Forward, faster shot the monster iron

tember 13, 1862, Hollins said: "I seized the *Manassas* and paid for her afterwards."—*NWR*, II, 1, p. 472.

sea-reptile toward the outline of a ship rapidly gathering form out of the darkness.

The most advanced ship in the enemy's line was the *Preble*. The flagship *Richmond* was anchored about 150 or 200 yards away on the port side. The first intimation of an attack was received on board of the *Preble*. Her watch discerned an object coming downstream, without a particle of light or smoke, and looking for all the world like a huge whale. The next moment this strange thing emitted clouds of the densest smoke, and made a rush at the *Richmond*. A red light was hastily hoisted to the gaff to indicate the presence of danger. On board of the *Richmond* the *Manassas* was seen, but it seems that her oncoming was mistaken for an accident, and a pandemonium of fog bells broke out to warn her off. Quickly followed a terrific crash.

Three planks of the *Richmond's* port side were stove in, making a hole two feet below the water line. The collier schooner *Joseph H. Toone,* which lay alongside the rammed steamer, was torn from her fastenings and set adrift. At the first alarm the crew rushed to quarters, and shortly the entire port battery was discharged into the darkness. Needless to say, the broadside was too random to be effective. The *Manassas* backed to deliver a blow at the *Preble*.

Down to the engine-room again came the order; "Now let her out, Hardy, and give it to her." But the information was returned that the shock of the collision had deranged the machinery of one of the two engines, and that with only one working there was not enough power to run down a vessel. Bitterly disappointed, Warley was obliged to pass by the exposed side of the *Preble*, without attempting a wallop at her, and to haul off as best the one engine would permit. The *Preble* had now added her broadside. The fire of the *Vincennes* and *Water Witch* quickly followed. A veritable Jovian hail fell around the long black thing gliding away upon the dark water. She was so low that the guns of the enemy were not depressed enough to reach her. Only one shot struck the mailed deck, left a slight dent, and glanced off. Another broke the flagstaff, and a third took off one of the smokestacks.

In the meantime, the Confederate squadron was awaiting upstream the signal rockets that should tell them of a successful attack by the vanship. Now the after hatch was opened and a midshipman prepared to send up the rockets. In the excitement he burned his hand, dropped the stick, and the rocket went sizzling down into the hold. The crew thought that a shell had entered, and for a moment there was a comical rolling over each other and piling up in the corners that provided jests in the squadron for months to come. Promptly, however, the midshipman recovered his composure, and the three rockets trailed their message into the night.

Following this comedy came an act of heroism. The last one of the random shots to register upon the *Manassas* struck the remaining smokestack, and knocked it across the vent of the one previously carried away. With the updraft choked, the asphyxiating gases from the furnace—the burning tar, tallow, and sulphur—filled the fire room and spread through the vessel. Something must be done. Quickly Hardy, the engineer, dashed to the deck with an axe to cut away the guys of the fallen funnels and to clear the smoke openings. The executive officer, Charles W. Austin, was instantly at his heels to assist him to stand on the highly arched deck. Defying the dangers of shot and shell and of slippery foothold, the two officers worked until they accomplished their voluntary mission.[11]

The enemy was cannonading furiously. Now he saw wee lights moving down upon him. The lights grew rapidly in size and brilliancy. "Fire ships" rang the cry through the Union vessels. Rams and fire ships were too much for the nerves of the men and officers, not yet inured to war and rudely called from sleep. The blazing hulks, chained together, and towed in line abreast by the *Tuscarora* and the *Watson,* seemed angry infernos. Cables were slipped and the squadron was under way—not standing much on the order of going. There was considerable confused signaling, but there seemed no doubt anywhere that the thing to do was to get to the open sea. The senior officer present was Captain John Pope, U.S.N., on the *Richmond.* When the *Preble* came up with the flagship, her commander hailed and asked: "I can hear your orders; what are they?" "Proceed down the Pass," Captain Pope replied.

Then Commander Robert Handy, of the *Vincennes,* signaled to the *Richmond,* "Shall I anchor?" He was answered, "Cross the bar." Some distance from the bar,

[11] These privateer officers, together with the pilot, were mentioned in official reports for conspicuous services. They were rewarded by appointments in the navy, Austin as a master-not-in-line-of-promotion and Hardy (William H.) as a third assistant engineer. It is uncertain whether the pilot, a Mr. Mason, was a privateersman or a naval employee, but more probably the former. He may be the J. Stevens Mason whose name appears in the list of masters-not-in-line-of-promotion.—*NWR*, I, 16, p. 730a; and *Naval War Records,* Office Memorandum No. 8, List of Officers in the Confederate States Navy, 1861-1865 (Washington: Government Printing Office, 1898).

he grounded, head on. From this position he could bring none of his broadside guns to bear upon his pursuers; but, taking down the cabin bulkheads, he caused two of his eight-inch shell guns to be run out of the stern ports, and opened fire from them. His situation seemed critical and exposed to raking fire. At this juncture a signal shown on the *Richmond* was read on the *Vincennes* to "abandon ship." Handy sent an officer over to the *Water Witch* to verify the reading. Upon the young lieutenant's return he began at once to leave the ship. A train was laid to the magazine and a slow match lit. The men and officers got into the boats, some pulling for the *Water Witch*, the remainder, including Commander Handy, proceeding to go aboard the *Richmond*. Captain Pope was greatly astonished when Handy appeared. The latter had his ship's ensign, dramatically, wrapped around his body in large folds. The Captain at once demanded the meaning of this comedy, and was told that the *Vincennes* had been abandoned on signal. Pope was wild with anger. Such a signal had not been made. The ship did not blow up, and after waiting a while Commander Handy and his men went back to her.

Meanwhile, the two Confederate steamers had some difficulty in managing their blazing tows, which finally got out of line and grounded. Seeing the failure of the fire ships and the precipitate flight of the enemy, Commander Hollins commenced a pursuit, keeping the foe under the fire of his superior ordnance and yet not venturing within the range of his adversary's guns. The fight began at 3.45 A.M. and by nine o'clock the enemy had been driven to the mouth of the Southwest Pass. The Confederate vessels then returned to the anchorage at the forts, after having destroyed the incipient fortifications at the lighthouse, and taking with them as prizes the collier *Joseph H. Toone* and a large cutter belonging to the *Richmond*.

In his effort to get the *Vincennes* afloat, Commander Handy threw overboard fourteen 32-pounder guns, all his 32-pounder shot, and twenty-seven stands of grape. Though by ten o'clock it should have been obvious that the Confederates did not intend to press the pursuit to the open sea, yet orders were then issued for the destruction of the three supply vessels anchored in the Gulf at the mouth of the Pass. It was not until the next day that the panic among the would-be blockaders abated somewhat, and for several days the blockade of the river had no actuality whatsoever. On the seventeenth, two of the enemy's gunboats attempted to enter the river, but were met by the *Ivy* and the *Jackson,* and forced to draw off.[12]

The burden of administering the trouncing to the enemy had fallen upon the originally private-armed ships, manned and officered in considerable part by ex-privateersmen. The *Manassas* opened the ball, starting the panic; the *Calhoun* carried the commodore's flag; and the *Ivy* was the chief pursuer. The terrible gunnery of the last is mentioned, with emphasis, in the enemy's reports. This vessel was continued as the guard ship of the river, continually harassing the blockading vessels with her long range fire.

The repulse of the United States squadron was heralded throughout America as an humiliating defeat.

12 *NWR,* I, 16, pp. 703-730a; *Daily Picayune,* October 13, 14, 16, and 18, 1861; *Savannah Daily News,* October 21, 1861.

THE CONFEDERATE PRIVATEERS

Admiral David D. Porter, U.S.N., in writing his *Naval History of the Civil War,* twenty-five years later, speaks of the rout as a "ridiculous affair," as "mortifying," and (page 91) says that:

There is nothing that can equal the comicality of Captain Handy's performance—laying a train with a slow match to his magazine, and then hastening away in his boats with the American flag wound around him, and his remarkable antics when he found that his ship would not blow up. This presents an example unmatched in any navy in the world.

XIV

THE ONLY SUBMARINE PRIVATEER

THE people of the South, never having been greatly given to seafaring, approached the matter of maritime defense without any of the existing naval prejudices. They were constantly on the alert for any new scheme which promised them an advantage over an established navy. As an example, witness the intrepidity with which the New Orleans pilot embarked upon the construction of an ironclad privateer, partly following, partly going ahead of ideas which had stirred European naval circles during the preceding five years. The Confederates knew well that only by the adoption of naval machinery so improved and advanced as to render existing ships and means obsolete could they place their sea power upon a parity with that of the United States. The Confederate States Government had therefore embarked at the outset upon an ironclad program, which brought such splendid victories in the Hampton Roads on March 8 and 9, 1862.

Submarine warfare likewise received immediate attention at the hands of the army and the navy and civilians. Sub-surface torpedoes were not a new device. As the ram of the Confederate privateer *Manassas* was not a new weapon of offense in naval warfare but harked back over centuries of disuse to the tactics of the seafights between the ancient Mediterranean galleys, so the origin of submarine warfare was also, although not equally, remote. Some two centuries earlier the Dutch, in their war for freedom, had sent down upon the Spanish ships small water-tight boats weighted with stone so as to drift submerged and containing gunpowder and slow fuses. During the Revolutionary War, Bushnel, an American patriot, had experimented fruitlessly with the idea of an underwater attack; and in the early part of the nineteenth century Fulton had made important contributions to the development of the submarine. The latter offered the results of his work first to France, which rejected them; and then to Great Britain, which purchased them solely for the purpose of suppressing the submarine idea. It was not to the interest of the Mistress of the Seas to develop an implement which would give to a weaker navy an advantage over a stronger one. England wished to keep naval warfare on the surface where the tremendous broadsides of her ships-of-the-line were decisive. During the Crimean War, the Russians, weak in sea power, attempted to make use of submarine mines, but did not succeed in destroying any of the allies' vessels. For the same reason that Russia had resorted to this mode of warfare, the Confederacy took it up. From the very outset of the war, the Confederates, officially and privately, began to experiment. The efforts of the government agencies were directed principally toward the evolution of stationary and floating mines or torpedoes. Private enterprise brought out the first submarine boat, which, like the first ironclad ram, was a product of the Crescent City-on-the-Mississippi.

The builders were James R. McClintock and Baxter Watson, two practical marine engineers and machinists.[1]

[1] These men, under the firm name of Watson and McClintock, operated

They began work in the latter part of 1861 and completed their boat in the early part of 1862. She was launched at the Government Yard on New Basin in February. During her trial trip on Lake Pontchartrain she destroyed a barge placed as a target. Assured of her navigational and military qualities, the owners, who, in addition to the builders, were John K. Scott and Robbin R. Barron, applied for a letter of marque, appropriately naming her the *Pioneer,* and describing her as a submarine propeller. The commission, upon the security of H. L. Hunley and H. J. Leovy, was issued on March 31, 1862, listing Scott as commander, the number of crew as three, the tonnage as four, and the armament as a "magazine of powder."[2]

The building of both the *Manassas* and the *Pioneer* by private capital was certainly an indication that not all privateersmen were animated by the thought of gainful and easy cruising against defenseless merchantmen. It must have been quite obvious to everyone that neither the ironclad ram nor the diminutive submarine were cruising ships, which might expect to make rich prizes to compensate for the outlay of money and the hazards of the sea. Obviously they were limited to harbor or coast service. Their only source of prize-money lay in destroying the enemy's men-of-war in combat, for which, it will be remembered, the Government had offered a bounty in twenty per cent of the value of all superior

a shop at 31 Front Levee for the manufacture of steam gauges. They also invented a machine for the rapid pressing of Minié balls.—*Daily Delta,* August 17, 1861. But the construction of the submarine, according to local tradition,—of which there is a surprising dearth,—was performed at Leeds Foundry, on the corner of Fourcher and Delord Streets.

2 *NWR,* II, 1, pp. 399-401.

armed vessels destroyed, with an additional sum depending on the strength of the enemy's crew.

When David G. Farragut, flag-officer of the West Gulf blockading squadron, started up the Mississippi River in the latter part of April, 1862, to capture New Orleans, the *Pioneer* is said to have put out to meet him. But quickly she came to an untimely end. In making a submerged evolution she became unmanageable in some way that will never be known, and sank with all hands on board.[3] On came the enemy, defying the Confederate forts and fleet, humbled them, and took the city. The Union tars never knew how close to death they had come from an underwater attack. If the *Pioneer* had blown a barge out of the water, might she not have destroyed a man-of-war—even the flagship, and the brave admiral might not have been left to exclaim, two years later in Mobile Bay: "Damn the torpedoes! Go ahead!" or words to that effect.

The story of the *Pioneer* is differently told by Simon Lake in his *The Submarine in War and Peace,* in the chapter entitled, "Comedy and Tragedy in Submarine Development."[4] He says:

A friend told me the following story as related to him by a southern gentleman who was familiar with the history of the boat. It appears that this submarine was the conception of a wealthy planter who owned a number of slaves. He thought that it would add considerable interest to the occasion of her launching if, when the vessel left the ways, she should disappear beneath the waves and make a short run

[3] W. O. Hart, "The Submarine Boat at the Soldiers' Home," in *Louisiana Legal News,* May 29, 1923.

[4] Pp. 39-40. Published by J. B. Lippincott and Company, Philadelphia and London, 1918.

beneath the surface before coming up. So he took two of his most intelligent slaves and instructed them how to hold the tiller when the vessel slid down the ways, and in which way to turn the propeller for a time after she began to lose her launched speed. He told them when they got ready to come up they should push the tiller down and the vessel would come to the surface to be towed ashore.

A great crowd assembled to see this novel launching, "When things were all ready," said the old Southern gentleman, "sure enough, them two negroes got into the boat and shut down the hatches; and do you know, suh, that at that time them niggers was worth a thousand dollars apiece." Well, it seems that the boat slid down the ways and disappeared under the water just as had been planned. The crowd awaited expectantly, but the vessel did not reappear. Eventually they got into boats and put out hooks and grappling lines, but she could not be found. The designer of the craft stated as his opinion that he "might have known better than to trust them pesky niggers anyway," and he was willing to bet that they had taken the opportunity to steal the vessel and run away. He asserted that very likely they would take the boat up North and give it to the Yankees, and that they could expect to hear of the "Yanks" using it to blow up some of their own [Confederate] ships.

Her disappearance remained a mystery for a great many years—until long after the war closed, in fact, and the incident had been forgotten. Years afterward, during some dredging operations to deepen the harbor, the dredge buckets one day got hold of something they could not lift. A diver was sent down to investigate, and he reported that there was some metal object buried in the mud which looked like a steam boiler. They set to work to raise this, and putting chains around it they lifted it on to the wharf. The gentleman, in closing the narrative, remarked, "And do you

169

know, suh, when they opened the hatch them two blamed niggars was still in thar, but they warn't wuth a damned cent."

This amusing tale is a canard. Without doubt it was invented and repeated for the amusement that old gentlemen, not only of New Orleans and the South, but of wherever old gentlemen may be found, get from imposing "all that the trade will stand" upon the credulity of the younger generation or of strangers.

In fact, the writer must admit that he is by no means satisfied with any of the stories of this remarkable privateer. The first account, shown in the footnotes as based on an article by Mr. Hart, of New Orleans, is logical and plausible. Mr. Hart's informant was "the late Captain William Youngblood, who was long an inmate of the Home and a gallant Confederate soldier, and for some years inspector of vessels at the Port of New Orleans," and "was a friend of the men, who built the boat." Preference, it would naturally seem, should be given to this account. But an article in *The New Orleans Picayune* of June 29, 1902, written while the *Pioneer* still lay "half submerged in the weeds and flowers growing on the bank of Bayou St. John," denies, by implication, that the *Pioneer* was dispatched against Farragut's fleet. In referring to the builders of the submarine privateer, it stated that "the city falling into the hands of the federals before it was completed, the boat was sunk, and these gentlemen came to Mobile." The writer of this article was W. A. Alexander, who, while on army detail at an iron works in Mobile, had been associated with the erstwhile builders of the *Pioneer* in the construction and operation of two other submarines. While working together in the shops, Alexander probably had the story of the *Pioneer* from McClintock's own lips. His article was devoted primarily, however, to the last and best known of these vessels—which was called the *Hunley*—and his reference to the New Orleans vessel is only casual.

Seven years later[5] the *Picayune* carried another story, which, in mentioning the *Pioneer,* said: "However, it was never used, for in a test made just before the Federals took this city it sank in the Bayou St. John, three sailors losing their lives in trying the boat. It was not until many years after, when the bayou was dredged, that the boat was raised, and ever since it has been lying at Spanish Fort."

A little more light is shed on the history of this privateer by a letter, undated but probably written in 1870 or 1871, from one of the builders, McClintock, to Matthew Fontaine Maury.[6] McClintock now considered himself an authority on submarines and he wanted the great Confederate geographer, scientist, and naval officer, to advise him as to how he might sell his services to some European naval power. But, to quote that part of the letter germane to the present subject, he wrote: "This Boat demonstrated to us the fact that we could construct a Boat, that would move at will in any direction desired, and at any distance from the surface. The evacuation of New Orleans lost this Boat before our experiments were completed."

[5] April 2, 1909.
[6] "Maury Papers," Manuscript Division, Library of Congress, vol. 46, items 9087-9094.

171

THE CONFEDERATE PRIVATEERS

With a commendable military prudence—though deplorable from the point of view of the historian—all mention of the building and testing of the *Pioneer* was kept out of the newspapers of the day. But there is no doubt, and this is really all that is important, that a submarine war-vessel was actually built in New Orleans in 1862, commissioned with a letter of marque, and proved in the water, though never tried out in battle.

After continuing some sixteen years lost under water, this forgotten submarine was accidentally brought to the surface by a channel dredge. Placed on the bank out of the way, it remained there in corrosive mud and weeds for about thirty years, until further public improvements required its second resting place. Then, at last, a little interest in this most interesting relic awakened and the Beauregard Camp of the United Sons of the Confederate Veterans caused it to be removed to Camp Nicholls, the Louisiana State Home for Confederate Soldiers. The Home is also on the bank of the Bayou, near Esplanade Avenue. There the *Pioneer* was mounted on a concrete base, and "presented" with appropriate ceremonies on April 10, 1909.

Compared with the great cruising submarines of today, their Confederate forerunner appears a child's toy. She is an even twenty feet in length over all, her greatest inside width is but three feet two inches, and her maximum depth is six feet. In plan view her curves are very pleasing. In midship cross-section, she suggests a racing yacht model. She is fabricated of one-quarter inch iron sheets, fastened with five-eighths inch counter-sunk rivets.[7] The deck plates are curved to conic surfaces.

[7] Measurements made by the author.

172

THE WORLD'S ONLY PRIVATEER SUBMARINE,
THE PIONEER *OF NEW ORLEANS*

Upper View: Port Broadside.

Lower Left: Port Quarter.   Lower Right: Starboard Bow.

The little vessel seems the product of true crafts-manship; and Mr. Lake, a recognized authority on sub-marine design, quoted earlier, said that her form in-dicated that she should have been very stable and suc-cessfully navigable under water.[8]

Accident, neglect, and vandalism have conspired to despoil her. No account of the mechanical details has been discovered; but from the remnants of the machin-ery and appliances, together with Alexander's excellent account of the *Hunley,* these can be surmised with rea-sonable certainty.

The propeller—the blades are now broken off—was turned by cranks operated by two men, sitting on little iron brackets fastened, opposite, on each side of the ves-sel, immediately under the hatchway. There were rud-ders on either end, connected for single control. The bow rudder is gone, the stock being snapped off just below the rudder-post. The stern rudder is buried in the concrete base, but a photograph taken before the em-placement shows it to be an equipoise-rudder. The div-ing was accomplished by two side vanes, or fins, 35 inches long by 16 inches wide, placed about on the level of the propeller and over the forward rudder. They both worked on the same shaft, rotated by a lever arm, which directly pointed the angle of the dive. The port vane has been twisted off.

The sole entrance to the vessel is through the eighteen-inch hatchway amidships. The edge of the opening is reinforced with an iron collar, three-eights of an inch thick and two and a half inches wide. The cover is gone, but the indications are that it was simply a lid hinged

---

[8] *Submarine in War and Peace,* pp. 152-153.

aft and closing on a gasket fastened directly to the curved roof or deck; for the rivet holes surrounding the hatch are only one-eighth of an inch in diameter. It does not seem probable that the cover stood high enough, as in the *Hunley,* to serve as a conning tower with eye-ports. In fact, little provision seems to have been made for light or observation. In the roof, forward of the hatch, there are two groups of eight three-quarter-inch holes, each, arranged in circles one foot in diameter. These holes may have been glassed, serving as small light-ports. Surmounting the center of the more forward set of holes is a cuff, five inches in height and in diameter, which seems to have been a stuffing box through which an air shaft passed. This pipe was not more than an inch and three-quarters in diameter; and, as in the later submarine, was probably rather short and intended only for the in-take of air when the vessel was operating near the surface—at which time it resembled the present-day periscope travelling through the water. An interior stop-cock would prevent the admission of water when the submergence was deep. There is in the prow or nose of the vessel a two-inch circular opening, which, I am inclined to believe, was used for forward observation rather than as a socket for a torpedo spar.

There is little doubt that the torpedo, or "magazine of powder," as it was called in the letter of marque, was carried on a tow-line, the attack being made by the submarine diving under the enemy craft and the floating torpedo exploding upon being trailed into contact with its hull. This method was employed in the first trials of the *Hunley,* which, however, before being taken into action, was equipped to carry her torpedo on a spar outrigged from the bow. The method in the spar attack was to approach the victim at slow speed so that the cranks were ready for instant reversal upon the explosion of the torpedo against the sides of the enemy. Incidentally, it should be remembered that the time was yet several years in advance of the invention of the self-propelling torpedo.

The station of the commanding officer of the *Pioneer* was well forward and within easy reach of the diving lever, the rudder control, the depth gauge, and the air cock. The course was laid on the surface, and held by a set screw on the rudder-head. A magnetic compass, lighted by a candle, was used to detect variations from the desired direction; but due to the slow action of the needle the submarine could get considerably off the course before the deviation would be discovered—a difficulty which has been fully solved only by the recent invention of the gyroscopic compass.

It is regrettable that there is left to conjecture so much that concerns the mechanical details and the operation of this *Pioneer* among submarines, and also that her poor remains are left so unprotected that every rain enters her hull, which is now rusted through in many places. Mosquito-like in size, relative to the modern submarine, she is veritably mosquito-inhabited, being the perennial home of countless insects of the stalwart Gulf Coast variety, who resent the intrusion of an inspector—as the writer found to his discomfort in February, 1926.

Notwithstanding that the *Pioneer* had not accomplished her mission, three of her promoters, McClintock, Watson, and Hunley, convinced of the practicability of their ideas, transferred their activities, upon the fall of New Orleans, to Mobile. There, at the shop of Parks and Lyons, they built a second submarine, of about the same midship section as the first one, but with longer, tapering ends to reduce the water resistance. They spent much time and money in fruitless efforts to invent an electro-magnetic engine; but finally were forced back on hand propulsion, increasing, however, the number of crankers from two to four.

This vessel, which might be called *Pioneer II*—though as far as the writer has discovered she was never named—foundered in rough weather as she was being towed down the bay to a station off Fort Morgan, whence an attack was planned on the blockading vessels. No lives were lost.

A third submarine, named the *Hunley,* but more often called the *Fish Boat,* was at once begun. A different model was adopted and again the "strong-arm" motive power was doubled. The new ship was elliptical in cross-section, with the ends flattened to fit straight stem- and stern-posts. A false keel of cast iron, quickly detachable, served as the main ballast. Water compartments at each end provided trimming and auxiliary ballast. The ship's complement was one officer, one petty officer, and seven seamen. It has been said that she lacked longitudinal stability, and had a bad way of diving unexpectedly nose-on into the muddy bottom and sticking there until the crew was suffocated; but McClintock, in his letter to Commander Maury, quoted earlier, said that all her accidents were due to the crews' carelessness, induced by the very simplicity of her operation. At any rate, she earned the sobriquet, "The Peripatetic Coffin." After a fatal trial in Mobile Bay, she was taken on a flat car to Charleston. There four more crews successively gave their lives in the cause of adventure and their native land. The fifth one, on the night of February 17, 1864, accomplished the destruction of the U.S.S. *Housatonic,* which lay about five and a half miles off Fort Sumter; but the submarine never returned.[9]

The *Hunley* was not commissioned as a privateer, and, though private in origin and ownership, was under military control while in Charleston Harbor. The crews were mixed civilian, army, and navy. Hunley himself was in charge of the fourth unfortunate crew, and lost his life. At the time of the successful attack on the blockading squadron, Lieutenant George E. Dixon, Artillery, Alabama State Troops, was in command, but the crew was predominately from the navy.

The names of some of those daring souls, veritable members of a suicide club, who volunteered as her crews, are memorialized in bronze on South Battery, at the foot of Meeting Street, Charleston, South Carolina; but the identity of many is unknown. From the sinking of the U.S.S. *Housatonic,* in 1864 until 1914, the lapse of half a century, during which there were numerous wars and sea-fights, no other submarine succeeded in sinking a hostile war vessel.

These submarines have been sometimes confused with the steam torpedo boats also originated by the Confederates. These boats were almost wholly submerged, little more than the small smokestack showing above the water. They were called *Davids,* taking this name,

9 *NWR,* I, 15, pp. 332-335. Years later she was located and raised.

as did the *Monitors,* after the first one of the class to be constructed. The original *David* was the product of the private enterprise of Theodore Stoney of Charleston. She was never commissioned as a private-armed vessel, but was placed under the jurisdiction of the Confederate navy.[10]

[10] *The Evening Post* (Charleston), May 7, 1898. *NWR,* I, 15, p. 719.

XV

THE DRAMATIC CAPTURE OF THE
ST. NICHOLAS

A MONG the statutes of the Confederate Congress, approved on February 15, 1862, one may read that the Government of the Confederate States relinquished all claim to any portion of the proceeds of sale of certain vessels and cargoes captured in the Chesapeake Bay and the Potomac River, on or about June 29, 1861, by Captain George N. Hollins, and certain officers of the navy and private citizens under his command, "said prizes having been made without the participation of any vessel of the Confederate States or other government aid."[1]

This act makes of a bold exploit of individual coolness and pluck a privateering venture. The idea upon which the captures were based, seems to have occurred to several persons at about the same time. Credit has been given to Lieutenant Henry H. Lewis, C.S.N., to Richard Thomas, a citizen, and to Captain George N. Hollins, C.S.N.; but credit for the inception of the enterprise probably belongs to the last named.

In notes[2] left by Captain Hollins he tells how the idea occurred to him as he was going from Baltimore to Richmond, after having resigned his commission in the United States navy. Arriving in the Confederate capital he was speedily recommissioned on June 22, as a captain in the new navy. At the Office of Orders and Details,

[1] Statutes-at-large, C.S.A., Prov. Cong., Sess. V, Ch. 72.
[2] *NWR*, I, 4, pp. 553-555.

he found many old naval friends, with whom he discussed his project. They told him that the Secretary of the Navy, Stephen R. Mallory, would have nothing to do with the plan, but that Governor Letcher would be a ready listener. Accordingly the captain asked and obtained the Secretary's permission to broach the subject to His Excellency. The Governor of Virginia acceded, without a moment's hesitation, to the proposal and offered an advance of $1,000 to put the scheme through. He then introduced Richard Thomas, a gentleman from Maryland, whose sympathies were thoroughly Confederate and who wished to do something "to illustrate the spirit and purpose with which the sons of Maryland espoused the Southern Cause."

That afternoon Captain Hollins with his new acquaintance started out for Point Lookout, Maryland, *via* Fredericksburg.[3] On the way they were joined by the captain's two sons and five other men. The next evening the party crossed the Potomac in an open boat, landing in St. Mary's County. Going thence by wagon, "in a pouring rain, a nasty dirty night," they arrived at Point Lookout about an hour before the Washington-Baltimore packet, the *St. Nicholas,* docked on her trip to Washington. Hollins signed the Governor's draft and gave it to Thomas, who then took a steamer for Baltimore, under instructions to purchase certain arms and work up a party of trusted Marylanders before the return of the *St. Nicholas* to that city.

[3] The authorities for the following narrative are *NWR,* I, 4: *Richmond Enquirer,* June 20, 1861; *True Delta* (New Orleans), July 7, 1861; and a paper on the life of Colonel Richard Thomas Zarvona, by his brother, James William Thomas, in possession of the Maryland Historical Society, Baltimore.

THE ST. NICHOLAS

When the *St. Nicholas* started again down Chesapeake Bay on Friday evening, June 28, there was among the passengers a French *modiste,* registered as Madame la Force, who had large millinery trunks with her. This vivacious person soon had lured a United States army officer, who was also among the passengers, into a conversation, which the latter seemed to find delightful. Thomas, small of stature, having put his disguise to the acid test, remained in *tête-à-tête* until midnight. At this hour, the packet touched at Point Lookout, where several passengers came aboard. Among these was a distinguished-looking elderly gentleman. The hour was late and Madame said goodnight. It was bedtime and the other voyagers began to retire. But in a few minutes, Madame's stateroom door again opened. The *modiste* was now in the full regimentals of a colonel of Zouaves, with belted sword and revolver. Quickly the vessel was alive with Zouaves and naval officers. Captain Hollins, the distinguished-looking, elderly passenger of a few moments before, ran up to the steamer's captain with a brace of pistols and informed him that the ship was a prize to the Confederate States.

The trunk loads of Parisian hats, apparently destined for the fine ladies of Washington, proved to contain arms and equipment from Baltimore, with which seventeen of the passenger list had transformed themselves into men-at-arms. For the moment these men were purely volunteers, though electing to call themselves the Maryland Zouaves. Shortly afterward Richard Thomas, the erstwhile *modiste,* and leader of the men-at-arms, was commissioned as a colonel in the volunteer forces of the State of Virginia and was authorized to utilize this group of adventurous souls for the formation of a regiment to be called the Potomac Zouaves. Of this, more later.

Captain Hollins at once caused the captured steamer, with lights extinguished, to be turned toward the Virginia shore, and entered the Coan River, where a rendezvous had been arranged with Lieutenant Lewis, C.S.N., who should be in waiting with a detachment of soldiers from the First Tennessee Infantry and sailors from the Confederate States cruiser *Patrick Henry*. About an hour after the *St. Nicholas* had tied up at the landing, the reinforcements arrived, and were taken on board. Then, those passengers who wished to return north having been put ashore, the Confederates started for the bay again.

It was Captain Hollins' plan to capture by night attack the United States gunboat *Pawnee,* which usually patrolled these waters. The *Pawnee* was in the habit of receiving supplies from the *St. Nicholas* as she passed on her regular trips. It had been observed that the latter was never required to stop but was permitted to approach the man-of-war without challenge. Relying on this lax state of discipline, Hollins expected to lay alongside the *Pawnee,* and take her by boarding before the enemy knew what it was all about. However, getting a breathing moment, Hollins now read in the Baltimore papers, captured on the ship, that the *Pawnee* together with practically the entire Potomac River flotilla had gone to Washington to attend the funeral of Commander James H. Ward, U.S.N., who had been killed in the engagement at Mathias Point on the twenty-seventh.

Disappointed at not finding the enemy's war-vessel on the accustomed station, Captain Hollins, having no artillery, deemed it unwise to remain in open waters long after daylight should come. He, therefore, resolved to go up to Fredericksburg on the Rappahannock River.

Rounding Smith's Point into Chesapeake Bay, a schooner was passed, which might have been made a prize. But this apparent neglect was simply because two vessels were sighted together a little way out in the bay. The fine brig *Monticello* was first brought alongside and easily taken. The brig was up from Rio with 3,500 bags containing 17,500 arrobas, net weight, of coffee for the Baltimore market and dispatches for the United States Navy Department from the Brazilian squadron. The crew was taken off except the master and his wife, who were allowed to remain in their cabin; and a prize crew was placed on board with orders to take her to Fredericksburg. The schooner *Mary Pierce,* containing New England ice for the juleps of the Washingtonians, quickly followed in her wake. Then, turning back toward the mouth of the Potomac River, the Confederates bore down on the schooner first seen, the *Margaret,* from Baltimore for Boston, laden with coal; and made her a prize. Having replenished his bunkers from this unexpected collier, Captain Hollins took her in tow, and followed his two other prizes to Fredericksburg.

It had been a good day's work and fat prize-money had been earned by all on board. The *St. Nicholas* was condemned in the District Court in Admiralty sitting at Richmond, and yielded a net sum of $18,924.73. The Navy Department purchased her and converted her into the gunboat *Rappahannock*. Incidentally, Lieutenant Lewis became her commander.

The brig *Monticello* proved to be owned in Baltimore, and was released, but the cargo of coffee shipped by British merchants,[4] was seized by the Confederate Government. As the Richmond market for this commodity stood at a premium of about fifteen cents over the price brought at Baltimore, which was twelve cents a pound, the Confederates paid the Baltimore consignees for their coffee and yet earned a neat profit.[5]

The arrival of the ice schooner was timely, for it brought comfort to the sick and wounded lying in the hospitals as the result of the first of the many Virginia campaigns that were to come before the southerners could be subjugated. Not only welcome to fevered brows, this capture added some $8,000 to the prize-money.

[4] *NWR*, II, 1, pp. 374-377.

[5] From the report of Commander Samuel Lockwood on the U.S.S. *Daylight*, stationed off the mouth of the Rappahannock River, August 26, 1861: "This morning about 5 A.M. four fine-looking negroes, contraband of war, slaves from Lancaster County, Va., came alongside and delivered themselves up. I send them for your disposal. They informed me that two schooners were in a creek about 12 miles up the river loaded with grain for Fredericksburg, and that the brig *Monticello*, of Baltimore, which had been captured by the piratical steamer *St. Nicholas*, was lying at Manaskin [Monaskon] wharf, about 20 miles up the river. I determined to go in pursuit of them, and on going up, found that the schooners had disappeared, but on nearing the wharf discovered the brig lying there, and on our approach she hoisted her head sails and left the wharf, standing down for us under fore-and-aft sails. We went to quarters, took the usual measures to repel an attack or surprise, and on boarding her Lieutenant Lynch found she had been given up by the rebel authorities to her owners, which appears by the decree of the court herewith forwarded with the brig's papers, and I would call your attention to the decree and the reasons therein assigned for releasing the brig (the owners are not aliened [*sic*] enemies), and also to the fact of the cargo of coffee (which the captain says belonged to English subjects) having been sold in Richmond, Va., for 23 cents per pound."—*NWR*, I, 6, pp. 113-114.

THE ST. NICHOLAS

The Yankee captain of the schooner attended the sale, [recited Captain Hollins in his notes,] and seeing the fine prices paid for the ice he came to me and proposed that he should go to Boston, get another vessel loaded with ice, bring her down and let me know precisely when to meet him that I might capture him, take the vessel to Fredericksburg, sell the ice and divide the proceeds.

On the ice-laden *Mary Pierce* there had been found the huge flag of a "seventy-four," from which several ladies among the passengers on the *St. Nicholas* cut and made, as Captain Hollins tells, "a goodly number of secession flags."

Thomas, in whom the love of the dramatic seemed constitutional, in accepting the commission of colonelcy in the Virginia State Line, got the legislature to add Zarvona to his name. Under this *nom de guerre* he had served with Garibaldi in Italy. Love of adventure and an impulsive temperament had led Thomas to resign his cadetship at West Point and to go to California on government surveys. Thence he had gone to China to aid in the suppression of piracy. Therefore, the slow service of recruiting and organizing his regiment of Potomac Zouaves, now imposed upon Colonel Zarvona, was not the service suited to his dynamic nature; and he very soon set out upon another expedition to capture a sister ship to the *St. Nicholas*.

This time the enemy was more wary; and, when he attempted to take the *Mary Washington* by a *coup de main,* he and his party were taken prisoners. In the disturbance, it is said, Zarvona hid in a bureau drawer in the ladies' cabin. He carried on his person the Virginia commission, but that did not prevent his indictment for

185

piracy and for treason and his imprisonment in an unventilated dungeon. Upon this becoming known in Richmond, the criminal procedure against him was brought to an end by the institution of retaliatory measures; but he was kept in close confinement until the war was half over, and it was only upon the threat of severe retaliatory measures that Colonel Zarvona was exchanged as a prisoner-of-war.

During his long imprisonment, the little colonel made repeated efforts to escape. Once he threw himself from the sea-wall of Fort Lafayette into the water below, and swam toward the Long Island shore. The guard was called and in a rowboat overtook him. After he had been imprisoned a few months, it was stated in the press of Baltimore,[6] in which city Zarvona was very prominently connected, that he had lost his reason during his incarceration. Finally such pressure was brought to bear on the United States Senate, by influential friends and relatives, that the Committee on Military Affairs was directed to inquire into the alleged cruelties being practiced upon him. The report returned to the Senate was that he was found to be "sound and rational, but somewhat eccentric," though his peculiarities were "perfectly consistent with sanity of mind." However, it should be said that this picturesque character, when restored to the South, was so completely broken down in nervous system by the long imprisonment and severe treatment, that, at the age of only 30, he played no further part in the war, but betook himself to France where he spent most of the time until his death in 1875.

---

[6] *Baltimore Clipper*, November 13, 1861; *Savannah Daily News*, December 3, 1861.

XVI

SOME REPRISALS WITHOUT LETTERS

*D*URING the early days of the war, bodies of civilians, militia companies, and newly formed volunteer military organizations, acting upon authority, sometimes from their governor, more often very vague in character and source, and not infrequently with no authority at all, effected "reprisals" upon northern-owned vessels. When an embargo was placed at Cincinnati and Cairo upon arms moving down the Ohio and Mississippi Rivers to southern points, it aroused much resentment in the lower Mississippi Valley. The citizens of Helena, Arkansas, in the latter part of April, planted a cannon on the river bank and proceeded to retaliate by bringing to the *Queen of the West* and the *Mars*. The cargoes of these two steamboats were seized, and word was sent to the Cincinnatians that they might have their goods if and when the arms were sent down. Presently along came the *Skylark,* steaming laboriously up the river, carrying the United States flag. In response to the second shot from the Arkansan shore, she turned her prow across the river; but she came gaily playing her calliope, and confidently, for she had just been engaged in the transport of munitions of war for the account of the Governor of Arkansas, Henry M. Rector. The next steamer to pass was the *Silver Wave,* flying the Confederate colors; and though Arkansas was still in the Union, she came direct to Helena and was well received.[1]

[1] *True Delta,* April 30, 1861. Arkansas did not secede until May 6.

THE CONFEDERATE PRIVATEERS

As might be expected, there was much partisan warfare in the border states under the name of reprisals. A small party of enterprising Alabama steamboatmen came up from Mobile to Kentucky to see what could be done about the war. One Captain Gid B. Massey, who seems to have been the leading spirit, went over to Cairo to make a reconnaissance, and formulated a plan for the capture of the steamboat *Cheney,*—which was quickly and easily put into operation. Those of the crew who were Illinoisian were sent ashore, and, with the Kentuckian remainder, the *Cheney* was run down the Mississippi River, stopping at New Madrid to report to General Pillow, C.S.A., and in due course arriving safely at Memphis.[2] A few days later, James M. Irwin, late captain of the *New Uncle Sam,* captured the *Equality* from her wharf at Cairo, and escaped south.[3]

In retaliation for these seizures the U. S. Gunboat *Lexington* came up from Cairo to Paducah, Kentucky, and made fast to the stern-wheel steamer *W. B. Terry,* which was owned at Eastport, Mississippi, and returned with her as a prize. All the Mississippians escaped ashore, vowing vengeance. Accordingly the captain and crew of the *Terry* got into action and captured the *Samuel Orr,* a river packet owned in Evansville, Illinois, and having on board a valuable cargo of coffee, bacon, and whiskey. The *Orr* was one of the fastest packets on the river and made an abundant reprisal, being a valuable addition to the Confederate river marine.[4] She was taken by the army as a hospital ship;[5] but later she was used as a

[2] *True Delta,* August 9, 1861.
[3] *Memphis Avalanche,* August 16; *True Delta,* August 18, 1861.
[4] *Memphis Appeal,* August 23; *True Delta,* August 25, 1861.
[5] *NWR,* I, 22, p. 565.

minelayer in the Tennessee River and in that service met her end on February 7, 1862, when her crew destroyed her in order to prevent her capture by a Federal squadron.[6] The exchange of steamboats went merrily on, and before the end of the month the Yankees got the *S. H. Tucker* of Memphis.[7]

As the *Orr* proved not to be a permanent acquisition to the Confederates, so the Federals a few months later lost the *Terry*. This vessel had been taken into the United States service by General Grant as an armed dispatch boat, when she was captured, and burned, in the Tennessee River by a small force of Confederates.[8]

A short while before the *Terry* was destroyed and at about the same place in the river, one Captain Roddy effected a reprisal. On February 9, 1862, he had been obliged to destroy the stern-wheel steamboat *Julius H. Smith,* which he commanded in the Confederate transport service, in order to escape capture. The captain bided his time, and six months later to the day, with a band of so-called guerrillas, he surprised and burned two of the enemy's steamers, the *Callie* and the *Skylark,* as they lay tied up to the river bank changing cargoes.[9]

Meanwhile, down in Alabama life had not been without excitement. On April 25, 1861, the brig *Belle of the Bay* and the schooner *Daniel Townsend* were seized in Mobile Bay by David J. Files and some fifty other citizens in a night raid. Two days later a party of the Continentals, an artillery organization, chartered the steamer *Gunnison,* and captured the bark *R. H. Gamble,* down

[6] *NWR,* I, 22, pp. 572 and 821.   [7] *True Delta,* August 28, 1861.
[8] *NWR,* I, 23, pp. 332-333.
[9] *Report of Committees,* 2d Sess., 39th Cong., 1866-1867, vol. 4, pp. 348-349.

the bay. The *Mobile Daily Advertiser* in telling of these captures said: "We have inquired concerning the authority under which these seizures were made, and learn that the instructions, though only permissive, were ample." Nevertheless, the prizes were released.[10]

Exactly a month after the seizures made by the Files party, the Gulf City Guards executed a more fruitful reprisal in the same waters. The ship *Danube* had arrived on May 18 from Liverpool with the United States flag flying and with contraband reported to be stowed away in her hold. Toward midnight of Thursday, May 25, the guards went aboard the river steamer *Baltic;*[11] and, in the early black hours of Friday morning ran alongside and captured her at her anchorage in the bay. They met with no resistance, and found and took out one 8-pounder cannon and some military equipment.[12] The *Danube* was libeled in the name of the Confederate States of America; and, in the District Court for Alabama, was duly condemned as to the three-quarter interests which was proved to be alien owned.[13] This interest was put up and sold, on September 7, for $10,-200 to Messrs. Duplat and Company of Mobile.[14]

Late in June, fifteen Mobilians equipped themselves with sundry small arms, provisioned the oyster sloop *Creole,* and put out into the Mississippi Sound to see what wrongs might be reprised. The valiant gentlemen

[10] *Mobile Daily Advertiser,* April 27, 1861; *True Delta,* April 27 and 28, 1861.

[11] Some months later the *Baltic* was purchased by the State of Alabama, prepared for gunboat service, and presented to the Confederate States navy.—*NWR,* III, 1, p. 244.

[12] *Advertiser,* May 25, 1861.   [13] *True Delta,* August 28, 1861.

[14] *Ibid.,* September 11, 1861.

cruised over to New Orleans, and upon the return leg of the expedition they chanced upon a launch from a blockading vessel. The man-of-war's boat opened fire, and the Mobilians decided that no wrongs had been committed, and "skedaddled" for home.[15]

A resident of New Orleans, one S. Plassan, owned the brig *Hope,* which was captured by the U.S.S. *Brooklyn* while trying to enter the Pass à l'Outre. Plassan had wanted so much not to lose his vessel that, when he sent her on a voyage to Martinique, on April 1, he did not change the United States registry, though himself a Confederate citizen—a little April Fool's joke which was by nature a boomerang. In his vexation at the seizure of his brig he wanted the Governor of Louisiana to effect a reprisal to recoup his loss. However, he was politely informed that the state had no power in the matter, that the Central Government alone had authority to cause reprisals, and that, furthermore, he was due to lose the *Hope,* for while her Confederate States ownership had made her subject to capture by the United States, her United States registry would have subjected her also to capture by the Confederate States.[16]

This attempt to straddle the market, recalls an amusing story that appeared in the press not long after the *Hope* episode, of how the schooner *G. F. Keeland* of New Orleans had arrived in Minatitlan, Mexico, flying the British flag at the peak, the Stars and Bars at the main, and the Palmetto State in her rigging. The master of the Keeland was suspected of intending to fit her out

[15] *Advertiser,* July 3, 1861.   [16] *Daily Delta,* June 28, 1861.

as a privateer, and it was so reported in New York;[17] but such intentions, if they existed, bore no fruit.

Schooners, however, which aroused suspicions did not always get away with them. On the evening of May 7, the schooner *William A. Atwater* arrived in Apalachicola, and the next morning sailed without a clearance. The circumstance indicated that she was probably not on friendly business, and caused a movement on the part of the citizens. Captain Hunter, of the Beauregard Rifles, at once organized a party of some thirty men, and on the steamer *Spray* set out in pursuit. The following morning the Confederates put into Cedar Keys for observation. They remained all day, and at daybreak of the tenth their patience was rewarded. The *Atwater* was descried coming into harbor. The *Spray* got up her steam and ran down to meet her. Captain Hunter went aboard the schooner and demanded her surrender. The master, in his turn, demanded to know by what authority; and the captain replied by pointing to his armed force on the steamer. Without further ado the *Spray* took her prize in tow and returned to Apalachicola, where steamer and schooner arrived on Sunday afternoon, the twelfth. The captors kept a guard on the *Atwater,* while she was being libeled and condemned in the Confederate States District Court for Florida. It was shown that the prize had been chartered by the United States Government as a transport, and was returning to Key West after carrying lumber to the enemy's garrison at Fort Pickens, near Pensacola. Fifteen hundred dollars in gold was found on board of the

[17] *Daily Delta,* August 2, 1861.

schooner, which itself brought $2,400 at the marshal's sale.[18]

The purchasers used her in blockade-running, under the name of *Lizzie Weston*. While thus engaged she was recaptured during the following winter. At this time she had on board a cargo of 293 bales of cotton, and was bound for Jamaica or a market.[19]

It might be interesting to recall that the original master of the *Atwater,* one Henry Allen, had occasion to write to his shipowners in New York, begging them to contradict the rumors that he had been hanged by a mob in Apalachicola—for he was very much alive and well.[20]

About the same time, some East Coast Floridians at St. Augustine, hearing that the enemy was down the coast taking on a cargo of Florida live oak, determined to break up this trespass and organized a double party to go thither, by boats and by horses. They were successful in their mission and brought back as prize the towboat *George M. Bird* and $20,000 worth of timbers.[21]

A little later, over in the Mississippi a couple of army lieutenants (J. V. Toulme and J. Colley), with a detachment from the Shieldsboro' Rifles, forsook their normal element and made prize of the schooner *Vigilante* in punishment for supplying provisions to the blockading fleet.[22]

In the meantime the blockaders had done a little seiz-

[18] *Apalachicola Times,* May 15 and October 18, 1861; *Pensacola Observer,* May 18, 1861; *L'Abeille de la Nouvelle-Orléans,* 25 mai, 1861; *True Delta,* November 2, 1861.

[19] *NWR,* I, 17, pp. 54, 55, 120. [20] *True Delta,* June 15, 1861.

[21] *Savannah Republican,* May 16, 1861; *L'Abeille,* 23 mai, 1861.

[22] *Daily Delta,* July 23, 1861.

ing themselves. On June 23, the small boats belonging to the U.S.S. *Massachusetts* overhauled and took possession of the Mexican schooner *Brilliante* and four schooners carrying the coasting licenses of the Confederate Treasury Department. It is with the latter that we are concerned. They were the *Trois Frères, Fanny,* and *Basilide,* of and from New Orleans for Mobile, carrying cargoes, respectively, of salt and oats, railroad iron, and brick; and the *Olive Branch,* of Mobile, sailing from Fish River to New Orleans with a hundred barrels of spirits of turpentine on board. The four Confederate coasters were herded together under Lieutenant George L. Selden, U.S.N., with combined prize crews of nineteen men; and ordered to the United States Admiralty Court at Key West.[23]

"The schooners were six days knocking about in the Gulf," is the story of Master Smith, of the *Olive Branch,* as later related in *The Daily Delta,*[24] "Lieut. Selden meantime under spirituous influence having lost his reckoning and not knowing whereabouts they were. At last they made land at Cedar Keys. They then lay off and on two days, just long enough for the gallant Floridians to come out and take them into a safe harbor."

The "gallant Floridians" were under the command of Colonel Waite Smith, and for the purpose of investigating the suspicious looking craft in the offing had secured the use of the steamer *Madison.*[25] The four recaptured schooners were taken into the Suwanee River,

23 *NWR,* I, 16, pp. 560, 566, 568.   24 July 12, 1861.

25 This vessel is erroneously described by the *Atlanta Southern Confederacy,* quoted in *The True Delta,* of New Orleans, July 14, 1861, as a privateer. The capture was made without letter of marque and reprisal.

and held there pending their adjudication in the District Court. A decree of sale, to provide the salvage money, was entered against them, and they were ordered to be sold on December 21, 1861.[26] In the meantime, Lieutenant Selden—who in his official report blamed the weather—and his men were prisoners of war. They were first sent to Tallahassee, where the men were kept in jail and the lieutenant was allowed the freedom of the town on parole. Later they were sent to Richmond to await exchange.[27]

On June 12, 1861, Commander Poor of the U.S.S. *Brooklyn,* unwittingly, made a very just reprisal and then let it slip. The beautiful yacht *Gypsy,* of 50 tons, duly registered under the British flag, left Biloxi, Mississippi, by the way of Ship Island Pass, which was not blockaded, ostensibly on a fishing and pleasure excursion. Out in the Gulf of Mexico the yacht fell in with the frigate, which took possession of her, charging a violation of the blockade and placing a prize crew on her. The owner and captain of the *Gypsy* was a wealthy Englishman, John G. Robinson, resident in New Orleans, and Commodore of the New Orleans Yacht Club. He was indignant at being taken on board the *Brooklyn* as a prisoner under armed guard. He protested vigorously; and was allowed to go, with his colored body servant, to the Head of the Passes in order to communicate by telegraph with the British Consul in New Orleans. This official replied: "I can give no advice. . . . If you have addressed Captain Poor that you are a pleasure yacht, and merely sailing on an excursion, I

26 The *Savannah Daily News,* November 26, 1861.
27 *True Delta,* July 14, 1861; *Daily Delta,* July 28, 1861.

think he will release the *Gypsy*. Tell him that you have this from me." So after some further parleying Commander Poor released the *Gypsy*, but not without requiring her crew to take an oath not to take up arms against the United States during the course of the war. Commodore Robinson was forced to guarantee their good faith; but when he got back to New Orleans he wrote to the British Minister in Washington, Lord Lyons, a long letter of complaint, asking that his lordship would cause to be canceled the oath taken under compulsion.

To the newspapers, the yachtsman said that Commander Poor justified the detention on the ground that the "*Gypsy* contained a large amount of contraband articles, to-wit: 5 gallons of best French brandy, 1 basket champagne, nearly consumed, a box of ice, several boxes of pâté de foi gras, and a large amount of fishing tackle." While the press said that Commodore Robinson was only "enjoying one of his usual summer fishing excursions," as a matter of fact he was engaged upon a secret and very unneutral mission known only to the Collector of Customs at New Orleans and to the Secretary of War in Richmond.

The ship *Windsor Forest* had sailed from Liverpool on April 27 with a valuable cargo of arms for the Confederate War Department. Her charter read to Quebec, but her real destination was New Orleans. Secretary Walker wired Collector Hatch on May 24 that "she will be near Cape San Antonio by first of June. She should be advised of blockade. Can't you put pilot boat on this duty?" Commodore Robinson volunteered "without expectation of fee or hope of reward, but from pure devotion to the Confederate States," to seek out and "to give this vessel timely warning to make a port of safety." He was furnished with a carefully prepared chart showing the probable track of the *Windsor Forest.* He also agreed to look out for another cargo transport, the *Bamberg,* in which the Confederacy was very much interested. On this mission, he sailed, about June 6, down Lake Pontchartrain into the Mississippi Sound, calling at Biloxi. If Commander Poor had but known the true objective of the adventurous *Gypsy*—

Though Robinson failed in his mission, neither munition transport was captured by the blockaders; and the Confederate War Department tendered its thanks for the "heroic spirit of self-sacrifice and devotion to the great cause."[28]

Another venture did not fare so well. The yacht *Wanderer,*[29] referred to as "the notorious yacht *Wanderer,*" because of her past connection with the illegal African slave trade, arrived in Key West from Havana on April 5. Her papers were good, apparently British, and Lieutenant T. Augs. Craven, commanding the U.S.S. *Crusader,* on the Florida station, after consulting with the United States District Attorney, was satisfied that no libel could be sustained against the vessel. It was known that she had been for sale in Havana; and it was rumored that certain parties of New Orleans,

[28] *NWR,* I, 16, pp. 564, 573, 820-825; *Daily Picayune,* June 14, 15, 20, 1861; *Daily Delta,* June 16, 1861.

[29] This vessel should not be confused with the British schooner *Wanderer* which was regularly captured by the U.S.S. *Sacramento* off Murrell's Inlet, S. C., May 2, 1863, for violation of the blockade, and which was sent to Philadelphia for adjudication, where she was condemned and sold.— *Report of the Secretary of the Navy for 1865,* pp. 488 and 518. *NWR,* I, 8, p. 837.

having plans for privateering, were negotiating to purchase her at a high price. Being fairly new and stout and a remarkably fast sailer, she was admirably adapted for conversion into a privateer or light cruiser.

"While aware that I have no legal grounds for detaining the vessel," wrote Craven to the Secretary of the Navy in Washington, putting the case up to the Department, "I do not feel justified in permitting her to escape to the rebels." The Department seems to have been too busy to answer such details. The *Wanderer* appealed mightily to the United States naval authorities at Key West, so, after eyeing her covetously for a while, they simply took her, without formality, armed her, and made of her a light cruiser in the Gulf blockading squadron. At the end of the war she was sold in Key West at public auction, bringing $2,760—which was, of course, so much clear gain to the Government. She brought further profit to the United States navy in the shape of four duly adjudicated prize vessels.[30]

[30] *Report,* 1865, p. 534. *NWR,* I, vols. 1, 4, and 16; II, vol. 1.

XVII

CERTAIN ADVENTURES MORE OR LESS
PRIVATE

THE sparsity of maritime resources in the Confederate States and the literal enforcement of the letter of marque act having resulted in a restriction of privateering, there was, nevertheless, an irrepressible spirit for private adventure in many of the citizens. To take advantage of this force for the public weal, the Navy Department conceived a plan which cost the Government nothing. It was to receive these men into the Navy without pay, and to permit them to undertake their conceived enterprise against the enemy under blanket orders, with equipment largely furnished by themselves. Thus nominally in the public service, they were protected against the charge of being guerrillas, pirates, and the like,—and they were not obliged to forego compensation, for, being entitled to prize-money under the general law for the navy, their pay was proportionate to their resourcefulness.[1]

Though the privateersmen, considering the owners and crews collectively, got almost the entire proceeds from their prize, the Government only taking a twentieth part, the naval crews, in the case of a captured merchantman or an armed prize of inferior strength,

---

[1] Statutes-at-Large, C.S.A., Prov. Cong., Sess. I, Ch. 1, 1861, continued in force U.S.A. Statutes of 1800, Ch. 33, which provided that thirteen-twentieths of the prize money was distributable among the officers and petty officers in shares prescribed according to rank, and the remainder among the seamen, marines, and other persons on duty on board.

199

got one-half the value; and, when the prize was an armed vessel of equal or superior strength to the captors, the Government allowed them full value. The privateersmen were restricted to operations on the high seas, but the navy people might take prizes on the coasts and in the rivers as well. There are many ways in which captures may be made at sea by the play of personal ingenuity and courage and without involving elaborate equipment or paraphernalia. Thus, avoiding the capitalists share in the prize-money, the division of profits among the actual adventurers yielded about as much under navy enrollment as when operating under letters of marque; and the plan of licensing volunteers, economical to Government and to individual alike, proved a substitute for regular privateering that was most attractive.

One of the first adventures under this plan fell to the lot of George C. Andrews, who had been commissioned as a master-not-in-line-of-promotion on February 21, 1863. Acting Master Andrews organized a party of fourteen watermen from the docks of Mobile, and proceeded, on April 6, to the mouth of the Mississippi in quest of an enemy steamer. They had no equipment but side arms. On the night of Saturday, the eleventh, they found the United States army transport *Fox,* lying at a coal yard in the Pass à l'Outre; and, when all was quiet during the first hours of Sunday, they stealthily boarded and captured her, without a fight. In fact it would seem that the master[2] and crew of the steamer were quite willing captives, for, in spite of numbering

[2] Master Walker "was formerly captain of one of the Mobile Bay boats."—*Mobile Tribune,* April 16, 1861.

half as many again as their captors, they helped the latter to navigate the prize. So quietly was the affair handled that the *Fox* put to sea without exciting suspicion, and made the voyage to Mobile without mishap; though, as she entered by the Swash Channel, at 3 A.M., the fifteenth, she was greeted with a fusilade of some thirty shots from the blockading squadron. The adventurers did not hesitate under the fire, but went on and were soon safely under the guns of Fort Morgan. The *Fox* arrived at the city wharves at six o'clock that evening, and the next day her capture was acclaimed in the *Mobile Tribune* as "certainly one of the most daring and well-managed exploits of the war."

This was the second time that the *Fox* had been under the Confederate flag, for prior to the capture of New Orleans she had been registered in the Confederate merchant navy as the *A. J. Whitmore*. Again under the Stars and Bars she reëntered the freighting business as the *Fanny,* running the blockade between Mobile and Havana. On August 21, she arrived in the latter port,[3] three days out, with a cargo of cotton, which sold at thirty-six cents a pound. For the return trip she loaded with government supplies. It was her last trip, for, as she was entering the home waters on September 12, she was chased by three blockaders, who pressed her so hard that the crew set her on fire and escaped ashore.[4]

The cutting out of the *Fox* set the blockading squadron on its ears. So when, in the following fall, one of Andrews' men happened to be in Havana, at the same

[3] *El Siglo* (Havana), 22 Agosto 1863.
[4] *NWR*, I, 20, pp. 120, 141, 155, 160, 583-586, 707, 809.

time as the blockade-runner *Cumberland,* it was at once concluded that the runner was fitting out as a privateer. This was a fast, though old, steamer of 700 tons, and was undergoing suspiciously extensive repairs. The United States Consul-General at Havana became quite excited over her, and the admiral commanding the East Gulf blockading squadron caused a warning against her to be read from the quarter-deck of every vessel in his squadron. The caution to extraordinary vigilance was not without fruit, for on February 5, 1864, the U.S.S. *De Soto* fell in with the *Cumberland* as the latter was trying to make Mobile, and captured her. However, the latter was still only a freighter, though she had on board a valuable cargo of arms and ammunition.[5]

The *Fox* exploit stimulated the Mobile adventurers to an even more daring accomplishment. One James Duke, sometime blockade-runner captain and afterward captive in Union hands, secured a commission as a master-not-in-line-of-promotion, and enlisted a party of about eighteen men. With high enthusiasm but not very definite plans, they set out from Mobile in a launch on May 28, 1863, working their way down the Mississippi Sound and around to the Pass à l'Outre—for they had chosen the scene of their exemplars' success. For some days they hid in the marshes bordering the principal mouth of the Great Father of Waters, undergoing rather hard fare. The enemy patrol boats were constantly moving up and down within view. Then at dusk on June 9,[6] their opportunity came. A gunboat passed up close to them. Half an hour later came the seagoing tug *Boston* towing the ship *Jenny Lind,* laden with ice,

[5] *NWR,* I, 17, pp. 643-645.   [6] *NWR,* II, 2, p. 530.

up to New Orleans. The launch slid out from her concealment and was oared alongside the tug. Duke hailed and was allowed to come aboard. The raiders, piling over the rail, took by surprise the tug's crew, who surrendered to the pretty display of Confederate revolvers. The tow line was at once cut, and the tug, free of encumbrance, was swung round and out to sea. So skillfully and quickly did the adventurers act that they escaped interference from the U.S.S. *Portsmouth,* a sailing sloop-of-war of eighteen guns, which was within speaking distance all the while.

Standing out into the Gulf they met the bark *Lennox,* from New York, loaded with an assorted cargo, to which they helped themselves, and then fired the vessel. The captain and mate of the bark were taken prisoners, but her people, of which there were about forty, were sent ashore in small boats. Scarcely an hour later they fell in with another bark, the *Texana,* also of New York, and treated her likewise. Leaving their last prize burning splendidly, the privateersmen turned their tug homeward. About 2 o'clock in the morning of the eleventh, they passed old Fort Morgan and, proceeding up the long bay, arrived before the city at eleven in the forenoon, with the Confederate flag flying and amid great hurrahs along the water front.[7]

In November, Duke undertook to repeat his performances. This time he made his base in the mouth of the Perdido River on the Florida coast near the Alabama line, being provided with a lugger mounting one boat howitzer and manned by a crew of sixteen. On the fourteenth, three schooners sailing together toward

[7] *Richmond Enquirer,* June 17, 1863.

Pensacola lured him from his hiding place. The wind filled the lugger's sails and away she sped, soon overhauling the flotilla, which proved to be three chartered transports bound from New Orleans to the Pensacola navy yard for coal. A prize crew was put on the *Mary Campbell* and Duke himself went on board the *Norman.* Before the third schooner, the *Venice,* could be secured the U.S.S. *Bermuda* appeared on the scene, and the Confederates made a hurried departure. The *Mary Campbell* and the lugger stood seaward, and were captured. The *Norman* ran for the shore, where Duke set her afire and escaped with ten of his men.[8]

About ten days after this adventure, the blockaders off Mobile were agitated by a report that Duke was coming, on the night of the twenty-seventh, in the torpedo boat *Gunnison,* to attack the squadron. In fact, it was Midshipman Edward A. Swain who was ordered to the *Gunnison* for this attack. For some reason, probably because the Confederates had learned that the enemy was informed of their plans, the sortie was abandoned.[9]

Incidentally, Swain shortly afterward secured a three months' leave of absence upon the termination of which he resigned from the service.[10] However, it was not long before he succumbed to the lure of an adventure projected against shipping in the Pacific, and got for himself an appointment as an acting master's mate—but more of that in another chapter.[11]

To emulate the shining examples of Andrews and

[8] *NWR,* I, 20, pp. 674-676.   [9] *Ibid.,* pp. 697 and 848.
[10] *Officers in the Confederate States Navy* (Washington: Government Printing Office, 1898), p. 133.
[11] See pp. 273-275.

Duke, another Mobilian, David Nicols, secured an acting master's commission and a crew of nineteen; and, having been duly sworn at the provost marshal's office, was allowed to pass the forts and obstructions and to proceed to sea in a cutter upon his adventurous undertaking. Cruising westward from Mobile, ever on the lookout for such of the smaller craft of the enemy as might be captured or destroyed, Master Nicols and his men reached the South West Pass of the Mississippi River, some days later, empty-handed. Hauling the cutter into the marshes, they set out on foot, wading through mud and high grass, for the coal dock near the lighthouse. There they found the fine, new quartermaster steamer *Leviathan;* and during the black hours of the morning of September 24, 1863, boarded her and made her an easy prize, standing to sea in her without loss of time. With daylight the news of the capture was spread among the blockaders, and the chase was soon begun. The *Leviathan* with all her canvas set kept ahead of her pursuers for two hours and a half after the latter had gotten her track; but at 10.30 in the morning the shells of the U.S.S. *De Soto* brought home to the Confederates the futility of further flight, and they surrendered. The enemy put them in irons and took them to New Orleans, for these raids on unarmed steamers had aroused the ire of Admiral Farragut, who vehemently called them piracies.[12]

After the *Boston* had been so easily carried through the blockading squadron into Mobile, the irascible old admiral had written from New Orleans to the commodore commanding at that station: "I cannot understand

[12] *NWR*, I, 17, pp. 556-559; 20, pp. 20, 237, 302, 597-599.

how the blockade is run with such ease, when you have so strong a numerical force."[13]

While the adventures of Andrews, Duke, and Nicols had the sanction of public authority, although privately organized, the adventure of one Thomas E. Hogg was wholly private. Hogg, a citizen of Maryland, had come South upon the declaration of war but had not naturalized himself in the Confederate States. November, 1863, found him on the Mexican frontier, as he says in affidavit, "for his health." A plan to capture one or more of the merchant vessels of the United States occurred to him, and he lost no time in putting it into execution. Through a Mr. Bell he obtained from Brigadier General Hamilton P. Bee, commanding Confederate troops in Brownsville, a paper sanctioning the undertaking. From the collector of customs at that port he got a blank for a ship's register, signed and sealed, only wanting to be filled in with the description of any vessel that might be captured.

Thus forearmed, Hogg crossed the Rio Grande and at Matamoras enlisted the coöperation of five Irishmen, named Wilson, O'Brien, Riley, Clement, and Brown. On the sixteenth day of November, the party took passage in the United States schooner *Joseph L. Gerrity,* laden with 122 bales of cotton, and bound for New York. The second night out, the adventurers rose against the captain and crew; and, without inflicting any injuries upon them, made themselves masters of the schooner in the name of the Confederate States. The course was now altered and the helm turned from the

[13] *NWR,* I, 20, p. 309.

Florida Straits toward Yucatan Channel. Arriving off Cape Catoche on the Yucatan Peninsula, the Yankee captain and crew and the one *bona-fide* passenger were sent ashore in a small boat; and the schooner proceeded into the Carribean Sea, putting in at Belize, British Honduras. By the aid of the blank register, Hogg passed his prize off to the port officials as the Confederate blockade-runner *Eureka,* of Brownsville, Texas, and sold the cargo. But he had been delayed in transit by light and contrary winds; and, in the meantime, the rightful captain of the *Gerrity* had reached Sisal, a small Yucatan port, where he laid full complaint and charge of piracy before the United States Consul. The latter got into communication with the British authorities, but before any action could be taken Hogg and one man escaped to the Pacific coast. Thence the fugitives doubled back across the Isthmus of Panama, and eventually arrived in Nassau. Here, late in the following April, the Maryland adventurer learned that three of his men had escaped to Liverpool, but had been apprehended in that port through the efforts of the United States Consular Service and imprisoned under charge of piracy. Hogg at once sailed for the Confederacy and repaired to Richmond, where he laid the case before the State Department.

The Secretary of State, Judah P. Benjamin, interested himself in the fate of these three unfortunate Irishmen, and wrote to the Confederate Commercial Agent, Henry Hotze, in London, disclaiming sanction of "such irregular and illegal warfare," inasmuch as the parties were neither citizens of the Confederate States nor in their service, but at the same time directing that nothing be spared that can properly be done to alleviate their condition and to save them from punishment for what was not an intentional offense. [For] we are informed that two of the men now prisoners in England had been in service in our Army and had been honorably discharged in consequence of wounds received in our service. It is believed by us to be apparent that all parties engaged in the enterprise were deceived and led into error by the sanction of local officials who were at too great a distance from the seat of government to obtain orders or directions for their conduct, and that all concerned were laboring under the honest delusion that they were engaged in a legitimate, belligerent act, justified by the law of nations in time of war, and were quite innocent of any felonious intent, without which their act can in no just sense be characterized as piracy.[14]

Counsel was employed to defend the three prisoners —at a cost of £458 1s. 4d. to the Confederate Government. It developed that the men were held in custody at the instance of Mr. Adams, the Minister of the United States, for extradition on the charge of piracy. A habeas corpus proceeding was resorted to, and the prisoners were discharged by the Court of Queen's Bench on May 25, 1864. The case turned on the construction of the extradition treaty between the United States and England. The defendants' counsel claimed that the capture was an act of war. Both belligerents were represented by eminent legal talent. The court held—the three associates overruling the Chief Justice—that the offense of piracy declared extraditable in the treaty was only that offense which was especially created by the domestic statutes of either country; for piracy *jure gentium* was

[14] *NWR,* I, 20, pp. 727-728; II, 3, pp. 1082, 1083, 1111-1113.

triable in the court of any nation and hence was not extraditable. The seizure of the *Gerrity* was held not to be a violation of United States law. Nor did the British consider the affair as an act of international piracy. The decision was hailed as a very satisfactory precedent by the Confederates. But in the meanwhile the British colonial authorities had restored the *Gerrity* to the custody of the United States commercial agent at Belize.[15]

However, the irregularities in the remote Military Department of Texas were not always confined to matters of judgment. A case of fraud committed upon the C.S.S. *General Rusk* led to the dismissal of a Confederate army officer and also a United States naval officer, under circumstances suggesting double piracy.

Under Special Order No. 381, March 28, 1862, all the Government vessels employed in the Department were placed, by Brigadier General Paul O. Hébert, commanding, under the charge of Major T. S. Moïse, Assistant Quartermaster. Among these was the *General Rusk,* a large steamer formerly a merchantman. Presently, under color of obtaining supplies for the Government, the major dismantled her as a man-of-war and entered into a fraudulent combination with four civilians to put her under the British flag by collusive transfer to some Englishman, and to employ her in trading between the Confederacy and Cuba. The transaction was without authority; and no payment or consideration to the Government, freight or charter money, was stipulated. Only a nominal bond signed by the civilians themselves was given for the return of the vessel to the army.

15 *NWR,* II, 3, pp. 1136, 1137, 1147, 1153, 1184, 1216, 1231; *Diplomatic Correspondence* (Washington: Government Printing Office, 1864), part 2; pp. 490, 594-595.

In July the stolen steamer brought her first cargo of cotton into Havana, and was provisionally registered at the British consulate as the *Blanche,* George Wigg, of Liverpool, owner. On the return trip supplies were carried in, which were sold to the Government at a heavy advance over Cuban prices. The robbery was working splendidly and yielding handsome profits. Late in September, the *Blanche* took on a cargo of 583 bales of cotton and cleared from Port Lavaca, on Matagorda Bay, Texas. It seems that no blockaders had been off the bay for some weeks, nor were any met on the trip. On the sixth day out, the coast of Cuba was made, and, the next day, La Mulata was put into for coal. One day was spent in refueling, and then, having taken on a coast pilot, the *Blanche* leisurely steamed, close inshore, toward Havana.

On Tuesday, October 7, 1862, El Morro Light was in view. In the early afternoon a large Spanish frigate passed under the castle into the Havana harbor. When the Spaniard had disappeared, another man-of-war in the offing bore down on the surreptitious trader. The Stars and Stripes unfolded on her and a blank cartridge sang out. The *Blanche* was well within the marine league of Spanish neutrality, but her captain deemed it more prudent to get even closer inshore and ran into Marianao Creek, anchoring within about three hundred yards of the beach. Perceiving the hostile intent of the enemy, the Cuban pilot went ashore, and brought on board a Spanish civil officer (an *alcalde de mar*), who hoisted the yellow and red flag of Spain over the British flag to show that the vessel was under the protection of Her

Most Catholic Majesty, Isabella II. But the Yankees paid no attention to requirements of international law and comity. A shotted gun was fired at the *Blanche*—though, by reason of defective ammunition, the shell fell far short—and two boats' crews were dispatched to cut her out. The *Blanche's* captain, Robert Nelson Smith, now deemed it advisable in order to preserve his ship and cargo to slip his cable and to run her upon the beach.

It was about three o'clock when Acting Master Charles G. Arthur, in the first cutter from the cruiser, boarded the blockade-runner. He asked the captain why he beached his ship, and was answered by a shrug of the shoulders. Arthur then inquired what was the cargo, and received the laconic answer: "Cotton."

"Don't you know that cotton is contraband of war?" queried the boarding officer.

"No; not that I am aware of, on board a British ship, and in a neutral port," responded Captain Smith.

It was now Smith's time to ask a few questions, and he demanded to know what right Arthur had to board a neutral ship in neutral jurisdiction. The naval officer replied that he belonged to the United States steamer *Montgomery,* that he had orders to take the ship, that he didn't care about the protection of flag or authorities, and that he wouldn't discuss his rights in the premise. The *alcalde* attempted to remonstrate—in Spanish—against the violation of his country's honor; but the boarding officer peremptorily ordered him to leave the ship, using force in compelling him to get into his boat.

Acting Master Arthur declared the ship to be his prize and the crew his prisoners. He stationed sentries in all parts of the ship with orders to shoot anyone who moved, and extended an invitation to the sailors to join the United States navy. He got no recruits, however. In the meantime, he had ordered a naval engineer to go down into the engine room, and back the steamer off the ground. Presently smoke began to issue from below. The ship was afire and the flames were spreading rapidly. Someone yelled that there was gunpowder on board, and the boarders made a mad scramble for their boats, only taking away with them the Spanish pilot and a passenger, a British subject named Robert F. Clement,[16] as prisoners. The ship's crew escaped to the shore, which was less than a hundred feet away.

The two cutters pulled a discreet distance away to avoid the effects of the explosion—which did not occur, there being no gunpowder on board. The boarding parties watched the flames lick up the masts and burn the two neutral flags; then returned to the *Montgomery*.

The destruction of the *Blanche* produced great indignation in Havana, being denounced as piratical. Both the Spanish and British ministers in Washington made vigorous protests to the United States Government. The Secretary of the Navy had received no report, and, on October 28, he wrote Admiral Farragut a curt request for information. On December 9, the Secretary had not yet received an explanation, and he again wrote the admiral, this time directing him to depose Commander Charles Hunter from his command of the *Montgomery*, and to send that vessel to New York under the charge of the executive. Upon his arrival in New

[16] Clement was one of Major Moïse's civilian associates in the enterprise.

York, the unwise Hunter was court-martialed and dismissed the service.

Meanwhile, Major Moïse had been tried by a Confederate States army court on charge of defrauding the Government, and had been dismissed; and the Richmond authorities had instituted civil proceedings to recover from the fraudulent combination the value of the services of the vessel on her first and only round trip. Diplomatic representations were made to Spain by the Confederate commissioner in Paris, John Slidell, through the Spanish Ambassador to France, Señor Isturitz, for indemnity in the value of the steamer. Conversations on the subject were held in Washington between the Spanish minister, Señor Tassara, and the State Department—and a year later they were still discussing it. The Confederate States Government considered it impolitic to press the Spanish Government until after peace should be established.[17] The United States Government eventually made reparation to Spain in the sum of $200,000.[18]

If one man in the western departments of the army proved treacherous and a defrauder to the service, there were countless brave, true men who preferred saddles to swivel chairs, who loved hazard, and who, if anything were to be taken, only took it from the enemy. Many such individualistic souls found their place in the partisan rangers, whose operations in small bodies within

[17] *NWR*, II, 3, pp. 725, 727-728, 781, 810, 855, 884, 932. *NWR*, I, 18, pp. 838-840; 19, pp. 267-286. *Diplomatic Correspondence,* 1862, pp. 476, 532, 536; 1863, pp. 418, 432, 436, 440, 444, 611, 617; 1864, part 2, pp. 391, 497, 635, 636; 1866, part 1, pp. 234, 235.

[18] James Morton Callahan, *The Diplomatic History of the Southern Confederacy* (Baltimore: The Johns Hopkins Press, 1901), p. 78.

the enemy's lines made life full of thrills. The rangers were organized under an Act of Congress, passed April 21, 1862, which granted to them not only the pay of their grades but the full value of all arms and munitions of war which they should capture and deliver to the Quartermaster's Department—forming a sort of land privateering.

Captain James H. McGehee, who commanded a troop of such unattached cavalry in Arkansas, seems to have had a penchant for forays upon the water. Early in January, 1863, he appeared on the west bank of the Mississippi River opposite Memphis, which was then occupied by the enemy. Finding the steamboat *Jacob Musselman* lying on the Arkansas side, he made her a quick and easy prize, and ran her some fifteen miles upstream to Bradley's Landing. At this point he found a flatboat loaded with stock, and captured it. Then, having taken the stock and such things from the steamer as were valuable, he burned both vessels, and disappeared into the interior. A few days later McGehee and a dozen of his men boldly crossed the Mississippi; and about midnight, Sunday, the eleventh, under the very nose of the U. S. gunboat *Conestoga,* boarded the towboat *Grampus No. 2,* at her moorings near the city wharf. They surprised the watch, and at the point of their revolvers made the crew get up steam and proceed up the river some five miles to Mound City Landing on the Arkansas side. The towboat had with her five coal barges, which the raiders cut adrift. The crew, after being paroled, were allowed to go into a vacant house near the landing and to make themselves as comfortable as possible for the remainder of the night. Afterward they reported themselves as having been "not unkindly used," though the master, one Thomas Chester, claimed to have been robbed of nearly one thousand dollars in green-backs and a very valuable gold watch. At any rate, the captors stripped the steamer of all valuable fixtures, loaded them into a six-horse wagon, and drove into the interior with their booty; but not before setting fire to the *Grampus*, which floated down the river, a magnificently blazing mass.

The commanding officer of the *Conestoga* avenged himself for the exploit that was carried out under his sleeping eyes by ordering the light-draft gunboat *Linden* to scourge the country in the vicinity where the *Musselman* and the *Grampus* were burned. The *Linden* took on a battalion of Indiana infantry and proceeded to the theatre of reprisal, where several citizens were made prisoners and some houses were burned, as a warning against "harboring guerrillas"—but none of the rangers were taken.

A month later Captain McGehee resumed the terrorizing of the river. On February 16, about thirty miles below Memphis, he fell upon and captured a flatboat laden with certain medicines much needed in the Confederacy and some naval ordnance. The next day, having rapidly changed positions, he came upon the United States army tug *Hercules* tied up to the Arkansas bank, opposite Memphis, on account of a fog. The rangers boarded her, killed one of the crew in the mêlée, took the others prisoners, set the tug on fire, and also burned one of the seven coal barges in the tow.[19]

These and other successful attacks on the river com-

---

[19] *NWR*, I, 24, pp. 134-137, 423.

munications of the enemy, greatly annoyed, vexed, and irritated Acting Rear Admiral David D. Porter commanding the Mississippi squadron; and he ordered, on February 13, that anyone who should fire on an unarmed vessel should be hanged on "the nearest tree," causing a notice of this intention to be published. The excitement in the squadron reached such a high pitch that a week later Captain E. W. Sutherland, commanding the U.S.S. *Monarch* shot and killed in cold blood a Confederate private, a prisoner in his hands, who admitted that he had been one of the party which attacked the U.S.S. *Dick Fulton,* one of the Ellet rams, on February 10. The Confederates had a long line of wronged women and pillaged plantations to avenge. Captain Sutherland himself in his report to the admiral, February 20, admitted the atrocities committed by the demoralized command of Brigadier General Stephen G. Burbridge, U.S.A. On the same day Lieutenant General John C. Pemberton, commanding the Confederate Department of Mississippi and Eastern Louisiana, ordered "retaliation in the fullest measure." Porter came to his senses; and, on March 2, in a conciliatory reply to a communication from the Confederate general said: "If General Pemberton is desirous that the war should be conducted on the principle of humanity and civilization, all he has to do is to issue an order to stop guerrilla warfare."[20]

The murder of prisoners does not seem to have been confined to one side—according to reports found in the Quartermaster Department at Washington. During most of the year 1863, there was constant warfare along

[20] *NWR,* I, 24, pp. 362, 364, 367.

the Cumberland and Tennessee Rivers between the Federal gunboats and transports on the one hand and small bodies of Confederate soldiers—to whom the enemy indiscriminately referred as guerrillas—on the other. On April 8, 1863, "a band of guerrillas, 1,200 strong, with two pieces of artillery, under Woodward," destroyed the propeller *Saxonia* and the stern-wheeler *R. M. C. Lovell.* These boats were on the Cumberland River, and were engaged in transporting sutlers' stores for the United States army. Woodward was a regularly commissioned lieutenant colonel in the Confederate army, and his command was the First Kentucky Cavalry.[21] Woodward, "after the surrender of the boats, took out eight negroes and shot them by the light of a lantern. Captain Lane, of the *Lovell,* expressing strong disapprobation of the act, was taken and shot in the same cold-blooded manner."[22]

It seems strange that no reference to this incident is found in the Naval War Records, nor is any made in such semi-official histories as Porter's *Naval History of the Civil War* or Mahan's *The Gulf and Inland Waters* (in *The Navy in the Civil War* series). However, it is interesting to note that at this time the Confederate Congress had had under consideration, for about two months, a plan to repress the use of slaves against the Confederacy. This measure was passed on May 1, 1863. It provided that any comissioned officer of the enemy taken in command of negroes or mulattoes should be deemed guilty of inciting a servile insurrection; and should, "if captured, be put to death, or be otherwise

---

[21] *Journal,* C. S. Cong., v. 1, p. 647.
[22] *Report of Committees,* 2d Sess., 39th Cong., 1866-1867, v. 4, p. 350.

punished in the discretion of the court." The negroes
themselves were to be turned over to the state authorities
to be dealt with according to the laws of the state.[23]

The river wars of the West were characterized by one
retaliation after another. Two days before Colonel
Woodward is said to have destroyed the steamboats and
shot the negroes, the nearby town of Palmyra had been
burned by the orders of Lieutenant Commander LeRoy
Fitch, U.S.N., as a lesson to the guerrillas. Not a house
had been left.[24] Similarly, on May 23, Brigadier General
Alfred W. Ellet, U.S.A., commanding the Mississippi
marine brigade, burned to the ground the town of Austin, on the Tennessee River, as a reprisal for an attack
which had been made upon his commissary boat some six
miles upstream.[25]

At the end of the war the Quartermaster General of
the United States army reported that the steamboats on
the Mississippi River and its tributaries "captured and
burned by guerrillas" numbered 28, with a total tonnage
of 7,065 and a value of $335,000; and those "burned by
rebel incendiaries," 29, with a total of 18,580 tons, and
a value of $891,000. The report also stated that 19
steamers, totalling 7,925 tons and valued at $518,500,
had been "captured and burned by the enemy."[26]

The attempt to differentiate between the "enemy"
and the "guerrillas" is of doubtful propriety; for, as a
matter of fact, all attacks on the river shipping, made
under the Confederate flag, were quite regular and con-
formable to the rules of war. The river was the enemy's

[23] Conf. Statutes, 1st Cong., Sess. III, Res. 5.
[24] *NWR.* I, 24, pp. 66-75.   [25] *Ibid.,* p. 530.
[26] *Report of Committees,* 39th Cong., 2d Sess., vol. 4, pp. 356-357.

line of communication, upon which he transported his troops and supplies of war. However, during the last year of the war the Mississippi Valley became infested with gangs of armed desperadoes, who attacked and robbed both sides alike; and the world was presented, in March, 1865, with the unique spectacle of the belligerents, in the Baton Rouge area, entering into a ten-day truce during which to clean up the "jayhawkers."[27]

Comedy and tragedy are companions of war. The United States ironclad *Essex* was stationed in the Mississippi River off Donaldsonville, Louisiana, on September 23, 1863. At about two o'clock in the morning of that day an unusual noise was heard on the opposite shore in the direction of the army telegraph station. A boat was dispatched to a point within hail of the station to inquire into the cause of the disturbance. The young officer in charge hallooed and received in reply, as from the guard: "Some guerrillas are at the Bringier plantation and we are going down after them." This answer was satisfactory, and the man-of-war's men pulled back to their ship. But with the coming of day, they found that they had been tricked. A party of Confederate raiders had taken the telegraph station, catching the garrison napping. The hail had been answered by a Confederate—whose sense of humor, or audacity, had been irrepressible—just as the raiders were in the act of making off with their prisoners and captured property.

The next night there was another and similar disturbance on shore. Again the navy hailed. The information came back over the water: "The guerrillas have returned and are in camp." The ironclad's guns then opened upon

27 *NWR*, I, 27, pp. 70-76.

the station. Only a few pistol shots replied. But in response to specific directions from the shore a rolling barrage was laid down on the line of retreat of the supposed enemy. After some little time, the ship's people became suspicious and ceased firing. An hour or so later, they learned that the affair had been staged by three drunken sergeants, to while away the tedium of guard duty at the expense of their compatriots in the navy.[28]

The Confederates may have been regular troops or they may have been only partisans. But the craving of the drunken sergeants for excitement must be classed as a purely private adventure.

[28] *NWR*, I, 25, pp. 432-433.

XVIII

JOHN Y. BEALL, PARTISAN SEA-CAPTAIN

*J*OHN YATES BEALL, twenty-eight years of age, a graduate of the University of Virginia and an invalided soldier, aspired, in the spring of 1863, to be upon the Chesapeake Bay what John Singleton Mosby was then in the interior of Virginia and Maryland.[1] The feats of Mosby and his partisan cavalrymen were upon the lips of everyone.

Early in the year Beall came to Richmond to present his views to the Government. He had just returned from Canada, though the reason for his having been in Canada does not appear. In one of the early skirmishes of the war, down in the Shenandoah Valley, while commanding a company of volunteers, he had received a musketry wound in the chest, which seemed to aggravate a consumptive tendency. During his convalescence he had toured the Confederacy, spending some time in Louisiana. Then he had wandered through the western part of the United States, at length arriving in Dundas, Canada West, in November, 1862. Two months later, he turned southward, and, after some adventure, arrived again in Virginia, having made the last lap of his jour-

[1] The sources for this chapter are: *NWR,* I. vols. 3 and 9; John W. Headley, *Confederate Operations in Canada and New York* (New York and Washington: The Neale Publishing Company, 1906); Daniel B. Lucas, *Memoir of John Yates Beall; His Life; Trial; Correspondence; Diary* (Montreal: printed by John Lovell, St. Nicholas St., 1865); Isaac Markens, *President Lincoln and the Case of John Y. Beall* (New York: printed for the author, 62 Beaver St., 1911); *Trial of John Y. Beall as a Spy and Guerrillero by Military Commission* (New York: D. Appleton & Co., 1865).

ney from Baltimore by a pungy operated by petty blockade-runners.

He had two bold but not impractical ideas. One was the formation of a secret expedition on the Great Lakes to capture the single United States gunboat allowed upon those waters by the treaty with Great Britain. As this man-of-war was stationed at Johnson's Island where there was located a large camp of Confederate prisoners of war, it would be an easy matter, having taken her, to release these captives, and create an army within the country of the enemy. The other was a project to carry on a species of privateering on the waters of the Chesapeake and the Potomac. The Secretary of the Navy informed Beall that his schemes were feasible, but that the one for operations on the Great Lakes might embroil the Government with Great Britain, and was, therefore, not to be thought of at that time. The second proposal, however, was acceptable.

Beall and a comrade, also an invalided army officer, were given on March 5, 1863, commissions as masters-not-in-line-of-promotion in the naval service. They were authorized to receive the enlistment of men not subject to the provisions of the conscription laws, and to draw equipment for them from the naval storekeeper. Thus Beall and his men, like Andrews, Duke, and Nicols in the last chapter, became legally a part of the naval establishment; but as with the Mobile expeditions, it was their partisan or private character which was more conspicuous. They must contrive their own boats, and pay themselves out of prizes taken from the enemy.

The first two recruits to be signed up were a couple of young Scotchmen, a Lowlander named Bennett G.

Burley, and a Highlander known as John Maxwell. At length the expedition numbered some ten men, and about the first of April it set out from Richmond for Mathews Court House which was established as the rendezvous. Nothing much was accomplished until the fall. During their first month, the would-be privateersmen surprised a camp of runaway negroes, killing one of the "contrabands" and capturing another. In July they cut the United States cable to the eastern shore of Virginia, and in August despoiled the lighthouse on Smith's Island. Then, his comrade having been restored to the active list in the army, Beall was left without commissioned assistance. The appointment of Edward McGuire and the young Scots as acting masters followed. By September the force had reached a total of eighteen, and owned two boats, a black one called the *Raven* and a white one named the *Swan*.

The time was now ripe for a real exploit, and on Thursday, September 17, the sea-partisans left the rendezvous and put out into the bay from Horn Harbor, Mathews County. "Captain" Beall commanded the *Swan* and McGuire was in charge of the *Raven*. The little squadron stood across the Chesapeake to Cape Charles for operations on the Atlantic side of the eastern shore. At Raccoon Island, the sloop *Mary Anne* and two fishing scows were encountered and captured; and were taken up the coast into Wachapreague Inlet in Accomac County. The following night, the *Alliance,* a large sloop, laden with sutlers' stores for the enemy's occupational forces at Port Royal, South Carolina, was made a prize. The equinoctial storms had set in, and a heavy sea was running when the Confederates attempted to board the *Alliance,* the *Raven* on the starboard and the *Swan* on the port. The little *Raven* lucklessly was slammed against the side of the big sloop, then drawn back by the roll of the water, her tiller broken and her captain overboard. McGuire regained his boat, which had now washed around to the port side, and both parties boarded together. Beall led his men to the forecastle and McGuire to the cabin. Master Ireland would have put up a fight for his sloop, but the Confederates had him covered and he yielded.

Although the rough weather continued, the Confederates set out in their boats, on Sunday morning, and took the schooner *J. J. Houseman.* On Monday night, they added to the collection the schooners *Samuel Pearsall* and *Alexandria,* and decided it was time to go home. The crews of the *Mary Anne* and the fishing smacks were paroled, and the captives from the other vessels were placed on the *Raven* and the *Swan.* The prizes, except the *Alliance,* were stripped of valuables; their sails were set, and they were sent derelict to sea. One of them, however, the *Houseman,* was later picked up by the enemy. Master McGuire with the prisoners arrived safely at Horn Harbor and proceeded with them to Richmond.

In the meantime, Beall had remained aboard the *Alliance,* which had a most valuable cargo, worth probably $200,000 on the Richmond market. He determined to run the blockade with her, and stood in to the bay and for the Piankatank River. Arriving at the mouth of the river without having suffered misadventure, he had the bad fortune to miss the channel and to ground the vessel. In this predicament an enemy's man-of-war was seen approaching. Quickly taking off such of the cargo as he could, Beall set fire to the sloop and landed. The goods saved brought about $10,000 in prize money.

The operations of the marine coast guard or the Confederate volunteer coast guard, as Beall's men had come to be known in the countryside, was a humiliation to the army and navy of the United States; and aroused the ire of both services. Early in October a joint expedition was arranged for their capture. On the morning of the fifth, General Wistar, U.S.A., left Yorktown with the Fourth U.S. Colored Infantry and with detachments from Pennsylvania and New York cavalry and artillery regiments. The infantry and artillery were disposed so as to hold the neck of Mathews County, and the cavalry was sent into the interior on a sweeping reconnoissance. At the same time six navy and five army gunboats were stationed so as to command all water avenues of escape from the peninsula between Mobjack Bay and the Piankatank River (which constitutes Mathews County).

To break up the sea-partisans proved not so easy a matter; for, upon the approach of the cavalry they would disperse in the woods and, knowing every path, elude pursuit. On one occasion a Confederate named Smith was taken just after having fired upon the pursuers and having killed one of them. The feeling of the United States troopers was so excited that they gave no quarter and at once hanged the unfortunate man. After three days, the expedition succeeded in capturing Acting Master McGuire and three other Confederate naval officers. The enemy's War Department report of the affair states that "about 150 boats and schooners were destroyed"; but his navy report says that "one large boat pulling twelve oars, was captured," and "quite a number of canoes were destroyed," though the two cutters belonging to the volunteer coast guard were not found.

Following this raid all was quiet in the country for a month. Then Beall and his men took boat again. In the *Raven* and the *Swan* they struck across the bay and entered Tangier Inlet on the eastern shore, capturing there a schooner. Beall now divided his party and sent a detachment away in a boat, remaining on the prize. Through carelessness the boat party was captured, on November 14, and in affright one member of it divulged the plans of the expedition. Forthwith detachments from the First Eastern Shore Maryland Volunteers, in pungies and boats, began to scour the coast; and Beall and the few men remaining with him were discovered, the next day, and overwhelmed.

The capture was held, in official United States, to be "highly important," and to have been only effected by "bravery and determination." General Henry H. Lockwood, U.S.A., commanding the area in which they were taken, asked the War Department what status should be accorded to the prisoners, fifteen in number. He did not think that they were properly prisoners of war, and suggested that they be tried either by a military commission or by a civil court under the Virginia code of 1860, in Northampton or Accomac Counties, which were occupied by United States forces. The general thought that the latter procedure would be a very clever *coup d'état;* and, further, he did not doubt that "twelve men at least in the county of Accomac can be procured who will be disposed to deal with these fellows as their outrages deserve." The reply was returned, on November 21, that the prisoners "will be held for the present, not as prisoners of war, but as pirates or marauding robbers," awaiting the further pleasure of the Secretary of War.

In response to this attitude the Confederate Government renewed the retaliatory measures that had effected the release of the crews of the *Savannah* and other privateersmen, nearly two years before. The reprisals were not long in effecting the desired result; the captives were accorded the amenities of war, and, in course, were exchanged.

Returning to Richmond, Beall received no immediate assignment from the Navy Department, and became very restless. For a short time he attached himself to a detachment of engineers, under command of a Lieutenant Henderson, a personal friend. In this he seems to have been animated by the desire to draw rations. Soon, however, the inactivity of the army life palled on him; and he took French leave for Canada, passing through the lines by the way of the Eastern Shore, the scene of his hugely enjoyed escapades. Arriving in Canada, Beall reported himself to the Confederate High Commission, and was assigned an important rôle in just such an attempt upon the Great Lakes as that in which he had tried to interest the Navy Department a year and a half before. This enterprise was in every respect a public armed affair, and the recital of how "Captain" Beall came within an ace of making the Confederacy mistress of the lake front is a tale of the regular naval service. In it he had as his lieutenant, Bennett Burley, one of his tried and trusted comrades of Chesapeake days.

Beall remained on the Canadian border and engaged in several secret service exploits to the embarrassment of the northern states. In the middle of December his career as a raider came to a close with what is known as the Buffalo-Dunkirk expedition. This was an attempt to release some Confederate general officers, who were being transported across New York for reimprisonment at Fort Lafayette, in New York Harbor. The expedition proved a fiasco and Beall was taken prisoner, and carried to and incarcerated in the same fortress with the generals. Again he was charged with criminal acts, and was brought to trial before a military commission and sentenced to hang. The matter was kept very quiet and Beall was not allowed to communicate with his Government for aid in his trial. No chance was taken for the Confederacy to institute her unfailingly coercive weapon of retaliation. Beall was sentenced to hang and was hanged on February 18, 1865.

In the meantime, two of his comrades in the secret service in Canada, Colonel Robert M. Martin and Lieutenant John W. Headley, had escaped into Kentucky, and were at Louisville. A few days after Beall's execution and while his friends were in ignorance of his fate, these two officers conceived a reprisal to effect his release. Observing in the daily paper that Andrew Johnson, Vice-President elect, was stopping at the Louisville Hotel, they planned to capture him and hold him hostage. They took three or four Confederate refugees into their confidence on a well-laid scheme for the Tennessee-an's abduction from his room in the hotel; however,

Johnson "checked out" a little earlier than the hour set for the kidnapping, and never knew how close had been his escape.

When the conspirators learned that their intended victim had left by steamboat two hours earlier, they gnashed their teeth in the bitterest of disappointment. Headley in his memoirs laments that they had not known that the Vice-President elect was taking passage upon the river; for, he wrote:

On the boat was the very place of all others to get Johnson. Our party of five could have taken passage on the boat, some for one place, some for another. At an auspicious moment we could have captured all on board in detail, and had the boat landed at a convenient place in the woods, after securing all the firearms on board and all that might have been worn concealed by passengers. We could have camped in the woods until three of the party went out and secured five horses by fair means or force, and by riding all night we would have been at least twenty miles from the Ohio River in a friendly country.[2]

2 *Confederate Operations in Canada and New York*, p. 410.

XIX

LETTERS OF MARQUE STILLBORN

THE records of the several executive departments of the Confederate States Government were partially, and in some cases totally, destroyed at the end of the war. The files of the letters of marque and reprisal issued by the Confederate Department of State, as now deposited in the Manuscript Division of the Library of Congress, are incomplete.[1] They were found among the so-called Pickett Papers, which were purchased in Canada after the war by the United States Government from ex-Confederates through Colonel John T. Pickett, a former Confederate diplomat and staff-officer. These files often contain applications for letters of marque together with the requisite bonds, but no record of the issuance of a commission when there appears no reason to suppose that one was not issued. Again, private-armed ships are known to have been at sea when no reference to them can be found in the existing Confederate archives. Although the Confederate law on privateering required that the commanding officer of each letter of marque should deposit with the collector of customs at every home port visited a detailed journal of the cruise since last in home waters, verified under oath, the historical data existent are very fragmentary, for no one of these journals has been located. Some complete accounts of private-armed cruises are to be found in the newspapers

---

[1] The *Picket Papers* are largely reprinted in *NWR,* II, vols. 1 and 3, and constitute the general source of data for this chapter.

231

of the day, but often the secrecy which properly surrounds the conduct of war prevented any notice of privateering operations from being taken by the press.

The matter of tracing out the history of the southern privateers is complicated also by the indiscriminate tendency of the enemy to refer to all high seas craft of the Confederacy as privateers, if not as pirates. An instance in point is the destruction of the Confederate schooner *Judah* at the dock of the Pensacola navy yard, on September 14, 1861, by a boat expedition from the United States frigate *Colorado*. One Union report of this occurrence refers to "the piratical schooner *Judah*," and another calls her "the rebel privateer *Judah*."[2] There are no Confederate reports in the naval records, nor does the *Judah* show in the existing list of letters of marque. However, the very circumstance that the schooner was lying in the navy yard should have indicated clearly her public nature. The facts in the case are well developed in the press of the day, however.

The *Judah,* before the war, was in the Gulf coasting trade.[3] During the summer of 1861 she was chartered for duty as the harbor police-boat at Pensacola. When the attack was made there were few men on board of the schooner, and the watch seems to have been lax. But after recovering from the surprise the Confederates are said to have fought "like Turks" and to have driven off the enemy, but not before the latter had succeeded in setting the vessel aflame by throwing fire-balls aboard her.[4]

On the other hand, when the Union reports of the

[2] *NWR*, I, 16, pp. 670-675.   [3] *True Delta*, May 10, 1861.
[4] *Ibid.*, September 21. 1861. *Daily Picayune*, September 20, 1861.

attack on the *Royal Yacht* in Galveston harbor on November 7, 1861, prefix the descriptive "privateer," the facts set out in the reports do not so patently deny the private-armed character. But in this instance the Confederate records are unusually complete, and clearly show her to have been chartered in the regular naval service and under the command of a navy officer.[5]

The schooner *Agricola* of Ellsworth, Maine, arrived in Boston about August 27, and reported that she had been chased and boarded by a privateer called *Freely,* of Charleston, at a point only twenty miles off Cape Ann.[6] The master of the schooner said that they released his vessel because the privateersmen did not wish the cargo which he was carrying. Now it happens that the name *Freely* does not occur among existing letters of marque, nor is there any local press report of such privateer having sailed from Charleston. The only privateer definitely known to have been in New England waters is the *Jefferson Davis,* which, however, had sailed southward more than a month earlier.

At this time there were current reports of privateers all over the Atlantic Ocean, eastward to the coast of Africa and southward to Rio de Janeiro.

In the face of all this, one rather hesitates to regard as stillborn those letters of marque about which no record of cruise survives. It tempts the imagination to ponder their unchronicled fate, and to complete the dreams of those who pledged their bond and ships— for surely they had dreams and perhaps performed deeds.

[5] *NWR,* I, 16, pp. 755-762, 844, 862.
[6] Dispatch, dated Boston, August 27, in *Courier,* September 3, 1861.

THE CONFEDERATE PRIVATEERS

As a suggestion, there appears in *The Record,* a weekly journal published in Richmond, October 8, 1863, a report that "Edgar L. Lambert, late of Alexandria, Va., has been appointed by the President a 'lieutenant for the war' in the Confederate States Navy, and has been ordered to the steamer *Richmond* at Drewry's Bluff. Lieutenant Lambert has displayed great bravery as the commander of a Confederate privateer." Yet there can be found no record of this gentleman as a captain of corsairs.

The earliest applicants for letters of marque were William Hone and B. S. Sanchez, both of Savannah. They came forward eagerly, April 18, immediately upon the heels of President Davis' invitation. Hone asked for a commission to arm the *Gallatin,* a topsail schooner of about one hundred and fifty tons burden. He intended to place two 12-pounders on the main deck and to carry a crew of forty men, well armed with rifles, cutlasses, and revolvers. He seems to have offered bond, but there the trail ends. Sanchez' story is different. He wrote that his vessel, the brig *Hallie Jackson,*

built of the strongest material (white and live oak), copper fastened, built under my own direction, would carry two large, or four small guns, with a crew of, say, 30 men.

Sanchez was somewhat satisfied with his brig, and continues, in his letter to the Secretary of State:

This vessel has the exalted honor of having hoisted the first Confederate flag within the limits of a foreign country, having by my instruction displayed our flag for one week while in the port of Matanzas, Cuba.

234

It was no fault of her proud owner that the *Hallie Jackson* did not become an active privateer. While returning from Cuba to Georgia to be outfitted for warfare, she was captured off the mouth of the Savannah River by the United States blockader *Union,* and was sent to New York for adjudication.

Georgia privateers seemed to have been ill-fated. Another Savannah adventurer, E. J. Black, applied fruitlessly on April 30, for papers for the schooner *Lamar,* which was to mount one 12-pounder swivel and to have thirty-five men with the necessary side arms and equipment. The first letter of marque actually to be granted appears also to have brought no result. It was issued on May 10, 1861, to three men from Brunswick, Thomas A. Hillier, James Houston, and James Spier, for the little schooner *Triton.*

A New Hampshire ship captain arrived in New York, on April 27, from Savannah, and reported to the commandant of the navy yard that a topsail schooner and a brig were fitting out in the Savannah River for privateering. The United States Navy Department lost no time in ordering, on May 2, two war steamers to watch the mouth of the Savannah. Therein probably lies the reason that the Savannahian privateers never took the sea.[7]

It is clear that during the early months of the war a great wave of enthusiasm for privateering swept over the country. But often this lure of sea-roving, combined with the surge of patriotism, impelled the imaginations of the impecunious, who were desirous of obtaining special privileges from the Government. Even for ready

[7] *NWR.* I, 1, pp. 17-18.

money, good ships and guns were hard to find. No provision had been made in law for public assistance to private-armed enterprises, nor would the state of the Confederate armories and navy yards have permitted it.[8] The very value of privateering to the Government lay in the lifting of burdens from the public bureaux or agencies; and it was out of the question for the Confederacy to go to extremes in encouraging private armaments after the fashion of Louis XIV, who farmed out French men-of-war on shares,[9] and of Louis XVI, who lent ordnance from the royal arsenals to the corsaires.[10]

Sometimes those who wished to have the letter of marque served up on a silver tray made indirect overtures to the Government. Sanford Kingsbury, of Carrollton, Georgia, wrote to the Secretary of the Navy, on April 29, 1861, that he had been

applied to for information respecting letters of marque and reprisal from our Government by citizens and residents of the New England States who represent to me that they are willing to engage in that business in behalf of our Confederacy providing our terms are such as to be "inducements" for them to embark into that kind of warfare, [adding that they are] prepared to commence operations at an early day.

[8] However, in the instance of the *Manassas*, the Confederate Government made an exception, furnishing to the outfitters a 9-inch gun with ammunition.—*NWR*, I. 1, p. 792.

[9] *Ordonnances de 1674 à 1709—Nouveau Code des Prises, par Lebeau* (Paris, an VII), tome I, pp. 64, 109, 193, 339. Cited by Francis R. Stark, *The Abolition of Privateering and the Declaration of Paris* (New York: Columbia University, 1897), pp. 98-99.

[10] *Ordonnance du 24 juin, 1778—Recueil général des anciennes lois françaises, par Isambert, Jourdan et Decrusy* (Paris), tome XXV, p. 314. Cited by Charles La Mache, *La Guerre de Course dans le Passé dans le Présent et dans l'Avenir* (Paris: A. Pedone, Editeur, 1901), p. 45.

Among the early applicants was one John Brass of Monticello, Florida. He wrote to the Attorney-General of the Confederate States on April 24, requesting that a commission be sent to him, saying that:

> In view of the present crisis of our country, our most prominent citizens are exceedingly anxious to do service to the country by the fitting out of a privateer, the command of which they are desirous of placing in the writer's hands.

But such a vague application did not conform to the general practice and law that a vessel must be actually fitted out before a letter might be granted; and nothing came of it. In the latter part of August, Brass addressed the Secretary of State asking that a blank commission be issued to him prior to his departure for England, whither he was going with the intention "of procuring and fitting out a vessel for the purpose of privateering upon the enemy's commerce." This, again, was out of order; and he was courteously informed that when he had purchased, armed, and equipped a vessel he might obtain a letter of marque from the Confederate High Commission in London. A few days later, on September 2, he wrote to the State Department that he "owned and commanded" and had "armed and equipped" a vessel described as "the *Monticello,* of St. Marks, Florida, an ironclad steam propeller of 460 tons burthen." The Collector of Customs at St. Marks was then directed to issue a commission if the transaction were really "a *bona fide* one"; and a letter of marque was granted on September 30. Later the Department received information from Charleston that Mr. Brass was in that city trying to equip a privateer. Whereupon the Assistant Secretary wrote to the collector at St. Marks to investigate the case, directing him to "promptly revoke the letter of marque," if he should find that Brass was "merely using the commission issued as a means of procuring a vessel and equipping her as a privateer." There the data end.

The scrupulous care with which the State Department guarded its letters of marque probably at times caused the loss of privateers to the Confederate flag. On May 4, William R. Miles, of New Orleans, wrote to the Department that he had made arrangements to put a fleet of private-armed ships to sea from European ports, and asked for some twenty or thirty letters of marque in blank. The request, being contrary to law, was denied; but Mr. Miles, being genuinely interested and financially able, subsequently appeared as part owner in several New Orleans privateers.

The powers attaching to a letter of marque and general reprisal were quite generally misunderstood. Two Louisianians, E. J. Delany and P. J. Holstein, applied in May for letters under which to operate a company which they were then raising "for the purpose of privateering on the Mississippi River." Even the next year, with the decisions of the District Court for Louisiana in the cases of the *Jarvis* and the *Marshall* standing as notice to all that letters of marque could confer rights only upon the high seas, we find, in a newspaper advertisement, that one "Captain Frobus" was raising a company for "inland privateering," in New Orleans. He asked that all those who were connected with the expedition and those who wished to join would report themselves at headquarters, No. 18 Canal Street, on Sunday, February 16, at noon between the hours of 12 and 1 o'clock.

An editorial in the same paper says that there is "no one better qualified to lead such an expedition than Capt. Frobus. Cool, decisive, prompt, and daring, he could soon make his presence felt among the prowling Feds."[11]

Foreigners were eager to get a bit of the cream of Confederate privateering. One W. J. Grazebrook wrote from Liverpool, on May 20, 1861, to the State Department, that he would undertake to get a squadron of iron-plated steamers to sea against United States commerce in eight to ten weeks, provided that the Confederate States Government would underwrite the cost and guarantee to him a profit of not less than ten per cent and under certain contingences as high as one hundred per cent. Nothing came of this modest offer.

Early in June, William C. Corrie wrote from Charleston to the Secretary of State, Robert Toombs, in Richmond, that an association of gentlemen, with which he was connected, proposed

to purchase in Glasgow, Scotland, an iron barque-rigged propeller of seven or eight hundred tons burthen, of great speed, and to fit, arm, equip, provision, and man her, either there or at some other port beyond the limits of the Confederate States. [He asked for a] conditional commission, to be exchanged for a regular one as soon as the vessel was purchased, armed, and manned.

But he was simply referred to the commissioners in Europe, and there were no further developments.

About a month later the Secretary received another communication from Charleston, signed David Riker. This gentleman desired to organize a party to proceed

11 *Daily Delta,* February 15, 1862.

to Cedar Keys, Florida, from which place the expedition would go by a fishing smack to Havana. Reaching Cuba, it was the plan to take passage on board of a New York steamer, which was to be captured in the open sea and converted to privateering. The State Department advised the would-be privateersman to secure a captaincy in his state militia and special orders from the Governor.

It not infrequently happened that those already in the army desired to get into privateering. Undoubtedly, amid the monotony of the training camps of the early months of the war, the picturesque appeal of privateering strongly attracted imaginative and restless minds. Generally the soldier lads had only vague ideas about this form of service. Here is a specimen letter received by the Secretary of State from a Virginia camp:

I desire to obtain some information in regard to privateering; the course to be pursued by persons wishing to enter this arm of service; whether they will be received as companies or only individually, and the point of rendezvous; also any other information which you may deem necessary.

The soldiers remained soldiers.

Little chance had mere landsmen of becoming successful privateersmen, when many sea folk failed in making their letters of marque and reprisal active. The largest privateer commissioned by the Confederate States, the *Phenix,* of Wilmington, Delaware, appears among the stillborn. This steamer planned to leave the North secretly and to proceed to Apalachicola, Florida, at which port the formal commission was to be delivered. The commander, Eugene Delany, wrote to President Davis, on May 18, 1861; "If I find the latter place blockaded, and cannot cope with them, you may then expect me at Caillou River, Louisiana." As this ship would have been a valuable acquisition to the service, the State Department instructed the collector at both Apalachicola and New Orleans to be on the lookout for the *Phenix*, and to receive bond without insisting "too much on slight formalities." But what became of this private frigate does not appear of record.

There were two vessels fitted out in Baltimore, early in June, as privateers. One was the *Lorton*, a schooner of 95 tons, manned by a crew of twenty-five. The other was a brig of 179 tons burden, called the *Sealine*, and carrying a ship's company of thirty-five men. Both vessels were armed with one pivot gun. They were owned by W. T. Kendall, a Baltimorean. Though their names show in the list of Confederate privateers published by the United States Navy Department in Volume I, Series 1, of the Official Records, one might suppose that they were active, but there is no other indication that they should not be classed among the ventures that failed to materialize.

The schooner *Josephine*, of Gloucester Point, Virginia, never cruised as a private-armed vessel because of a private difficulty between the owners and the bondsmen.

The application for a letter of marque for the *Onward*, a schooner of seventy tons burden, was made by George Robinson, at Apalachicola, August 20. The armament is given as one 32-pounder Dahlgren, and the strength of the crew at thirty men. On the same day and place, Joseph L. Dunham and Thomas Stokes applied for a commission for the *William P. Benson*, re-

241

naming her the *F. S. Bartow* in honor of the Congress-
man from Georgia who fell at Manassas, July 21, while
leading a brigade of Georgians into battle.[12] This
schooner was of 74 tons, carrying one 24-pounder pivot
gun and one brass 6-pounder, with a company of thirty
men. No record of the issuance of a commission for
either of these schooners has been found, but it is certain that the *Bartow,* at least, was armed and equipped.
A description of a lively combat, on September 11, between this privateer and the U.S.S. *R. R. Cuyler* is
found in the *Apalachicola Times* of September 18; and
a somewhat apologetic report, by Captain Ellison,
U.S.N., for not having captured the "rebel schooner"
appears in the Official Records. When next the *Onward*
and the *Bartow* (the latter's name having reverted to
Benson) are seen, they have just run through the blockade into Havana with a cargo of turpentine.

The abandonment of the idea of cruising warfare
seems a prudent decision from the financial point of
view, for the profits that the owners made as blockade-
runners probably exceeded considerably the gains that
might have come to them through prize-money. The
Benson was never captured; and the *Onward,* with her
name changed to *Emma,* enjoyed a successful career in
commerce until the spring of 1863. While she was lying
in the mouth of the Ocklockonee River with a cargo of
cotton stowed away, ready for an opportunity to break
through the vigilance of the blockaders, a boat expedition from the United States bark *Amanda* descended
upon her. The assault was warmly opposed, from the
shore, by a mixed detachment of Confederate infantry

[12] *Daily Delta,* August 6, 1861; *Journal, Cong., C.S.A.,* I, 279-280.

and cavalry. The enemy's seamen succeeded in gaining possession of the schooner; but the severity of the Confederate fire obliged them to abandon their valuable prize. Consigning the *Emma* to the flames, they barely escaped with the loss of one of their two boats and with seven casualties.[13]

More letters of marque were issued at New Orleans than at any other Confederate port, but only those vessels which promptly got to sea waged an active *guerre de course*. The *Joseph Landis,* a high pressure steamer, of some 400 tons, was the first for which a letter was asked, on April 22 by Peter Marcy and others. She was to carry two large caliber guns and one hundred men, but her destiny was not the private-armed service; instead, she became the tender to the Confederate ironclad *Louisiana*. Next, applications together with bonds were filed for the *A. J. Whitmore,* by W. B. Becker, and for the *Yankee,* by Thomas McLellan. The latter steamer was taken into the naval service as the gunboat *Jackson*. The former was examined by a naval board, but was rejected on account of the vulnerability of the boilers and machinery and for the further cause that there was no room to mount guns.[14] She was then employed in blockade-running, a game at which she played successfully until the fall of the Crescent City, after which she became the United States army transport *Fox*—with what fate we have already seen.

On May 14,[15] the steamer *W. H. Webb* arrived in New Orleans from Havana, and on the seventeenth her owners applied for a letter of marque. She was a very

13 *NWR,* I, 17, pp. 390-394.   14 *NWR,* I, 16, p. 828.
15 *L'Abeille de la Nouvelle-Orléans,* 15 mai, 1861.

fast packet steamer, of 656 tons, and well-conditioned. The commission was issued on the following day, specifying an armament of four 12-pounders and a crew of one hundred men with Joseph Leach, one of the owners, as captain. The *Webb,* however, never sailed as a privateer; but remained in the transportation business until the middle of January, 1862, when she was impressed into the military service by Major General Mansfield Lovell, C.S.A., under orders from the Secretary of War. She was converted into a staunch man-of-war, which victoriously carried the Confederate ensign through numerous engagements in the so-called River Wars of the West. As one of the vessels in Major General Richard Taylor's gunboat expedition, which captured the United States ironclad *Indianola,* on February 24, 1863, in the Red River about thirty miles below Vicksburg, the *Webb* was skillfully navigated by a civilian steamboat captain and fought by a detachment of soldiers.[16]

With the war virtually at an end, the *Webb* was ordered to proceed to sea to wage a *guerre de course* against the enemy's commerce. She was again in the Red River below Shreveport. Under the dashing Lieutenant Commanding Charles W. Read, famed for his Clarence-Archer-Tacony exploits in commerce-destroying off the New England coast in 1863, the gauntlet of enemy fleets and forts was run. New Orleans was passed at noon on April 24, 1865. It was two hours and a half before Admiral Thatcher's squadron off that city recovered sufficiently to start pursuit, and it was another hour and a quarter before the first chaser from Admiral

16 *NWR,* I, vols. 17, 19, 20, 23, 24, 25, 26.

Lee's Red River squadron appeared. However, at four o'clock, well below the city, the sortie was brought to a close by the U.S.S. *Richmond,* which was standing up from the sea. The latter took such position in the channel that the *Webb* would have to pass close under the powerful broadsides of the man-of-war. Read saw that he must lose his ship; and, preferring to save his and his men's lives, he took the bank, setting fire to his grounded vessel and fleeing into the swamp. There the Confederates were rounded up by cavalry. What a privateer the *Webb* might have made![17]

But to return to what was happening in New Orleans in 1861, the Collector of Customs issued commissions on June 4, 8, and 10, respectively for the steamer *Isabella,* the bark *Matilda,* and the steamer *Governor A. Mouton.* James I. Bard was part owner and commander of the *Isabella,* and was part owner in the *Matilda.* His associate in the ownership of the steamer was one W. R. Adams, and of the bark, one Flavel Belcher, who was also captain of the *Matilda.* The *Mouton* was owned and commanded by Samuel E. Parker. Bard's vessels have left no trace of activity. Parker's ship, however, it is known, went into blockade-running, at which she was successful for about a year. She ended her career under the Confederate colors on May 11, 1862, when she was captured by the U.S.S. *Hatteras,* while running between Sabine Pass and Berwick Bay.[18]

The letter of marque which was issued on October 10 to Joseph Barbiere, an army captain, for the steamer *General N. S. Reneau* brought forth upon the Gulf of Mexico no privateer, armed with five guns and carrying

[17] *NWR,* I, vols. 2, 22, 27.   [18] *Ibid.,* vol. 18, pp. 486-488.

150 men, as had been the intent of the applicant; but met a very contrary fate. On December 3, the agent charged with the outfitting of this vessel was captured by the enemy off the coast of Mexico; and, in order to avoid being taken as a pirate, threw the letter overboard, sinking it in the warm waters of the Gulf.

Only one letter of marque seems to have been issued in Mobile in 1861. This one, dated May 25, constituted authority for an association to send to sea the steam tug *A. C. Gunnison,* with two 6-pounders and fifteen men under Captain Peter G. Cook. However, the *Gunnison* had another destiny; she was taken into the public service, becoming a torpedo boat in the regular navy.

Despite the practical difficulties that had developed in the way of privateering, the year 1862 continued to bring in applications for commissions. In October, a group of western gentlemen, Amos Pierce Chamberlain, of New Orleans, John D. Freeman, of Jackson, Mississippi, and Andrew McKee and Thomas B. Power, of Texas, went to Richmond to arrange for the sending of a squadron to sea. Four steamers and one schooner were in the group, and of these only the schooner is known to have had a cruise. The steamers were splendid vessels, and doubtless engaged in blockade-running. The *Pelican* was of 1,479 tons burden, and rated 10 guns and 150 men. The *Mocking Bird* of 1,290 tons, the *Dove* of 1,170 tons, and the *Bonita* of 1,110 tons, each had an armament of eight guns and a ship's company of 150 men. The schooner, the *Retribution,* has a chapter of her own.

In 1863, the stillborn letters of marque included the steamer *Texas,* the schooner *Chesapeake,* and the steamer *Charlotte Clark.* The *Texas* was an 800-tonner of much promise, with eight guns and 125 men. Charles de Montel, of Texas, "an old sailor who has seen service and is besides a very brave and energetic man," commanded and owned her. The owner of the *Chesapeake,* Thomas Smith, was a Baltimorean who had suffered loss at the hands of the United States and who wished to send out his schooner armed to effect reprisals. This vessel was said to be a fast sailer, mounting four guns and carrying fifty men. The owners of the *Charlotte Clark* were four residents of Memphis, Tennessee, but the place of outfitting of this steamer does not appear. The applicant for the commission, J. H. Edmonston, stated that she was "1,100 tons burden, drawing 12 feet water, capable of carrying three guns on pivot carriages," and would have a crew consisting of 125 officers and men.

Finally, the year 1864 brought five useless privateers into being. They were all schooners. The *Paul Jones* and the *Stephen R. Mallory*—names deserving better and more active namesakes—were Bahama Island craft. The first, of 160 tons, was commanded by John T. Gordon, who had served for a time on the privateer schooner *Retribution,* and was doubtless desirous of emulating the success of the privateer *Paul Jones* of the War of 1812. Her armament was two guns and her crew thirty men. The *Mallory* was a seventy-four—not a ship-of-the-line of seventy-four guns, but a little cockerel of seventy-four tons with three small pieces of ordnance and twenty men! Her commander was J. Samuel Jones. The *Gibraltar,* Captain William G. Ford, and the *Rescue,* Captain W. G. Hartfield, were of Mobile, and the

Stonewall Jackson, Captain M. W. de Bolle, was also of the Gulf coast.

The year 1865 brought no more ships to berth in the privateering service of the Confederacy.

XX

HOW SOME PRIVATEERS CHANGED
THEIR MISSION

*T*HE great activities under the Confederate letters of marque occurred in 1861. With the passing of that year the developments of the war were hastening the end of privateering. Supplies inevitably vanish during the times of national emergency, and the demand for every character of goods, manufactured and raw, waxes larger in disturbing ratio. The Confederate States not only were not exempt from the operation of war-time economics but, being an agricultural country, very quickly began to feel the exhaustion of certain stocks. This tightening of various commodity markets drew attention rapidly to the necessity of expanding the import business. The result was that marine transportation had become, by the beginning of 1862, more lucrative than privateering, if not equally patriotic as well. For the cargoes of munitions of war and of other necessities of military and civilian nature balanced, if they did not outweigh, in value to the conduct of the war, the embarrassment caused to the enemy by the depredations of the privateers upon his sea trade. Of course, the prize goods brought in by the private-armed cruisers constituted an increase in the stocks of the country, and the prize vessels were an addition to the commercial marine. But the character of the cargoes was always uncertain, and the latter were little suited to the war needs of the Confederate States. With a single exception, the prizes taken by the letters of marque had been sailing vessels, mostly slow and cumbersome, not adaptable either to conversion into naval vessels or to employment in blockade-running. Celerity of maneuver and strength in construction were paramount in ships of war, and high speed was an essential in the merchant service.

The privateersmen were not slow in sensing the trend of the times, or in following the lead of both patriotism and economics.

We last saw the little privateers *Dixie* and *Sallie* in Charleston harbor where they had been sold after successful cruises. When next we hear of them they are blockade-runners. The former changed her name to *Kate Hale* and again to *Success*. She sailed regularly between Georgetown, South Carolina, and Saint John, New Brunswick, Captain L. D. Benton, one of the old privateer lieutenants now commanding, until early one fine spring morning in mid April, 1862, she was captured by the U.S.S. *Keystone State*. Her last cargo consisted of 100 bales of cotton, 234 barrels of spirits of turpentine, 40 bushels of peanuts, and 3,000 pounds of rice.[1]

A correspondent for the *New York Times* saw the little *Sallie* in Nassau, and wrote to his paper, February 15, 1862, that "there have been several arrivals of small craft from Secessia with turpentine and cotton—one was the notorious privateer schooner *Sallie*. She is about the hardest looking vessel for a privateer I have ever seen."[2] But the *Sallie* was as successful a trader as she had been a privateer, and was never captured by the blockaders.

[1] *NWR*, I, 12, p. 679.   [2] *Ibid.*, p. 628.

The *Mariner*, of which we have seen a bit at Hatteras, was another privateer that turned trader and successful dodger of all blockaders.[3]

The *Gordon*, which we knew both at Hatteras and Charleston, passed from privateering into government service as a chartered coast and harbor patrol boat, at Charleston, and then into blockade-running. The latter change came about in consequence of the arrival of John Slidell, of Louisiana, and James M. Mason, of Virginia, and their suites, at Charleston early in October. These gentlemen were seeking passage to Europe, where high diplomatic duties awaited them in London and Paris, respectively. The State Department had at first intended to send them over on the C.S.S. *Nashville,* and Navy Department orders had been so issued. At this juncture heavy reinforcements were made to the blockading force. The *Nashville's* great draft made it difficult for her to get over the bar; and in face of the heavy naval odds, the two commissioners persuaded the Secretary of State, R. M. T. Hunter, to authorize the special charter of the extremely fast *Gordon.* The then charter was for local service only and carried a rental of $200 a day. The owners preferred to sell her for $62,000, but agreed to accept $10,000 for a round trip to the West Indies, provided the Government would pay the value in event of capture. These terms having been accepted, a favorable opportunity for sailing was not long in coming.

The night of Friday, October 11, 1861, began clear and moonlit, but toward midnight the skies became overcast and every promise was given that it would be a night to suit the most meticulous blockade-runner. At

[3] *NWR,* I, vols. 6 and 8.

two o'clock on Saturday morning, the *Gordon,* now disarmed and renamed the *Theodora,* was racing over the bar into a heavy rain. The darkness was impenetrable and she passed through the blockading squadron without discovery by the enemy lookouts. On the following Wednesday, when nearing Cuban waters, she fell in with a Spanish man-of-war, which with great courtesy escorted the High Commission into the port of Cardenas. Mason and Slidell went by rail to Havana, where they took passage in the English royal mail steamer *Trent* for St. Thomas on the second leg of the voyage to England. The *Theodora,* after recoaling, proceeded a few days later to Havana. There a cargo of cigars and other light articles was shipped for the account of a Charleston mercantile house, to whom the Government had sublet the return trip to the Confederate States. Shortly afterward the War Department purchased the sometime privateer, for $60,000, and put her into packet service between the South Atlantic ports and the nearby neutral islands belonging to Great Britain and Spain. As an army freighter she was never captured.[4]

In passing, it might be recalled that the experiences of Mason and Slidell again had contact with Confederate privateering. When they arrived prisoners in the United States, after having been forcibly removed from the *Trent* by Captain Wilkes, of the U.S.S. *San Jacinto,* President Davis had just inaugurated his retaliation for the mistreatment of the captive privateersmen. In a mingled flush of anger and joy, the House of Representatives at Washington passed resolutions to

4 *NWR,* II, vol. 3.

hold these diplomats as counter-hostages.[5] But the ardor of the United States Government was very soon brought under control by the unequivocal demands of the outraged British Ministry; and no executive action was taken on the resolutions.

Had the Confederate emissaries gone to England on the *Nashville,* as originally planned their journey would have been uninterrupted. The *Nashville* made her escape through the blockade and was at Southampton when the mail steamer *La Plata* arrived from St. Thomas. This was the vessel on which Mrs. Slidell and her daughters and Mrs. Eustis, wife of one of the secretaries of legation, had continued the journey to England. The ladies were received and entertained on board the Confederate man-of-war before taking train to London.[6] Less than a year later the cruiser *Nashville,* having been sold by the Government, became the privateer *Rattlesnake.*

The *Calhoun,* of New Orleans, like the *Gordon,* of Charleston, after a short tour of duty in the navy as a chartered man-of-war, became a vessel of cargoes again. On January 23, 1862, while returning to New Orleans from Havana with an important cargo of 50,000 pounds of powder, she was—according to General Lovell, who commanded Confederate troops at New Orleans—"unnecessarily and timidly," allowed to fall into the hands of the enemy. The general's report continues:

She will prove a great pest on the coast, as she is very fast and of light draft. Her crew tried to set her on fire,

[5] *Congressional Globe,* December 2, 1861.
[6] *Mercury,* December 21, 1861.

but in their fright and haste they failed to do so effectively. It was an unfortunate piece of business.

Lovell's prophecy was made good, for the *Calhoun* was immediately taken into the United States navy, and proved an efficient cruiser in the West Gulf blockading squadron.[7]

The privateer schooner *Savannah,* whose capture led to the famous piracy trial in New York, after being condemned in a United States admiralty court, was purchased by the navy, for $1,250, and became the U.S.S. *Chotank.* As a war schooner the enemy replaced the light armament of the privateersmen with a battery of two 9-inch and one 11-inch Dahlgrens.[8]

Then there were some privateers which became Confederate men-of-war. The *Ivy* and the *Music* were taken into the regular naval service. The *Ivy's* participation in the affairs at the Head of the Passes, has been seen. The *Music* took an important part in the battle of the Lower Mississippi, April 24, 1862, and afterward served as a consort to the famous ram the C.S.S. *Arkansas.*[9]

Like many of the private-armed ships which changed their mission to regular combat service or to the ways of commerce, so did many privateersmen. Captain Stevenson, of the *Manassas,* came to command the division of army gunboats at the forts below New Orleans in April, 1862. Captain McLellan remained upon the *Music* in the public service. Lieutenant Harleston, "pirate" of *Savannah* fame, turned to the army as an officer, successively in the cavalry, artillery, and infantry. Another of the *Savannah* privateersmen, Evans,

[7] *NWR,* I, 17.   [8] *NWR,* II, 1, p. 58.
[9] *NWR,* I, vols. 1, 16, 18, 19.

the prize master who successfully brought that letter of marque's only capture into port, later joined the navy on foreign service, yielding up his life as a warrant officer on board of the C.S.S. *Alabama* in the battle with the U.S.S. *Kearsarge,* off Cherbourg in the English Channel on June 19, 1864.

Other privateersmen reëntered the merchant marine, and some of them became famous blockade-runners. Among the latter were Captain Coxetter, of the spectacular *Jefferson Davis,* and Captain Moore, of the jaunty *Dixie.* These two had much in common; in that both attempted to fit out another privateer but failed to get it to sea, and both by their many successes achieved the epithet "notorious" at the hands of the blockaders. Thomas J. Lockwood, who had captained the private-armed steamer *Gordon,* acquired wealth and fame in the commercial navy. His commands included the well-known blockade-runners *Theodora, Kate,* and *Colonel Lamb.* Before the war he had been master of the *Kate,* then under the name *Carolina.* He made of this vessel one of the most renowned packet steamers of the beleaguered Confederacy. It is said that she made more than forty successful voyages into Dixieland before being wrecked, near the entrance of the Cape Fear River during the late fall of 1862. So great a thorn in the side of the blockaders did the *Kate* become that twice boat expeditions, under cover of night, were sent in to try to cut her out at her Wilmington anchorage. Lockwood was the unfortunate captain who brought the yellow fever plague to Wilmington in August, 1862. The epidemic raged for ten weeks and carried off 446 persons. The favorite cargo of Captain Lockwood was munitions of war; and, on one occasion when asked what he had carried on his last voyage, he humorously replied, "Food for the North." The Nassau correspondent of the *New York Times,* in reporting this witticism, expressed the hope that "he may dine upon a meal of the same food before he gets back."[10]

[10] *NWR,* I, 1, pp. 245, 406, 556, 570; 2, p. 193; 8, pp. 152, 153; 10, p. 602; 11, p. 744; 12, pp. 531, 629-630; II, 1, 406-407. *The True Delta,* September, 11 and 21, 1861; *Courier,* April 27, 1861. James Sprunt, *Derelicts* (Wilmington, N. C., privately printed, 1920), p. 115.

XXI

PRIVATEERING IN THE PACIFIC

*T*HREE hundred years before the War of Secession, the Anglo-Saxon and Huguenot ancestors of the Confederates had found the waters of New Spain a tempting field. The doughty sea-dogs of Queen Elizabeth and of Henry of Navarre, such as Hawkins and Drake and Têtu, took pleasure and profit in private warfare against the Spanish and Portuguese in the new Americas. Even when England, and France as Protestant, had been at peace with Spain and Portugal, the nobility and royalty had considered shares in these sea-roving ventures, which they called reprisals, as laudable and as good investment. The strong-hearted mariners who braved the dangers of the sea and religious and racial hatred to separate the Spaniard from his gold and silver, passed on something of their character to their descendent Confederates.

In 1861 there were still gold ships upon the Pacific. They belonged to the enemy and it was rightful that he should be despoiled of them. Upon that ocean the United States had also a valuable whaling industry, ships that dealt in the liquid gold, oil. Upon these the Confederates desired at once to descend in privateers; and it was through Mexico that this was sought to be brought about.

On May 17, 1861, John T. Pickett was handed by the State Department, in Montgomery, Alabama, his commission and instructions as special agent "of the

Confederate States near the Government of Mexico."
Pickett was a well-known southerner, and had a varied
past. At times he had been United States Consul at
Turks Island and at Vera Cruz. As a soldier of fortune,
he had held a general's commission under Lojos Kossuth
in the Hungarian insurrection of 1848; and had served
in one of the Lopez expeditions to Cuba, commanding
the revolutionary forces against the Spanish regulars in
the Battle of Cardenas. Pickett, by temperament and
experience, seemed eminently the man to further the
Confederate policy in Mexico.[1]

Mexico being coterminous with the Confederate
States, it was highly desirable that a friendly alliance
should exist between them. Pickett was authorized to
conclude a treaty of amity, commerce, and navigation.

There are many reasons [pointed out his instructions]
why Mexico should desire to form such an alliance. The
people both of the Confederate States and of Mexico are
principally engaged in agriculture and mining pursuits, and
their interests are therefore homogeneous. The institution of
domestic slavery in one country, and that of peonage in the
other, establish between them such a similarity in their sys-
tems of labor as to prevent any tendency on either side to
disregard the feelings and interests of the other. [Further,]
were the Confederate States to guarantee Mexico against
foreign invasion, it is obvious that they could do so more
promptly and effectually than any more distant nation.

For the success of its Mexican diplomacy, the Department of State depended largely upon the person-
ality of its agent and the judicious use of a large con-
tingency fund.

[1] *NWR,* II, 3, pp. 16, 29.

IN THE PACIFIC

The Mexicans [wrote Robert Toombs, the Secretary of State,] are not overscrupulous, and it is not our mission to mend their morals at this precise period. Retaining all the gravity and love of grandeur, peculiar to the Spaniards, they have a supreme contempt for meanness and parsimony in high official station, particularly in foreign agents. So also with regard to personal slovenliness and boorish manners.

But it was not so much formal recognition by and alliance with Mexico that the Confederacy desired—for the special agent was instructed not to stand on ceremony if his mission could not be accomplished otherwise—as an arrangement to promote privateering. Pickett was expected to utilize the facilities afforded by his long residence in Mexico and his extensive acquaintance in its commercial classes to

feel the pulse of merchants and shipowners on the subject of privateering. Should a desire be manifested to obtain letters of marque and reprisal from this Government [continued Toombs] you will make known the power vested in you by this Department to grant such commissions in conformity with the law of Congress authorizing the issue of the same.

Since Mexico had declined to accede to the Declaration of Paris abolishing privateering, it was

confidently anticipated [that the Mexican authorities] will accord to the armed vessels sailing under the flag of the Confederate States the right to enter the ports of Mexico with any lawful prizes that they may make on the high seas.[2]

In July, Pickett reported to State Department that he had

[2] *NWR*, II, 3, pp. 202-206.

succeeded in establishing friendly and confidential relations with Mr. de Zamacona, the new Minister of Foreign Affairs, and but for the unhappy condition of this Government (a new revolution being about to burst upon it, the English and French Ministers having suspended diplomatic relations, etc.) would feel confident, by this time, of having accomplished all the material objects of my mission.[3]

But matters did not develop favorably in Mexico; and, by August, there did not seem "the slightest probability" of obtaining from the Mexican Government concessions such as the great maritime powers had withheld.

In the meantime the Confederate commissioner had, on June 21, appointed C. Markoe, an American merchant resident in Vera Cruz, sympathetic to the South, "as agent to receive applications for letters of marque and reprisal," furnishing him with a sealed package of five blank commissions, which was only to be opened under certain conditions. But Markoe never found it practical to send a privateer to sea, for not long afterward Vera Cruz was occupied by the allied forces of England, France, and Spain.

Then the *Trent* crisis between England and the United States came along opportunely; and Pickett thought, in the event of the open rupture between those two governments, that England would immediately cause the occupied Mexican ports to be places of outfit against Union commerce. This rupture never came.

However, the Mexican Government itself gave Pickett an opportunity of which he quickly availed himself. When that Government, yielding to the request of

[3] *NWR*, II, 3, pp. 226-227.

the United States, gave its sanction to the marching of the enemy's troops across Mexican soil in order that Texas might be attacked through the back door, Pickett felt that this unfriendly act relieved him from the "strictest regard" for Mexican neutrality. Accordingly, on September 10, he issued agency credentials and five blank letters of marque to Don Mateo Ramirez, a government official in Sinaloa and Lower California. At the begining of 1862, he wrote to the Secretary of State at Richmond that he had not heard whether the Don had been successful; but that, as the latter, whom he had long known, was a man

of great sagacity and prudence, and was keenly desirous of capturing a California gold ship, we may yet hear of his operations in the Pacific.

I ought further to add [continued Pickett] that I furnished Mr. Ramirez with some loose memoranda on the law of maritime captures, which, if not strictly in consonance with the views of modern writers, can not fail to meet the entire approval of the brigand chiefs of the Pacific coast of Mexico. In a word, there would be no difficulty about the condemnation of any prize he may bring into those ports, especially if she have treasure on board. I have hoped thus to bring about a collision between the Mexicans and their allies, the United States.[4]

The ease with which a privateer might stow his guns below, or even throw them overboard, change his name, and resume his character as a merchantman, together with the undeveloped condition of the North American coast on the Pacific Ocean, cloaks the possible operations of Confederate privateers on the western seas in

[4] *NWR,* II, 1, pp. 394-396.

romantic uncertainty. Other than the five blank commissions which were given to Ramirez, none seems to have been issued for the Pacific coast of Mexico until early in 1864, when General William Preston was handed ten blank commissions along with his instructions as "Envoy Extraordinary and Minister Plenipotentiary" to the new Imperial Government of Mexico. What use, if any, Preston made of these letters of marque is not now known.[5]

Nevertheless, there were frequent reports of privateers on the Pacific side, and the shipment of gold from the Golden Gate to Manhattan was seriously interrupted. On the day that President Davis issued his Letter of Marque Proclamation, twenty-five merchants and bankers of New York memorialized the Secretary of the Treasury on

the exposure from depredations by Southern privateers of the California Mail Steamers, carrying $40,000,000 of gold annually from San Francisco to this port, and asked the Department to furnish each of said ships with two or more guns and sufficient artillerymen. . . . The capture of even one of these steamers by the enemies of the Government, either on the Atlantic or Pacific, would stop shipments of gold from San Francisco, or at any rate divert the flow of treasure from New York to foreign countries; would result in serious injury to our merchants and banks, and necessarily incommode our Government in any future loans it may deem necessary to apply for, while our plan would be attended with but trifling expense.[6]

Early in July, it was reported in the press that three million dollars in gold had accumulated in San Fran-

[5] *NWR*, II, 3, pp. 989-990.   [6] *Ibid.*, I, 1, p. 8.

cisco over and above the usual deposits, owing to the failure to make the accustomed shipments out of fear of loss to privateersmen. The trans-Continental route was likewise put in jeopardy by the land forces of the Confederates in New Mexico and Missouri.

The president, Allan McLane, of the Pacific Mail Steamship Company, wrote to the Secretary of the Navy, on April 24, beseeching protection for his steamers, their "mails, passengers, treasure, and merchandise freight" from "molestation and capture," by the stationing of naval force at focal points along their tracks.[7] This plan appealed to the Navy Department, which proceeded to order to that duty such war steamers as were available.

However, with the small force which could be assigned to this mission, it was something of the case of finding the needle in the hay stack.[8]

On July 20, 1861, J. B. Montgomery, the flag officer in command of the Pacific squadron, advised his captains that he had been "officially apprised of the probability that privateers under the secession flag have been fitted out for the purpose of intercepting the United States mail steamers, in their transit with treasure from San Francisco." Again on the twenty-ninth of August, the commodore issued a warning to "keep a vigilant lookout" for privateers; but, the next week, he came to the conclusion that there was "no reason to believe that any are fitting out, or likely to be fitted out, along this line of coasts." A few months later the United States Navy Department and the Pacific squadron were up-

[7] *NWR*, I, 1, p. 14. [8] *Ibid.*, pp. 48, 55.

set by confidential advices from Valparaiso that a privateer was being fitted out on the Chilean coasts. A cruiser was sent to investigate the report and found it without foundation. But at the same time it was deemed expedient to inaugurate a convoy system.[9]

In September, the press carried a story, based on a private letter received in San Francisco from Hong Kong, and dated August 11, that a Confederate privateer was fitting out at Shanghai for operations in the China Sea. The persons given as the organizers of the enterprise were two steamship captains named Allen and Lynch, one Ward who was said to have held a colonel's commission in the Imperial Chinese Army, and a United States naval storekeeper named Cleary. It was stated that the outfitting was to be accomplished with United States naval stores. Early in August, the rumor also reached the commanding officer of the U.S.S. *Saginaw,* a cruiser attached to the Pacific squadron. This officer, Commander James Findlay Schenck, fell in with the suspected vessel, the *Neva,* on the thirteenth, just outside of Wusung River. After a thorough examination of the suspect, Schenck was convinced that there was nothing in the rumor, and that its origin lay in the idle threats and boasting of Cleary, who was a passenger on board the *Neva.*[10]

About the same time, from a copy of the *Commercial Advertiser* of Honolulu—which had been received in New Orleans by the last overland mail—*The True Delta,* on September 12, 1861, reprinted a story fraught with privateering possibilities.

9 *NWR,* I, 1, pp. 54, 76, 77, 86, 220, 221.
10 *Ibid.,* p. 68; *Courier,* October 26, 1861.

IN THE PACIFIC

Under the caption, "A privateer in the Pacific," the tale reads as follows:

Captain Nichols of the clipper ship *Bald Eagle*, informs us that on the second day out from San Francisco, he observed a sail on his windward quarter. He kept on the same course till the vessel had approached near enough to show that she was a "long, low, suspicious looking black craft," of a schooner rig. Capt. N. went down and examined his chart, comparing the course of the schooner with the wind, and came to the conclusion that she was bound nowhere but to speak his ship. By this time she had approached somewhat nearer, close enough to show that she was well manned, and anything but a regular trader.

Having a large amount of specie ($530,000) on board, and suspecting that all was not right, and that the schooner might be fitted out for privateering, he changed his course, put his vessel in her best sailing trim, set every inch of canvas he could spread, and before nightfall left the black craft nearly hull-down astern, and in the morning nothing was seen of her. Capt. Nichols thinks there is no doubt that she was a privateer, but whether commissioned with one of Jeff. Davis' letters of marque or not, makes no difference. The *Bald Eagle* was armed with two ship's guns and plenty of small arms and Capt. N. says he would not have feared meeting the schooner, unless she had guns of longer range, which was very probable.

This story doubtless reminded the readers of *The True Delta* of a little squib, entitled, "No Apology Necessary," which had appeared in that paper some fortnight earlier.[11] It is illuminative as to the origins of rumors, and possesses enough flavor to warrant repeating.

[11] August 25, 1861.

While lying off Tangier Island, Capt. Jenkins of the schooner *Mary and Adeline,* saw a pungy schooner standing across Chesapeake bay, which he reported as a "pirate with a motley set of fellows on board." He afterwards ascertained that the pungy schooner was the *Indiana* used by Lieut. Crosby [U.S.N.] as a tender [to the steamer *Fanny*],[12] and that the men on board were twenty-five soldiers from a Massachusetts company, detailed for guard duty. Whereupon he got Gen. Butler to write to the navy department that the pungy schooner he saw "was not a pirate, with a motley set of fellows on board." The mistake was doubtless a very natural one, and did not demand an apology, unless he could have met some piratical craft.

In May, 1862, the United States Navy Department received advices that a privateer, carrying a heavy armament of eight rifled guns, had appeared in Chinese waters; and dispatched the screw sloop-of-war *Wyoming* from San Francisco to Manila to look after the reported Confederate. While the *Wyoming* found no privateer in the Orient,[13] it may be interesting to recall that this man-of-war got into a little private war of her own with a Japanese prince, and had an hour's engagement in the Shimonoseki Straits with a half a dozen land batteries and three armed vessels. This affair occurred on July 16, 1863. The *Wyoming* was hulled eleven times, and had four men killed and seven wounded. The Japanese sustained heavy damages.[14]

American papers reprinted an item from the Calcutta *Englishman,* stating that a Confederate privateer was cruising in the Bay of Bengal, and that her commander had declared to the captain of the British ship *Selim*

12 *NWR,* I, 6, pp. 73-74. 13 *Ibid.,* I, 1, pp. 391-392, 472-473.
14 *Ibid.,* I, 2, pp. 393-399.

that he would catch, and burn or destroy, every vessel leaving Calcutta under the United States flag.[15] At this time most traders in the Orient went armed against the Chinese and Malay pirates; and therein probably lies the foundation of many of the rumors concerning Confederate private-armed ships.

However, an undoubted instance of privateering, though a fiasco, occurred on the American side of the Pacific in March of the year 1863. But on account of its importance, the story of Captain Greathouse and the schooner *Chapman* at San Francisco is told separately and at length in the next chapter.

Close upon the heels of the *Chapman* incident, the commandant of the naval station at San Francisco was disturbed by the receipt of intelligence to the effect that "efforts are making at Victoria to fit out steamers and other vessels to deprecate upon our commerce in the Pacific, and that meetings have been held in that place for the object of raising means to carry out this infamous project." The commandant at once dispatched the U.S.S. *Saginaw,* Commander W. E. Hopkins, on a cruise in the Puget Sound; directing visits to the ports of Angeles and Townsend in Washington Territory, to Victoria on Vancouver Island in the British Possessions, and to "such other places in that vicinity as may be necessary for the purpose of obtaining information from the authorities, and from other sources, in relation to the equipment of rebel privateers in those waters." The orders stated that if no good reason were found for these apprehensions, Commander Hopkins would return to the station; but, "on the other hand, should these

15 *Courier*, March 17, 1863.

rumors be confirmed by observation and intelligence from authentic sources, you will remain and take such action in the premises as may prevent the escape of any vessel intended for a so-called Confederate privateer, or lead to her capture outside of British waters." At Victoria, Hopkins was informed that, after the seizure of the *Chapman,* the privateering proclivities of the Confederates or Confederate sympathizers had dropped out of the public eye; and, that though many of these schemers had departed for the gold mines, rumor had it that there was still in the city a secret organization, holding occasional meetings and merely awaiting the arrival of letters of marque from the President of the Confederate States.[16]

The alleged attempt to fit out a privateer at Victoria was the subject of considerable correspondence between the State Department at Washington and the British Legation. Secretary Seward wrote Lord Lyons, on March 31, 1863, that he was reliably informed that an attempt had been made

to fit out the English steamer *Thames* as a privateer, under the flag of the insurgents, to cruise against the merchant shipping of the United States in the Pacific. Fortunately [he continued], the scheme was temporarily, at least, frustrated by its premature exposure. In view, however, of the ravages upon the commerce of the United States in that quarter which might result from similar attempts, which will in all probability be repeated, [he felt] the expediency of asking the attention of his Majesty's colonial authorities to the subject.

His Lordship investigated the matter of the *Thames,*

16 *NWR,* I, 2, pp. 165, 259-261.

with the result that the idea appeared "to have originated in sundry articles in one of the Victoria papers, about two months ago, wherein it was stated that a Confederate commodore was in Victoria, and that proposals had been made to purchase the screw steamship *Thames* for a privateer." The supposed commodore, it seems, was Captain Manley, a representative of a San Francisco firm which was engaged in the Mexican trade; and it was he who was inspecting the *Thames* with the view to ascertaining her suitability for the purposes of his house. In this tenor Lord Lyon wrote to Mr. Seward, May 15, 1863; and the case was closed with the thanks of the latter on the twenty-second.[17]

Nevertheless, at this very time, the Confederate colony on Vancouver Island was in correspondence with James Mason, the Confederate Commissioner at London, in reference to obtaining a letter of marque. They were organized as the Southern Association of Vancouver and British Columbia, with Jules David as President. David wrote to Mason in April and received his reply in June. The diplomat referred his petitioner to the Secretary of State at Richmond. On October 16, David addressed a request for a letter of marque to the Secretary stating that the Association had at its disposal for privateering a first-class steamer of 400 tons burden, capable of doing 14 knots, and had ample funds with which to arm and outfit her. In conclusion he begged, if there should be any objections to the granting of a privateer commission, that the Government would send a public war vessel into the Pacific to destroy the extensive

---

[17] *Diplomatic Correspondence* (38th Cong., Sess. I, H.R., Ex. Doc. No. 1), 1863, part 1, pp. 535, 567, 604-606, 612, 614.

commerce of the enemy on this ocean. What action the State Department took in this matter is unknown.[18]

There were numerous Confederate sympathizers up and down the Pacific Coast, who were quite eager, for country and pocketbook, to do their bit at privateering; but countless difficulties were in the way in addition to the far-reaching espionage maintained by the several agencies of the United States Government, not the least of which was the policy of the Davis Administration to hew very closely to the technical requirements of the law concerning letters of marque.

In the summer of 1863, a small but strong and fast sailing steamer was being built at San Francisco for the command of one George Simpton, a former commander in the Texan navy in the days of the Lone Star Republic. This gentleman appealed to one A. J. Grayson as being "a faithful and reliable man to have charge of a privateer." Grayson, formerly a native of Louisiana, was now a resident in Mazatlan on the Pacific Coast of Mexico. He wrote to President Davis—dispatching his letter by a personal messenger—advising the far-away President on the state of the Cause in California and Mexico, and asking him to send back two or more blank letters of marque. However, the answer returned was characteristic. The Secretary of State, Judah P. Benjamin, replied for the President, four months later, transmitting a copy of the law on the subject, and referring him to the Confidential Agent of the Confederate States at Monterey. The time required to exchange communications with Richmond was so great—as were also the difficulties of making the crossing from the

18 *NWR*, II, 3, pp. 933-934.

Pacific to Atlantic side of Mexico in order to arrange a full compliance with the privateering regulations—that the venture of Señors Grayson and Simpton was stifled.[19]

About the same time, one James M. Tindell applied at Mobile for a commission under which to arm privately an indefinite ship at some unstated port; but the request, being contrary to the tenor of the law, was denied. He then asked for any sort of Government authority which would take from a wild scheme of his any odor of piracy, and offered bond that he would do nothing contrary to the laws of nations. His adventure comprehended the organization, at Shreveport, of a party of a hundred to a hundred and fifty men. There a caravan of cotton was to be formed and a trip made through Texas to Matamoras, Mexico, where the cotton, teams, and wagons were to be sold for the necessary gold with which to carry on the project. The expedition was then to divide, a part going overland to San Francisco, a part taking neutral passage to some port near Aspinwall, on the Isthmus of Panama, and a remaining few to go to Europe. The two larger parties had similar objectives. After reaching San Francisco and a Caribbean port, respectively, they were to go aboard some Union steamship as passengers and capture her at sea. In the event of a failure by either or both of the larger parties, Nassau was named as the rendezvous. The European party was to be charged with the duty of purchasing a steamer suitable for the purposes of war and sending her to the Bahamas. At the assembly point, it was supposed, enough of the original party would

[19] *NWR*, II, 1, pp. 421-423.

gather to form the crew for the purchased steamer. The plan was too loose and did not appeal to the Richmond Cabinet in 1863.[20]

But in the following year a somewhat similar scheme proposed by Thomas E. Hogg, of schooner *Gerrity* fame, was accepted by the Secretary of the Navy, who commissioned Hogg a master-not-in-line-of-promotion without pay, and authorized him, on May 7, 1864, "to strike a blow at the California trade and whalemen in the Pacific." The Secretary's orders directed Hogg to ship his men "regularly in the service of the Navy" and to make such acting appointments of officers as might be required, "reporting their names and, in all cases, the evidences of their fitness and character to the Department."

You will proceed with the men under your command from Wilmington by the shortest and safest route to the port of Panama [wrote Mr. Mallory, expressing as public direction the plans of the adventurous Mr. Hogg]. At that port you will take passage on board either the *Guatemala* or *San Salvador*, the two Federal screw steamers trading between Panama and Realejo. After reaching the high seas you will consider upon and devise means to capture the vessel in the name of the Confederate States, and effect the capture without fail. Your conduct toward the people of the captured vessel will be guided by that spirit of humanity which ever characterizes the conduct of our naval officers. Having secured the steamer, organized your crew, and hoisted the flag of the Confederate States, you will adopt prompt measures to arm your vessel and proceed to cruise against the enemy of the Pacific. If practicable, you will report or communicate with Captain R. Semmes, of the C.S.S. *Alabama*,

[20] *NWR*, II, 1, pp. 418-420.

and obey such orders as he may give you. The rights of neutrals must be strictly regarded. The importance of establishing and maintaining a wholesome naval discipline is enjoined upon yourself and your officers. Should you seek neutral ports for supplies or otherwise, you will be careful to observe the usual naval courtesies and customs toward those in authority, and upon all proper occasions you will seek to place the character of the contest in which we are engaged and the principles involved in it in their proper light. Should you at any time hesitate as to your course as a Confederate cruiser your judgment may be governed by the consideration that you are to do the enemy, in accordance with the rules of civilized war, the greatest harm in the shortest time, and you will enjoin upon your officers and men the performance of their duty in that spirit of humanity which ever distinguishes a Confederate naval officer.

Acting Master Hogg at once set about organizing his party. Edward A. Swain, lately a midshipman on the Mobile station, was given an acting appointment as master's mate; and was the only member of the expedition who had ever served in the regular naval establishment. Acting Master Frank M. Harris, of the regular navy, was ordered, at Hogg's request, to duty in the enterprise but he never joined, for he was captured on the blockade-runner *Young Republic* while making the voyage between Wilmington and Nassau. The other members of the party seem to have been picked up variously as to place and qualification. All were probably mariners, and at least one of them had served as a mate on a Pacific steamer. The expedition was held together by a written secrecy oath upon the penalty of "any punishment that my associates in this matter may adjudge."

The enterprise was organized in Havana with Hogg commanding and Swain as executive officer. A ward room personnel for the prospective cruiser was selected and the nucleus of a crew obtained. The party probably spent too much time under the seductive influences of the Cuban capital; for, despite the obligation to secrecy, the United States Consul General got wind of the expedition, and wrote to his brother consular officer at Panama a pretty complete exposé of the plans and personnel of this quasi-privateering venture.

About the last of September or the first of October, Hogg and his associates left Cuba for the Isthmus of Panama. Having arrived on the Pacific coast, they began making arrangements for coaling depots and points for taking on supplies after the prize should be made. The plans of Acting Master Hogg were expansive. He decided to capture both steamers, and accordingly divided his party: himself and six of his officers to proceed against the *Salvador,* and the remainder of his cohorts to undertake the seizure of the *Guatemala.*

Meanwhile the information from the consulate at Havana had been received in Panama. The admiral of the Pacific squadron and the officials of the Panama Railroad Company were warned of the plot; and a plan was concerted with Captain Dow, of the *Guatemala,* and Captain Douglas, of the *Salvador,* for the protection of the two packets.

On November 10, 1864, the *Salvador* sailed from Panama Bay with seven adventurously minded passengers on board. Just before the steamer cast off, Commander Davenport with a detail from the United States flagship *Lancaster* came aboard for the apparent purpose of making the ordinary police inspection. While the passengers were assembled in the cabin having their tickets examined, the navy people quickly searched the effects of the suspected raiders. They found a number of very interesting things, among them Hogg's commission and orders, the articles of secrecy, and a Confederate flag. Commander Davenport did not betray these discoveries, but essayed an easy attitude toward all the passengers. The *Lancaster's* steam was up when the passengers came on board of the *Salvador,* and while they were in the cabin the man-of-war had started seaward. Davenport casually requested Captain Douglas to overhaul her so that he might return to his ship. At daylight the next morning, when well beyond the territorial jurisdiction of the Government of Colombia, and within sight of the *Lancaster,* Commander Davenport ordered the American flag to be hoisted; and, by virtue of his commission as an officer of the United States navy, took charge of the ship and arrested the Confederates. The names and rank of the latter were found to be: Thomas E. Hogg, acting master, commanding; E. A. Swain, acting master's mate, executive officer; John Hiddle, acting chief engineer; T. J. Grady, acting first assistant engineer; William L. Black, acting assistant paymaster; R. B. Lyon, sailing master; and Joseph Higgin, paymaster's clerk.

In the meantime, the other raiders had gone to Salvador to make the attempt on the *Guatemala,* when that steamer should touch at the port of La Libertad. However, Captain Dow adroitly managed to checkmate his would-be captors, leaving them standing on the dock —enraged, but at least free.

It is probable that Hogg knew nothing of the history
of the failure of Francis Drake in a buccaneering expedition upon the isthmus some three hundred years
earlier—how the English, like himself, had secretly
landed on the Caribbean shore, crossed the mountains
to the Pacific side, and would have accomplished their
objective but also for an act of indiscretion on the part
of a member of their party; how the Spaniards, gaining
intelligence of the impending raid, in the nick of time,
set a trap for the raiders, into which they fell as neatly
as he had. But the English prototypes, more fortunate
than their Confederate exemplars, extricated themselves
from the ambush, preserving themselves for a return
and successful exploit; whereas, Hogg and his associates
shortly found themselves imprisoned in Fort Alcatraz,
California.[21]

Several times after the nipping of the *Salvador* affair,
the United States navy and the Pacific Mail Steamship
Company were disturbed by reports of privateering or
secret service attempts to be made on the commerce in
the Pacific. During the last months of the war this un-
easiness was increased by the knowledge of the insta-
bility of authority in the Mexican ports—due to the
kaleidoscopic capriciousness of the Republican and Im-
perialist factions—making for a condition very favorable to the development of Confederate privateering
ventures. The last of these disclosures reached the Navy
Department in Washington just about ten days before
General Lee's surrender. It came by the way of the
consul general at Havana, and told that a party of Confederates had just left Cuba on board of the schooner

[21] *NWR,* I, 3, pp. 352-368.

Transit, bound for Truxillo, Honduras, with intentions to prey upon the United States shipping on the West Coast.[22]

While private-armed enterprise by the Confederates accomplished little or no known destruction of commerce in the Pacific, the fear of it caused the enemy to divert much of his naval force from the real field of activity to those waters where, until the arrival of the Confederate man-of-war *Shenandoah* in the winter of 1865, it had no worthy opponent.

[22] *NWR,* I, 3, pp. 397, 409-410, 452, 459, 484-485, 511.

XXII

THE CASE OF CAPTAIN GREATHOUSE AND THE SCHOONER J. M. CHAPMAN

*W*ITH daylight the tide was sufficiently risen to float the schooner. During the night she had lain aground at her wharf, settled to the bottom at low tide by the heavy weights of her cargo, which, in part, consisted of boxes marked "oil-mill" and "machinery," and of lumber. It was Sunday morning, March 15, 1863. Three men were on the quarter deck, impatient and apparently waiting for someone. At length one of them wanted to sail without their dilatory friend, but the other two reminded him that they were still fast aground. Presently the tide ran strong and the rocking and thumping of the schooner told them she was lifting. Then she swung free, and the two could no longer resist the importunity of the other to sail. In fact the suspicions of all were thoroughly aroused by the delay of their partner to return aboard. It did not matter that he was the sailing-master, and had the Spanish translation of documents which were thought important to the success of the enterprise: there were cogent reasons for sailing without delay. The sun was coming up over the American continent and across the Bay of San Francisco, lighting up the water front to the observation of all who were awake. The mooring lines were cast off, the jib hoisted, and the mainsail loosed; and the schooner swung into the stream.

She was the *J. M. Chapman,* of 90 tons burden. The

man most eager to sail was Alfred Rubery; his companions were Ridgeley Greathouse and Lorenzo L. Libby; and the person awaited was William C. Law. There was a fifth principal, the originator of the adventure, Asbury Harpending. He seems to have been below deck.

The lure of privateering upon the Pacific had long pulled at the heartstrings of Harpending, a Kentucky gentleman living in California. He and Rubery—the latter an Englishman—dreamed, talked over, and planned a private-armed cruise and the capture of a mail steamer transporting gold from San Francisco to Panama. Then Harpending, to translate fancy into fact, undertook the journey across the continent to Richmond to obtain from President Davis a letter of marque. This being before the day of trans-continental railways, he went, perforce, on horseback across the great plains of the West. Reaching the Confederate capital he seems to have succeeded in doing what few, if any, others were successful in performing: he secured a letter of marque in blank. Perhaps the legal difficulty in the way of granting him a blank commission may have been overcome by appointing him as a prize-agent with authority to issue commissions. There is nothing in the records to show, and the present files of letters of marque in the archives at Washington fail even to mention Asbury Harpending's name in any connection. But when he returned to San Francisco he undoubtedly had a blank letter of marque with him, for he exhibited it to his associates.

Fortified with a Confederate commission, Rubery and Harpending set out to secure a vessel. They arranged for the purchase of a suitable craft, and Rubery gave a draft as the purchase-money. But, unfortunately, the draft was returned for lack of funds, and the privateers-men were refused the vessel.

Undaunted, they continued with their plans and made a voyage to Cerros Island off the coast of Lower California to ascertain the fitness of that place as a dèpôt and rendezvous for attacks upon passing steamers. Returning again to San Francisco, Harpending made the acquaintance of a ship captain who seemed a likely fellow. He broached the subject of privateering to him, showed him the letter of marque, and dwelt upon the value of the prizes to be taken. As a result, Captain Law agreed to join the enterprise as sailing-master and to assist the party in procuring a vessel. Soon Law pointed out the *Chapman* as a fast schooner, well adapted for the purpose in mind. There was still the question of funds, but shortly a capitalist was found in the person of Ridgeley Greathouse, a banker of Yreka, a town in Siskiyou County, on the Oregon border. This gentleman was introduced at a meeting of the would-be privateersmen, and agreed to finance the expedition. The schooner was promptly purchased, and the day following Law went on board and took charge of her. He moved her to a new wharf, induced Libby to join the party as a mate, and engaged four seamen and a cook.

Under the pretext that he was acting for the Liberal Party in Mexico, Greathouse purchased two brass, rifled 12-pounders with shells, fuses, powder, muskets, pistols, lead for balls, percussion caps, knives, and every necessary kind of ordnance equipment. He bought a number of uniforms such as were generally worn by man-of-war's men. These articles went on board of the schooner in the boxes marked "oil-mill" and "machinery." He purchased and shipped a large quantity of lumber with which to construct berths, a prison room, a lower deck, and to fit the vessel generally for her mission.

Out of consideration for his material aid, Greathouse was named captain. The others were to share in authority and in prize-money in the following order: Harpending, Law, Rubery, and Libby. Their plan of action was carefully worked out so as to avoid suspicion on the part of the local authorities, and to save their skins if it should miscarry. The schooner was "put up" for a voyage to Manzanillo, Mexico; and some freight was received. Law cleared her at the customhouse, signing and swearing to a false manifest. After nightfall on Saturday, March 14, the body of the crew, some fifteen in number, were brought on board of the privateer and concealed in the hold.

During the night they were to have gotten quietly under way and stood to sea. Once upon the sea the course was to be laid for Guadalupe, an island about two hundred miles off the coast of Mexico in latitude 29° N. There the guns and military stores were to be landed, together with the lumber; and Harpending and the fighting men left. Thus far no belligerent activity was to have taken place, so that it might not be said, should they fall into the hands of the United States authorities, that they had committed treason in fitting out a hostile expedition on United States soil. From Guadalupe the voyage was to be continued to Manzanillo, where the *bona-fide* freight was to be delivered. Then returning to the island, Captain Greathouse and his men would mount their guns, construct the decks and quarters required, and load the schooner with stores for her cruise. Having fitted out the *Chapman,* entered the appropriate data in the blanks left in the letter of marque, and duly enrolled the men, the expedition would return to Manzanillo, and from there the required forms would be dispatched to the Confederate State Department to complete the legal requirements. The privateersmen would then be ready to make their first prize, and they hoped to find a mail steamer shortly after they should depart the second time from Manzanillo. Having fallen in with and captured a gold ship, they planned to land the crew and passengers in Mexico; and convert the prize into a cruiser. In this larger and steam-propelled privateer they would seek other steamers. They thought to make of their cruise a veritable treasure hunt; intending, when the pursuit of the enemy's men-of-war should become too hot, to abandon commerce-destroying and to attempt the recovery of shipwrecked treasure. They had particularly in mind searching for the gold which had recently gone down when the California steamer *Golden Gate* burned upon the coast of Mexico.

The schemes of Greathouse, Harpending, and their friends extended afar. After securing much gold for themselves, they would set out to harry the far-flung commerce of the Union, going first to the Chincha Islands, off the Peruvian coast, to burn the guano ships, thence to the China Seas, and finally to the Indian Ocean.

Just as their dreams seemed about to begin to reach an alluring fulfillment, the breeze died, the sails of the *Chapman* dropped idly—becalmed. At this moment the belated Law appeared on the dock, waving wildly and calling to the schooner. He did not seem to notice that two boats were putting out from the sloop-of-war *Cyane* lying out in the bay. His last carousal ashore had a bit befogged his vision, and his one thought was to get to the schooner. But those on the schooner saw the movement on the man-of-war, and knew that the end of their cruise had come with the beginning. In a few direful minutes the boats lay alongside, and Lieutenant Arthur R. Yates, U.S.N., and his bluejackets sprang over the sides of the schooner. The privateersmen, seeing that escape was impossible and resistance useless, surrendered without a struggle. Scarcely had the seizure been made when the intoxicated Law climbed over the opposite rail, and was made a prisoner with his partners.

The customhouse officers had long been suspicious of the intentions of those in control of the schooner *J. M. Chapman,* and had maintained a strict surveillance over her and her people. On Saturday afternoon the watch was increased, and the commanding officer of the sloop was notified. The revenue officers, taking a squad of policemen, went on board of a tug, and took station behind an adjoining slip. They saw a large number of men go aboard the schooner and disappear into the hold. They were very eager to catch all the privateersmen, red-handed so to speak, and they too were awaiting the arrival of Law. They delayed to put out after the schooner so that the sailing-master might have time to reach his vessel. When the civilians came alongside the *Chapman,* the navy people were already the captors; but the tug gave the prize a line and towed her to Fort Alcatraz, located on the north side of the Golden Gate—through which the privateersmen should not pass.

THE CASE OF CAPTAIN GREATHOUSE

At the fort the schooner's cargo was unloaded and the prisoners were landed and incarcerated. She was then towed over and anchored under the guns of the *Cyane*. Thus ended the cruise of the *Chapman* and the hopes of Greathouse and Company.[1]

Upon taking possession of the privateer, the naval officer found a number of scraps of paper, partly torn and chewed. In the baggage of Harpending and Rubery they found a draft of a proclamation to the people of California inciting them to rise up and throw off the yoke of the United States and to join the Confederacy. A plan for the capture of the forts at San Francisco and a copy of the secrecy obligation taken by the members of the enterprise, disclosing the penalties, were found. The papers were in Harpending's hand writing.

The naval authorities were thrown into a panic by the disclosures. The U.S.S. *Saginaw* was ordered on a reconnoissance to Guadalupe, the privateering rendezvous; but before she could sail, it appeared to the commandant of the navy yard on Mare Island, Thomas O. Selfridge, that the plan for attacking and destroying the government property in and about San Francisco was well organized and about to be executed. The sailing orders were then countermanded and the gunboat retained for defensive purposes.[2]

While awaiting the attack, Selfridge telegraphed to the Navy Department in Washington, requesting au-

---

[1] Case of United States vs. Ridgeley Greathouse, *et al.—Report of cases decided in the Circuit and District Courts of the United States for the Ninth Circuit*, reported by L. S. B. Sawyer, Counselor at Law (San Francisco: A. L. Bancroft and Company, law book publishers, booksellers and stationers, 1878), IV, 457 *et seq.; NWR*, I, 2, pp. 122-123.

[2] *NWR*, I, 2, pp. 140-141.

thority to buy and arm two steamers to aid in checking privateering. The Department in reply authorized the charter, at Selfridge's discretion, of one or more steamers; "the owners of said steamers to run them and keep them in perfect order for sea; Government to furnish only the armament, coal, and fighting crew, with appropriate officers."[3]

The attack did not materialize; but in the meantime the Federal Grand Jury indicted Greathouse, Harpending, Rubery, Law, Libby, *et al.*, for treason, under the act of July 17, 1862. The indictment alleged in substance:

1. The existence of a rebellion against the United States, their authority and laws;

2. That the defendants traitorously engaged in, and gave aid and comfort to, the same;

3. That in the execution of their treasonable purposes, they procured, fitted out and armed a vessel to cruise in the service of the rebellion, on the high seas, and commit hostilities against the citizens, property and vessels of the United States; and that the vessel sailed on such cruise.

The case came up for trial in the October term of the Circuit Court with Mr. Justice Field and District Judge Hoffman on the bench. Law and Libby turned State's evidence, and the District Attorney entered a *nolle prosequi* as to them. The crew was held to have had no criminal part in the affair, and the proceedings were only directed against Greathouse, Harpending, and Rubery.

The counsel for the defendants alleged that no hostilities had been committed, that the voyage upon which

---

3 *NWR*, I, 2, p. 158.

they were about to embark was a peaceful one, and further that they had not actually sailed, being still within the harbor. It was also contended that the fitting out of a vessel under a letter of marque was a belligerent act and not a treasonable one.

However, the court held that: "Belligerent rights conceded to the Confederate States cannot be invoked for the protection of persons entering within the limits of a State which has not seceded, and secretly getting up hostile expeditions against the Government."

Mr. Justice Field charged the jury that: "When Harpending received the letter of marque with the intention of using it, if such be the case (and it is stated by one of the witnesses that he represented that he went on horseback over the plains expressly to obtain it), he became leagued with the insurgents—the conspiracy between him and the chiefs of the rebellion was complete; it was a conspiracy to commit hostilities on the high seas against the United States, their authority and laws. If the other defendants united with him to carry out the hostile expedition, they, too, became leagued with him and the insurgent chiefs in Virginia in the general conspiracy. The subsequent purchasing of the vessel, and the guns, and the ammunition, and the employment of the men to manage the vessel, if these acts were done in furtherance of the common design, were overt acts of treason. Together these acts complete the essential charge of the indictment. In doing them the defendants were performing a part in aid of the great rebellion. They were giving it aid and comfort."

Judge Hoffman disposed of the defense that the *Chapman* had not sailed and that the projected voyage to Guadalupe and Manzanillo was a peaceful one, by charging that:

> In general, a voyage is deemed to have been commenced when the vessel in readiness for sea quits her wharf or other place of mooring without intention of returning to it; [and that] it can hardly be contended that the mere postponement of actual hostilities can deprive the voyage of the character stamped upon it by its main purpose or design.

The jury returned a verdict of guilty; and, October 17, the three prisoners were fined $10,000 each, and were sentenced to imprisonment for ten years.

The trial created quite a stir on the entire West Coast. Sympathizers with the convicted privateersmen in Victoria addressed letters to influential friends in England to secure intervention in behalf of the prisoners. Someone wrote a letter to the London *Index,* dated San Francisco, November 15, 1863, and signed, "Friend," appealing to the Confederate authorities to institute the *lex talionis* which had been an effective stop in the piracy cases in Philadelphia and New York, two years before. This letter was printed in the issue of January 7, 1864, and was reprinted in the Confederate newspapers in March.[4]

However, it was unnecessary for President Davis to undertake retaliatory measures; for Rubery was pardoned by President Lincoln at the request of his British friend John Bright, a member of Parliament and ever a defender of United States interests. Greathouse and Harpending were brought before the Circuit Court on a writ of *habeas corpus;* and were released from im-

[4] *NWR*, II, 3, pp. 948-949; *Mobile Daily Advertiser and Register,* March 2, 1864.

prisonment, on February 15, 1864, upon taking the oath prescribed in President Lincoln's amnesty proclamation of December 8, 1863, and upon giving bond for future good behavior.

Meanwhile, the schooner was libeled in the District Court as confiscable to the United States under the acts of August 5 and 6, 1861. The privateersmen made no protest. The vessel was condemned by default, and sold, and the proceeds were brought into the registry for distribution. The commander of the sloop-of-war *Cyane* intervened, claiming for himself and his officers and men a share of the funds. The claim was disposed of on January 13, 1864, by the District Court refusing to entertain the idea that the *Chapman* had been the property of either enemies or pirates, and as such the proper subject of naval prize. It held that the vessel had been an instrument of treason and her proceeds were therefore only divisible between the Government and the informer of the conspiracy.[5]

[5] Sawyer, *op. cit.*, vol. 4, pp. 501-516.

XXIII

THE PRIVATEER RETRIBUTION AND THE CAREER OF THE ADVENTUROUS MR. BRAINE

THE first year of the war had been the banner year in privateering, but patriots were still willing to risk their fortunes in a war game whose day was passing— in fact had passed. In the fall of 1862, we have seen that a group of men, mostly Louisianians and Texans, applied in Richmond for letters of marque for four large steamers and one schooner, but that only the latter seems to have been actually at sea. The cruise of this schooner, the *Retribution,* fully kept up the terrorizing traditions of 1861.

This, the last of the letters of marque to harass United States shipping, like most of her predecessors, was a little vessel of checkered career. Originally the tugboat *Uncle Ben* on Lake Erie, she had been taken by the United States navy to form a part of the expedition to reinforce Fort Sumter, in April, 1861. On the passage down the coast she had been separated, by stress of weather, from the relieving squadron, and captured by the North Carolinians, who converted her into a small gunboat and in course turned her over to the Confederate States navy. Late in 1862, the latter abandoned her, removed the engines to the ironclad *North Carolina,* then being built at Wilmington, and sold the hull. The purchasers patched up the stern where the propeller shaft had penetrated, stepped masts and rigged her as a schooner, painted her black, and significantly renamed her the *Retribution.*

In her altered condition she arrived at St. Thomas, on December 7, 1862, with a cargo of cotton and turpentine from Wilmington; and soon had the West Indies squadron on its ears. The United States Consul suspected that the schooner was to be fitted out as a privateer with the proceeds from the cargo, and was very suspicious of the Danish schooner *Dixie,* which lay along side of the *Retribution.* On the night of the fifteenth, the *Dixie,* without clearance, ran to sea, and was followed on the eighteenth by the *Retribution.* They met at a small island off the coast of Venezuela. There a 20-pounder rifle and two 12-pounder smoothbores were transferred from the Danish consort.

The *Retribution* reappeared off St. Thomas, on January 3, 1863, chasing back into port the brig *Gilmore Meredith,* of Baltimore, and the schooner *Westward,* of Bangor, Maine. This incident made the United States merchantmen in the harbor timid about going to sea. A week later she took the brig *J. P. Ellicott,* of Buckport, Maine, bound from Boston to Cienfuegos. A prize crew was put on board, but during the night the men mutinied, captured the prize, put the prize master in irons, and sailed to St. Thomas. The prize master was Gilbert Hay, who, it has been seen, had twice before been unsuccessful as a privateersman: as prize master on one of the captures of the *Jefferson Davis,* and as commander of the *Beauregard.* The crew were aliens. The Danish port authorities gave the prize back to its original captain, and handed over the prize master as prisoner to the commanding officer of the U.S.S. *Alabama,* then lying at St. Thomas. So much for Danish neutrality.

In the meantime, the West Indies squadron was all agog looking for the *Retribution.* But the privateer was elusive, and the accounts reaching the Union men-of-war as to her whereabouts were conflicting. On the last day of January, she captured the schooner *Hanover,* of Boston, and took her to Fortune Island in the Crooked Island Passage of the Bahamas. There the prize cargo was reshipped to Nassau and sold. The prize herself was reloaded with salt and sent into the Confederacy—running aground in Cape Fear Inlet under the protecting guns of Fort Fisher. This procedure was quite irregular but as we shall see the captain of the *Retribution* was either ignorant or unmindful of the niceties of law. Resuming her cruise, the privateer made her third and last prize, the brig *Emily Fisher,* on February 19. The old tug-gunboat-privateer, formerly a steamer but now simply a schooner, had become unseaworthy, and was shortly afterward sold in Nassau.[1]

With the sale of his ship, Captain John Parker had now no longer, under Confederate law, any status as a commander of armed force. The right to carry on war was an appurtenance of the ship and not a right vested in the commander. Nevertheless, he proceeded to St. John, New Brunswick, and organized a party to capture some United States merchant steamer for the resumption of privateering. Having assumed the authority to make a number of naval appointments, on December 2, 1863, he issued an order to "Lieutenant Commanding John Clibbon Braine," to proceed with an assignment

[1] *NWR,* I, vols. 1, 2, 4, 6, 8, 14, 17, and 19; II, vols. 1 and 3.

of officers and men, numbering about fifteen in all, to
New York. Arriving there, the party would take ordinary passage on some steamer suitable for their purpose, and when at sea would throw off their disguise and
capture the vessel.

On Saturday, the fifth, the party boarded in New
York the steam packet *Chesapeake,* bound for Portland, Maine; and on Monday, when about twenty miles
northeast of Cape Cod, effected her capture in the name
of the Confederate States of America. Some resistance
being met with from the ship's crew, one of them was
killed and another wounded. The steamer put into the
Bay of Fundy on Tuesday night. Here Captain Parker,
who had remained to make recoaling arrangements,
boarded and took command, the prisoners being landed
at the same time. The next morning, while the *Chesapeake* was still close to the Canadian shore, the U.S.S.
Ella and Annie steamed straight in for her. The would-
be privateersmen abandoned ship and escaped ashore.
The man-of-war then took possession of the steamer
and towed her to sea. But before going very far, another
Union warship was met, whose commander realized the
gravity of the *Ella and Annie's* offense against Canadian neutrality. Being a superior officer, he remanded
the *Chesapeake* to the jurisdiction of the Provincial
Government of Nova Scotia.

The case was then thrown into court by the owners,
who claimed that the original seizure of the ship was an
act of piracy. At the hearing the captors did not appear,
and the court, with ill-concealed eagerness, ordered an
immediate restitution by default.

The Confederate Government sent a special commissioner to investigate the case, upon whose recommendation the affair was wholly "disclaimed and disapproved." It appeared that Parker's real name was Vernon G. Locke; that he was a British subject, and that all of his men with one subordinate excepted were also British subjects; and that Locke, *alias* Parker, had not been issued a letter of marque, but that he had purchased the schooner and her privateering rights from the original licensee just before commencing the cruise.

As long as Locke trod the quarter-deck of the *Retribution* it did not matter that he was not a Confederate citizen, for the letter of marque was negotiable without national restriction. But only a Confederate citizen had the right under international law, to effect purely private or personal captures at sea in the name of those States.

As it was, the Nova Scotian Court entertained a request from the United States Consul, for the extradition—on charges of piracy—of those of the expedition who had been apprehended. Though the affair had been repudiated and even lacked real color of being Confederate at all, the Confederate Government, allowing an honest belief of authority on the part of the sometime Captain Parker, lent its influence to secure him and his people immunity from criminal prosecution. Their extradition was denied.[2]

But this very private sequel to privateering was not without its repercussion. "Lieutenant Commanding" Braine, having gotten a taste of something which he longed to repeat, escaped to the Confederacy. At Wilmington he worked up a party to go privateering but

2 *NWR,* I, vols. 2, 3, 9, 17, and 27; II, vols. 1 and 3.

was unable to obtain a vessel. He felt sure of being able to capture one of the mail steamers running between New York and Havana; and asked the Secretary of the Navy for a commission as an acting master, with orders to go to New York, from there to effect a capture and to run the prize into a Confederate port. The Department acceded to the request, on May 26, 1864; authorized him to appoint three acting master's mates and three acting third assistant engineers; and enjoined that "the strictest regard for the rights of neutrals and neutral property must be observed, and discipline and subordination preserved among officers and men under your command." Instead of proceeding to New York, he took a partly organized party to Bermuda and thence by way of Nassau to Havana. There, in the middle of August, he applied to the Special Agent of the Confederate States for funds with which to continue the expedition. The Agent, Charles J. Helm, declined to assist in what appeared to be a violation of Spanish neutrality, and assumed the responsibility for breaking up the party. Twelve, all but Braine and one other who declined to go, were sent back to the Confederacy. In the meantime Helm wrote to Richmond to ascertain the position of his Government. The Secretary of State, in reply said that Braine had exceeded the authority given him by the Navy Department; and that "the attempt of Braine to organize a hostile expedition in the harbor of Havana was a gross outrage, and you very properly prevented its accomplishment."

But that statement was too quickly made, for Braine had not given up his schemes. On September 29, as a belated passenger, he boarded the outbound United

States mail steamship *Roanoke,* while it was standing out of Havana harbor. He had a secret party of some ten men among the passengers. His principal assistants were named Little and Parr. The *bona-fide* passengers numbered about thirty persons. The ship's crew consisted of some forty-five or fifty men. The *Roanoke* was a side-wheeler of 1050 tons, with two walking-beam engines and a single smoke funnel. She was brigantine-rigged and had an average speed of 12 knots.

The steamer had sailed late in the afternoon. By ten o'clock that evening most of the officers had retired, including the master, Francis A. Drew. It was the watch of the chief officer, Edward Dingle Nichols. A group of passengers were chatting near the pilot house. Two or three of them quitted the party and sauntered over to the mate. This worthy officer was amazed to find himself surrounded by revolvers. He was told to surrender without resistance, or be shot on the spot. He believed in discretion rather than rash valor, and complied with the demand. Handcuffs were dropped over his wrists and he was led to the saloon. There the raiders, acting quickly, soon brought, duly manacled, the others of the ship's officers. Some had been surprised in their staterooms, others at their several duties. Only two of the forward officers resisted. In a scrimmage the third engineer was wounded, and the carpenter was killed. His body was thrown overboard.

The crew continued to work the ship, variously under persuasion and compulsion, accepting the captaincy of Acting Master Braine, C.S.N. The ship's officers were permitted liberty on parôle in the day but were placed in irons at night. The Navy Department's instructions to Braine had been to run for a Confederate port with whatever prize he might make; but the adventurous Acting Master felt constrained to disregard his orders and to make for Bermuda.

On the afternoon of October 4, the *Roanoke* arrived off the islands and took a pilot. After dark she dropped anchor in Five Fathom Hole, and Braine went ashore in the pilot boat. At St. George he made arrangements for coal, provisions, and recruits to be sent out, and for a vessel to take off his prisoners. During the night he returned to his ship. With the coming of daylight the *Roanoke* got underway and proceeded to sea, keeping out of sight of land. For two days she stood off and on the islands. Then on Thursday night, the sixth, the brig *Village Girl* was encountered; and all day Friday was spent in company, taking on provisions and coal. Twenty or thirty men were added to the party. Coaling by means of the boats was slow and only ten or fifteen tons were transferred.

The pro-Confederates were now on the lookout for a brigantine with a black ball painted in her foretopsail. Once during the afternoon a sail was made and the transfer operations were suspended to chase her, but upon overhauling her she was found not to be the expected vessel. About eight o'clock in the evening, the Danish brigantine *Mathilde,* showing the black ball upon her canvas, arrived. The prisoners—crew and passengers—were transferred with their baggage to the Danish ship, which stood into Five Fathom Hole and sent the captives ashore in boats.

The released Yankees lost no time in getting to the American Consulate, and making affidavits concerning this "piracy." Charges were promptly filed with the Governor alleging a violation of the Foreign Enlistment Act.

In the meantime Braine is said to have transferred to the brigantine the specie taken on the steamer, amounting to approximately $20,000, and to have sent her on to Halifax. For some reason he seems to have considered that he had not enough coal in his bunkers to carry him into Wilmington. Though Bermuda was out of the route between Havana and New York, it would appear that if a steamer left Cuba with enough coal to take her to New York she should have been able to make the voyage to Wilmington *via* St. George. At any rate, on Saturday, October 9, 1864, Braine resolved to burn his prize, and sent his recruits on shore—where they were immediately arrested. On Sunday morning, the original raiders set fire to the steamer, abandoned her, and landed. They, too, were taken in custody by the police. Nevertheless, the raiders smuggled ashore a large consignment of Havana cigars, which the revenue officers discovered "in obscure nooks and cellars, and in empty tents in and about St. George."

The United States Consul filed a request for the extradition of Braine and his party on the usual charge of piracy. On the third day of the proceedings before the magistrates, Braine's commission and instructions were proved to be genuine, whereupon the Colonial Attorney-General refused to go further with the matter—for these papers made of the capture of the *Roanoke* a warlike and not a piratical enterprise.[3]

[3] *NWR*, I, vols. 3 and 17; and II, vol. 3. *Diplomatic Correspondence* (*U.S.*), 1864, part 2; 1865, part 1.

For some months nothing was heard of Mr. Braine. The Confederacy was on its last legs, but few fully realized the plight of the country. During the winter of 1865, Braine organized a party for another *guerre de course,* and in the latter part of March began operations in Chesapeake Bay. He had a yawl and some twenty men. On March 31, the fireworks began near the mouth of the Patuxent River with the capture of the *St. Mary's.* The prize, a Baltimore-built schooner of 115 tons, hailing from St. Mary's, Maryland, with an assorted cargo valued at $20,000, was larger and more suitable for cruising than the yawl. Accordingly, the Confederates transferred to her and that night put to sea. Promptly along came another schooner, the *J. B. Spofford,* bound to New York from Wicomico, Maryland. She was met off Hog Island and was made an easy prize. However, Braine did not want the vessel; and placed upon her the crew and passengers taken as prisoners from the first prize, releasing her as a cartel. The two schooners then parted company, the *St. Mary's* going south and the *Spofford* making for the Delaware Breakwater.

When the released schooner arrived at Lewes at the entrance to Delaware Bay, her master reported to the Inspector of Customs that during the night following his capture, he had seen a very bright light in the direction in which the "rebels" had departed. He supposed that they had captured and set fire to another vessel.

Several days later the *St. Mary's* put into Nassau under plea of distress. The United States Consul at once asked the Colonial Government to seize the vessel and "her piratical crew." The Governor of the Bahamas declined the request, saying that the schooner was a legitimate prize. Shortly afterward Braine returned to sea. The schooner was still unarmed, though the Consul insisted that some heavy guns had been taken on board while she was in port.

It was supposed that Braine was bound for Spanish Wells or Harbor Islands, there to pick up his old partner Parr. But the *St. Mary's* and Acting Master Braine turned up in the port of Kingston, Jamaica, in June. Again a United States consul attempted to secure his extradition—and failed. Braine now abandoned his prize—whether voluntarily or under compulsion it does not appear—and on the twenty-first, took passage for Liverpool. The consul sent a letter to his brother officer at that port giving such information as would enable him to identify Braine and to continue his prosecution. But here the adventurous Mr. Braine fades from the picture.

The *St. Mary's* was carried around to Anotta Bay on the north side of the island, and according to the last available account remained there. Mr. Seward wrote to Mr. Adams about it, and the latter addressed to Earl Russel a demand for the restitution of the schooner to her American owner. On August 15, the British Foreign Office replied to the American Minister that the case had been referred to the law officers of the Crown; and no more seems to have been said about her.[4]

[4] *NWR,* I, vols. 5 and 17; *Diplomatic Correspondence (U.S.),* 1865, part 1.

XXIV

THE UNITED STATES DABBLES IN PRIVATEERING

*W*HEN the United States went to war with Great Britain in 1812, the act of Congress declaring a state of war also empowered the President to issue letters of marque. However, the declaration of war against Mexico in 1846 carried with it no authorization for private-armed sea power, simply because Congress deemed it inexpedient in the face of Mexico's maritime poverty. The Confederate States, in recognizing a state of war and in the same act authorizing privateering against the United States, followed the precedent of 1812. On the other hand the United States not only, as in 1846, felt the inexpediency of resort to formal privateering; but, realizing the greater value of letters of marque to the enemy, attempted to neutralize them by discredit. However, the high moral pose struck by the Lincoln Administration on the subject of this immemorial institution of the sea was simply a strategical war measure —as later was the Emancipation Proclamation—and was varied and finally effaced to suit the material interest of the contest.

When the ink was scarcely dry on Lincoln's "Pirate Proclamation," and while his futile negotiations with England were going on for the acceptance of the Declaration of Paris, the *Quaker City,* a private-armed steamer of New York, went forth in the service of the

United States, with neither public commission nor letter of marque.

. This steamer was fitted out for war and sent to sea by means of a subscription raised at a mass meeting. This meeting had resolved itself into a committee of safety that came to be styled the Union Defence Committee of the City of New York.[1]

The news of the enforced evacuation of Fort Sumter had been announced in the New York evening papers of April 14, and the details appeared in the next morning's editions. At noon that day the *Tribune* published a call for a patriotic mass meeting, and at two o'clock in the afternoon a group of Wall Street financiers met at 30 Pine Street, forming a preliminary committee of ten. Daily and sometimes twice daily committee meetings were held, at which patriotic resolutions ran wild. Then a general mass meeting was held in Union Square at three o'clock on Saturday afternoon, the twentieth, amid a profusion of flags, bunting, rosettes, badges, cockades, and the like. Major Anderson and four other officers from the late Fort Sumter garrison were present. A fund of $21,000 was subscribed, and a mandate was given by the great crowd to an Executive Committee. On Monday morning, the Board of Aldermen appropriated half a million dollars for the work of the Committee, which organized the next day, and which thereafter met every day at 30 Pine Street and every evening at the Fifth Avenue Hotel.

The Committee blossomed forth in all manner of warmaking activities, which sometimes in the exuberance

---

[1] *Union Defense Committee of the City of New York—Minutes, Reports and Correspondence.* Published, 1885.

of patriotism seemed to constitute a usurpation of the functions of Government. But it is only with its relation to sea power that we are interested.

Following the mob scene in Baltimore on April 19, when the citizens attempted to oppose with stones and brickbats the passage of Massachusetts troops through the city, the Marylanders cut the rail communications with the North by burning bridges and destroying several miles of track. The news of this expression of sympathy with the secession movement greatly agitated the city of New York, and the first move of the Committee was to perfect arrangements for obtaining track materials and laborers to restore the rail lines. To provide transportation for this enterprise the steamer *Kill von Kull* was chartered, and loaded and sent, on the twenty-fifth, to Annapolis. The large Cunard liner *Kedar,* which had arrived from Liverpool on the twenty-second, was chartered by the committee, at $2,000 a day, armed, and on the twenty-seventh sent to Hampton Roads, where she did a brief tour of duty as a transport. But it was the committee's chartering of the *Quaker City* that brought forth immediate and permanent results for purposes of *la guerre de course.*

This vessel was chartered on the twenty-fifth, as a counterpoise to two Confederate privateers which were reported, in New York the day before, as fitting out in Chesapeake Bay. The *Quaker City,* schooner rigged, of 1,600 tons burden, owned by P. Hargous and Company, had loaded and was about to sail for Havana when the charter party was executed. The terms were $1,000 a day for thirty days, with option of renewal or of purchase at a price of $140,000. She immediately discharged her cargo and was moved to the Brooklyn navy yard where, at the expense of the Committee, she was fitted out and armed as a cruiser. A battery of two 32-pounder smooth bores and two rifled 6-pounders was put on board. Then on April 29, she sailed for Hampton Roads, with Samuel W. Mather in command. In her complement of officers there was not one who held rank in the United States navy.

Arriving off Fort Monroe, the private-armed cruiser reported to Flag Officer Pendergrast, commanding the home squadron, who assigned her to cruising duty in the Chesapeake Bay. She lay off and on the roads and the capes. On May 14, she made her first capture, the ship *North Carolina,* from Havre, in ballast, bound to Norfolk, her home port. On the twenty-fifth, she took the bark *Pioneer,* of Richmond, coming in from Liverpool; and on the same day shared with the U.S.S. *Monticello* in the capture of another Richmond bark, the *Winifred.* The latter was bringing in a cargo of coffee from Rio de Janeiro. Five days later she made a prize of a third Richmond trader, the schooner *Lynchburg,* also coming up from Brazil with coffee.

All of these captures were made without a shadow of commission for man or ship, and only by that precarious right vested in every citizen to make captures of the public enemy upon the seas in the name of his government. Nevertheless, in sending forward these prizes to the admiralty courts, the flag officer certified the roll of officers and men, 99 in all, as members of the naval establishment entitled to share in the distribution of the prize-money.[2] On June 1, Mather accepted a commission

2 Archives, U.S. Naval Library and Records, Washington, D. C.—*Prize Cases.*

UNITED STATES PRIVATE-ARMED STEAMER QUAKER CITY

From an aquarelle in the possession of the United States Naval Library and Records.

as acting master but it was not until October that any other of the officers of the *Quaker City* were appointed in the Navy.[3]

Upon the expiration of the first charter, the committee exercised its option to hire her for another month.[4] On June 4, the bark *General Green,* from Sagua la Grande, Cuba, for Baltimore, was encountered at the capes, and, as her register showed her to be owned in Charleston, South Carolina, she was made a prize. On or about the last day of the private charter, a fourth bark owned in Richmond, the *Sallie Magee,* up from Rio, was captured and sent to New York for adjudication.

The *Quaker City* now became an undoubted national vessel. It appears that the Navy Department continued the charter party for one or two months and then purchased her for the sum of $117,500. The Committee rendered a bill to the Department for the cost of the armament, $15,013.75; the Ordnance Bureau objected to its approval, saying that the cost was twice what it should have been; and there was a long drawn out dispute over the matter, which seems never to have been settled to the full satisfaction of the Committee.

The Union Defense Committee felt quite proud of its work, and itself, and at a meeting at 30 Pine Street

[3] Archives, U.S. Naval Library and Records, Washington, D. C.—*File of Acceptances.*

[4] Letter from the Secretary of the Navy to Flag Officer commanding squadron at Hampton Roads, May 25, 1861 (*NWR,* 5, p. 667), says that, "The steamer *Quaker City* has been rechartered for three months from the twenty-fifth instant, and will form a part of the Atlantic blockading squadron." However, the printed reports of the committee indicate that the steamer was rechartered by that body for another month, before the Government took her over.

on July 23, Charles H. Marshall, representing shipping interests, was reported, in the *Herald* of the next day, as speaking in the following tenor:

It is well-known that the ocean is swarming with privateers. The Secretary of the Navy had it in his power, if he had the ability, to have prevented these piratical vessels from getting out to sea. . . . The fitness of these merchant steamers for the work required of them was clearly shown in the case of the *Quaker City*, which was made ready for sea, armed, and equipped, in thirty-six hours. If these fine steamers had been taken up by the government, not a fishing boat would have been permitted to escape from a southern port. There would have been no necessity for the recapture of one of our vessels by the strong arm of a single negro[5]—absolutely the greatest and most heroic act he had heard of yet, nor would so much property have been stolen by the robbers who had escaped to sea. He was sorry to say that Mr. Welles was totally unfit to be Secretary of the Navy.

Thus, did the pot of unlicensed privateers call black the baking pan of regular letters of marque!

In the same edition the *Herald* printed an editorial recommending Cornelius Vanderbilt, of New York commercial shipping interests, to supplant Gideon Welles as Secretary of the Navy. Mr. Welles was not so impressed with Mr. Vanderbilt's superior abilities as to resign in his favor.

But the War Department was distinctly under the shadow of the Vanderbilt greatness; and, when the great Confederate ironclad *Virginia* defeated and demoralized the fleet in Hampton Roads on March 8 and 9,

[5] Refers to the recapture of the prize schooner *S. J. Waring* by her steward—see Chapter VI.

1862, it sought, by telegram, the aid of C. Vanderbilt, Esq., New York.[6] This was Saturday, March 15, and on Monday Vanderbilt came to Washington to confer with the Department.

As a result of the conference, "the great steamship *Vanderbilt*," of 3360 tons burden, was gratuitously sent to Fort Monroe as a means of "protection and defense against the rebel ironclad ship *Merrimack*." As authority for action, Vanderbilt received a sort of letter of marque from the Secretary of War, Edwin M. Stanton, reciting that:

Confiding in your patriotic motives and purposes, as well as in your skill, judgment, and energy, full discretion and authority are conferred upon you to arm, equip, navigate, use, manage, and employ the said steamship *Vanderbilt* with such commander and crew and under such instructions as you may deem fit for the purposes hereinbefore expressed.[7] [Namely,] to aid the protection and defense of the transports now in the service of this Department on Chesapeake Bay, Hampton Roads, and adjacent waters, and wherever the said transports may be bound.

The *Vanderbilt* was considered a formidable antagonist by Commodore Josiah Tattnall, C.S.N., whose flagship was the much feared ironclad *Virginia* (improperly but generally called the *Merrimack*). When the quasi-privateer arrived with the enemy's fleet, Tattnall wrote to the Navy Department in Richmond that the *Vanderbilt* was

as powerful in her lower frame as the *Virginia*, [and] had been fitted with a ram, very low down on her stern, for the

---

[6] *NWR*, I, 7, p. 129.   [7] *Ibid.*, p. 149.

purpose of attacking the *Virginia*. The enemy's plan obviously, [continued the Confederate Commodore,] will be to get me in close conflict with the *Monitor*, and, as in that event I must occasionally lose my headway entirely, to seize the opportunity to run into me with the *Vanderbilt* and other vessels, which, for that purpose, will keep out of the mêlée.

Nevertheless, the *Virginia* remained mistress of Hampton Roads, and, though offering combat without reserve, could never entice the ironclad *Monitor*, the ram *Vanderbilt,* or any of the enemy's fleet into engagement. On one occasion when the *Virginia* offered battle, and was refused, Commodore Tattnall sent the little wooden gunboats *Thomas Jefferson* and *Raleigh* within the enemy's lines to cut out three transports. The enemy suffered the two Confederate steamers to capture and tow away the brigs *Marcus* and *Saboah* and the schooner *Catherine T. Dix,* without responding to the taunt.[8]

The *Vanderbilt* was released by her owner and the War Department and received into the navy in September, 1862. She was then altered and armed for cruising in search of Confederate raiders and blockade-runners. Though she was never able to catch up with any of the elusive Confederate cruisers, she accomplished the capture of several merchantmen. One of these was the British steamer *Peterhoff,* alleged blockade-runner. This seizure brought on one of the most famous cases in admiralty annals. The prize was condemned in the District Court, but four years later the Supreme Court reversed the court of original jurisdiction; and the

[8] *NWR,* I, 7, pp. 221-224 and 330-338.

United States Government was obliged to compensate the owners.

In the meantime, sentiment in the United States seems to have turned in favor of privateering proper. The Confederate privateers had shown, not so much by the number of prizes taken as by the demoralization that was inspired by them in merchant marine circles, that privateering was still a potent influence in maritime warfare. Consequently a move was made in Congress during the winter of 1863 to vest power in the President to issue letters of marque, during the present or any future wars, without further authority from Congress. The proposal evoked considerable opposition, interesting to relate in a section of the country which had been in former wars the very hot bed of privateering, and which even at the beginning of this internecine contest had suggested it.

In July, 1861, the Board of Trade of Boston, seconded by the Governor of the Commonwealth of Massachusetts, had made to the Secretary of the Navy propositions looking to the "arming, equipping, and maintaining a fleet of small, light, swift-sailing vessels," explaining that "the whole blockade could be maintained by our New England coasters acting as a naval corps of volunteers, if only authorized and empowered by papers from the Government." The Governor added that our "skippers and men are keen and brave, the vessels strong and of light draft"—and doubtless prize-money seemed bright.[9]

At this time New England shipowners had already armed some of their steamers, notable among which

9 *NWR*, I, 1, pp. 44-45.

were the *Cambridge* and the *Pembroke.* The owners of both of these private-armed vessels were requested by the Navy Department to dispatch them in chase of the Confederate privateer *Jefferson Davis,* when the latter appeared on the New England coast in the middle of July.[10] Later the Government bought the *Cambridge,* for $75,000, putting her in commission as a third rate cruiser on August 29, 1861. The private armament had consisted of two eight-inch smooth-bores of 55 hundred-weight, two 12-pounder howitzers, and one 6-pounder rifle.[11] The *Cambridge* then joined the Atlantic blockading squadron. As to the *Pembroke* her owners would send her upon a *guerre de course,* and inquired of the Navy Department for a letter of marque.

The Secretary of the Navy, however, held on October 1, 1861, that

there are objections to, and no authority for, granting letters of marque in the present contest. . . . I am not aware, [he explained,] that Congress, which has the exclusive power of granting letters of marque and reprisal, has authorized such letters to be issued against the insurgents, and were there such authorization I am not prepared to advise its exercise, because it would, in my view, be a recognition of the assumption of the insurgents that they are a distinct and independent nationality. Under the act of August 5, 1861, "Supplementary to an act entitled an act to protect the commerce of the United States and to punish the crime of piracy," the President is authorized to instruct the commanders of "armed vessels sailing under the authority of any letters of marque and reprisal granted by the Congress of the United States, or the commanders of any other suit-

[10] *NWR*, I, 1, pp. 38-39.   [11] *Ibid.,* II, 1, p. 50.

able vessels, to subdue, seize, take, and, if on the high seas, to send into any port of the United States any vessels or boats built, purchased, fitted out, or held, etc." This allusion to letters of marque does not authorize such letters to be issued, nor do I find any other act containing such authorization. But the same act in the second section, as above quoted, gives the President power to authorize "the commanders of any suitable vessels to subdue, seize, etc." Under this clause letters permissive, under proper restrictions and guards against abuse, might be granted to the propeller *Pembroke.* . . .[12]

The owners, J. M. Forbes and Company, rejected the letters permissive. They clearly saw the international restrictions encumbering private-armed vessels endowed merely with the power to seize pirates, for such "could only stop and search suspected vessels at their peril, and with danger of interference from foreign cruisers. To be useful they must have powers of no doubtful character . . . as to the right of search or otherwise using the power of ships of war."[13] So the *Pembroke* went into the China trade. And the letters permissive fell flat.

Returning to the consideration of the privateering bill of 1863, we find that the Administration was apprehensive of how it might affect the sentiment of foreign powers if it came upon them "suddenly and without any explanations." Accordingly the United States Minister at London was instructed, on February 19, to pave the way for it.[14]

In the Senate, Sumner of Massachusetts was a bitter opponent of the measure. At length a compromise was

[12] *NWR,* I, 1, pp. 99-100.   [13] *Ibid.,* pp. 102-103.
[14] *Diplomatic Correspondence,* 1863, part 1, p. 135.

effected, and a bill was put through both Houses granting to the President authority to issue letters of marque and general reprisal in all domestic and foreign wars, but limited during the term of three years from the passage of the act, and permitting him to make "all needful rules and regulations for the government and conduct thereof, and for the adjudication and disposal of the prizes and salvages made by such vessels." The act was approved by President Lincoln and became law on March 3, 1863.[15] However, the Executive never considered it expedient or politic to take advantage of the power thus acquired.

In a discussion between the Secretaries of State and of the Navy shortly after the passage of the act, the latter was emphatically against the issuance of letters of marque. He held, in the formal memorandum of this conversation, that

to clothe private and armed vessels with governmental power and authority, including the belligerent right of search, will be likely to beget trouble, and the tendency must unavoidably be to abuse. Clothed with these powers, reckless men will be likely to involve the Government in difficulty, and it was an apprehension of that fact, and to avoid it, I encountered much obloquy and reproach at the beginning of the rebellion, and labored to institute a less objectionable policy.

Propositions for privateers, for yacht squadrons, for naval brigades, volunteer navy, &c, &c, were, with the best intentions in most instances, pressed upon the Department, regardless of the consequences that might follow from these rude schemes of private warfare. It was to relieve us of the necessity of going into these schemes of private adventure

15 U.S. Statutes-at-Large, 37th Cong., Sess. III.

that the "Act to provide for the temporary increase of the Navy," approved July 24, 1861, was so framed as to give authority to take vessels into the naval service and appoint officers for them temporarily, to any extent which the President may deem expedient. Under other laws, . . . These laws, therefore, were intended and seemed to provide all the advantages of letters of marque, and yet prevent in a great measure the abuses liable to spring from them. Private armed vessels, adopted temporarily into the Naval service, would be more certainly and immediately under the control of the Government than if acting only under a general responsibility to law.

It will be necessary to establish strict rules for the government of private armed vessels, as to some extent they will be likely to be officered and manned by persons of rude notions and free habits. . . .

The Department of State lost no time in publishing regulations, in sixteen paragraphs and largely based, as were the Confederate regulations, upon the experience of 1812. There were, however, several very essential points of difference between the rules promulgated by the two belligerents. The security bonds were doubled in amount by the Washington Government. The bounties to be paid for successful encounters with armed ships of the "insurgents" were enormously increased. When the armed vessel "burnt, sunk or destroyed" was of equal or inferior force, the bounty was fixed at $1,000 for each person on board of the enemy at the commencement of the engagement; and when she was of superior force the unit value was doubled. The pension deduction was placed at only 2 per cent—instead of five. Offenses committed on board of privateers were triable before a naval court-martial—rather than in the civil courts. The Government reserved the right to purchase any ship and her armament at the original cost plus a premium of 14 per cent.

In addition to the regulations, "Instructions for the Private Armed Vessels of the United States" were printed. At once a few applications for letters of marque were received, and filed—but none were granted.[16]

Though the United States refrained from issuing regular letters of marque during the continuance of the war, belligerent advantage was taken of private sea-power wherever possible. As an alternative to the convoy system, the Navy Department proposed to certain California and West Indian shipowners to give them protection for their vessels by placing on board navy guns and gun crews. The plan contemplated granting to the merchant captains commissions in the navy as acting masters, without pay. The naval complement to be allowed to each vessel was two petty officers and twelve men.[17] Thus without material loss in their commercial efficiency the armed merchantmen would become virtually auxiliary cruisers. The proposal does not seem to have taken well with the shipping companies, who preferred to have their vessels convoyed.[18]

On one occasion, the armed mail steamer *Northern Light,* was to carry from Aspinwall, Panama, to New York, an especially valuable cargo including more than two million dollars in gold. The C.S.S. *Sumter,* Commander Raphael Semmes, was terrorizing the West Indian waters, and the president of the steamship company

16 U.S. Naval Library and Records, Washington, D. C.—Naval Archives.
17 *NWR*, I, 1, pp. 85 and 393.   18 *Ibid.,* I, vols. 1, 2, and 3.

INSTRUCTIONS

FOR THE PRIVATE ARMED VESSELS OF THE UNITED STATES.

Department of State,

Washington, 186

To Captain .... Commander of the

private armed .... called the ....

....

Sir:

1. The tenor of your commission under the Act of Congress entitled "An act concerning letters of marque, prizes, and prize goods," a copy of which, and of the regulations of the President founded thereon, is hereto annexed, will be kept constantly in your view. The high seas, referred to in your commission, you will understand, generally, to extend to low water mark; but with the exception of the space within one league, or three miles, from the shore of countries at peace with the United States. You may, nevertheless, execute your commission within that distance of the shore of a neutral nation, and even on the waters within the jurisdiction of such nation, if permitted so to do.

2. You are to pay the strictest regard to the rights of neutral powers, and the usages of civilized nations; and in all your proceedings towards neutral vessels, you are to give them as little molestation or interruption as will consist with the right of ascertaining their neutral character, and of detaining and bringing them in for regular adjudication, in the proper cases. You are particularly to avoid even the appearance of using force or seduction with a view to deprive such vessels of their crews, or of their passengers, other than persons in the military or naval service of the insurgents.

SEWARD'S INSTRUCTIONS TO UNITED STATES PRIVATEERS

From an original in the possession of the United
States Naval Library and Records.

requested the Navy Department to furnish a special escort through the Mariguana Passage. The U.S.S. *Keystone State* was ordered to this duty and arrived on schedule, yet saw nothing of her valuable convoy nor of her enemy the *Sumter*.[19] Neither did the *Sumter* see anything of the *Northern Light* or the *Keystone State*. The seas are very broad. This recalls the fact that the private-armed schooner *Henry W. Johnson,* sent out by the New York Board of Underwriters for the protection of vessels in which they were interested as insurers, cruised about in the West Indies and vicinity for some months during the summer and fall of 1861, falling in with no privateers—which were, nevertheless, thereabouts.[20]

The activities of the armed merchantmen of the War of Secession were characterized by none of the brilliant exploits performed by their successors in the World War.

[19] *NWR,* I, 1, pp. 44, 48, 55, 75.   [20] *Ibid.,* I, 1, pp. 31, 37, and 203.

XXV

THE CONFEDERACY BEGINS THE MODIFICATION OF PRIVATEERING

*E*ARLY in the War of Secession, as we have seen, it became evident that privateering as a great factor in maritime warfare had passed. This a few Confederates discerned in the summer of 1861, while the great majority, with ideas built on the wars of the Revolution and of 1812, were still harboring extravagant expectations. These few were casting about to find some way in which to conserve to the public defense the valor and resource of private-armed sea power.

In May, 1861, B. J. Sage, a Louisiana planter and lawyer, addressed a communication to the Confederate Government on the subject of a modified form of privateering to meet the altered conditions in the world.[1] He proposed a navy of two classes. The first, of course, was to be and remain the regular navy; and the second was to be constituted of private ships, armed and manned with a certain amount of government aid but exclusively under government regulation and control. The rôle of this second-class navy was to be purely that of the commerce-destroyer, and its pay was still to be the prize-money. The proposal, however, would confer upon these private-armed ships a public status, and would

[1] Archives, U.S. Naval Library and Records, Washington—No. CXLVI, being the Papers of Master B. J. Sage, C.S.N., referring to the Confederate States Volunteer Navy. This collection constitutes the general authority upon which this chapter is written.

gain for the Government a very desirable control over their actions.

In August, Sage wrote again—and at great length. He set forth how the value of privateering as a remedy for naval disparities might be conserved through the reform and elevation of the institution. He urged upon the Government the necessity of preparing for a long war and especially the necessity of omitting no means to neutralize the naval superiority of the United States. If the peace should come quickly, he argued, then ships constructed or purchased for the second-class or volunteer navy, should they not be desired for retention in the peace-time naval establishment, would constitute a welcome addition to the commercial marine. Although one may suspect that the Louisiana planter was not without an appetite for sea-roving—for, in fact, he naïvely suggested himself for a high commission in such volunteer navy—he nevertheless saw the situation so clearly and supported his views so persistently, apart from his personal ambitions, that he should justly be considered the apostle of the volunteer navy idea.

The Government took no action on his suggestions during the summer session of the Provisional Congress; but when that body reassembled for the winter (fifth) session, Sage went to Richmond and sought to apply the pressure of public opinion. During December he published articles in the newspapers of the capital. It seemed to him that Confederate privateering had fallen far short of its possibilities and was seriously declining. In the Richmond *Whig,* one morning, he wailed: "Are we giving up privateering? Practically we seem to be; and it is giving up one of the most formidable means of harassing the enemy. . . ." Then his ideas began to be noticed. On January 6, 1862, the Secretary of the Navy submitted to the President a plan "to create a branch of naval warfare which shall enable us to unite and employ private capital and enterprise against the enemy, and which shall be free from the objections urged against privateering."[2] Three days later the proposal was transmitted to Congress, where it was referred to the Committee on Naval Affairs. Toward the close of the session it came back to the floor in the shape of "a

[2] *NWR.* II, 2, pp. 124-125.

About this time John Slidell, the Confederate Commissioner at Paris, had also seen the handwriting on the wall and had come to the conclusion that privateering was obsolete. On February 11, 1862, in the last paragraph of his first dispatch to the Department of State after taking residence in France, he wrote:

"I hope you will excuse me for making a suggestion that may perhaps be considered as savoring of supererogation. It is quite evident that privateering is an arm which can no longer be used to advantage. The chief, I may say the only, object of the owners, officers, and crews of privateers is prize money. So long as our own coast is blockaded, and our prizes are not admitted into any neutral port, there can be no inducement to fit out private armed vessels. Why not, then, abandon a system which experience has demonstrated to be an absolute failure, and which, while innocuous to our foes, is the subject of bitter commentary by our enemies, and warmly deprecated by our friends in Europe? The cruise of the 'Sumter' has shown what efficient services may be rendered by small national vessels, not looking for pecuniary profit, but seeking only to inflict the greatest possible amount of injury on the enemy's commerce. If twenty or thirty national vessels of the class of the 'Sumter' had been sent out with such instructions at the commencement of hostilities, the Federal flag would now be rarely seen on a merchant ship, and the whole of the immense carrying trade of the enemy would have passed into the hands of neutrals. It is not too late to pursue that policy, but I very much question the expediency of that mode of warfare if it be confined to one or two cruises. On a large scale it would command respect, and, by promoting the interests of the maritime nations of Europe, would naturally excite their sympathies in our favor; but with only the 'Sumter' afloat, no appreciable effect is produced on the carrying trade, and an opportunity is afforded for a great deal of hypocritical declamation about the wickedness of destroying private property."—*Messages and Papers of the Confederacy,* II, 179-180; and *NWR,* II, 3, p. 339.

bill to establish a volunteer navy," introduced by Deputy Colin J. McRae, of Alabama, a newly added member to the Naval Committee. The bill "was read first and second times, placed on the Calendar, and ordered to be printed"; and five days later, February 17, died with the Provisional Congress.[3]

The permanent Congress met the day following; and on March 10, Representative Conrad, of Louisiana, Chairman of the House Committee on Naval Affairs, introduced a similar bill. However, it fared badly; for, when Conrad took it up for consideration on April 16, it was tabled upon the motion of Henry S. Foote, of Tennessee.

In the meantime, the State of South Carolina had sought, by ordinance in Convention, on January 7, 1862, to stimulate private-armed warfare through the establishment of a system of bounties. The ordinance provided that to "any person or persons, for the time being not in the actual service of this State or the Confederate States," who should "capture or sink, burn or otherwise destroy, any armed ship or vessel belonging to, or in the service of, the United States, invading the waters within this State, or coming within three marine leagues[4] of its coast," the State would pay $20 for each person on board the armed vessel at the beginning of the engagement and $30 for each captive brought in. In the case of transports, bounties, similar but $5 less in amount, were authorized. If the enemy's ship were destroyed, the victors were to be rewarded at the rate of $10 for

---

[3] *Journal of the Provisional Congress of the Confederate States of America* (Washington: Government Printing Office, 1904).

[4] Probably intended as one marine league or three geographic miles.

each ton of burden. The ordinance also declared that unarmed vessels and cargoes captured from the enemy became the property of the captors; but, in this respect, the South Carolinians were legislating upon a ground delegated under the Constitution to the Confederate States.

At the same time that the Congress declined the Volunteer Navy Bill, it looked with more favor upon another project which had been advocated by Sage; namely, the encouragement of inventors and constructors of machines, engines, or contrivances for the destruction of vessels. On March 19, an amendment to the act concerning letters of marque was offered, so that such inventors might be paid 50 per cent of the value of each armed vessel of the enemy sunk or destroyed by his invention; and, on April 21, it became law. Nearly a year earlier Congress had enacted a law in connection with letters of marque, that anyone who invented "any new kind of armed vessel, or floating battery, or defence," was entitled to the exclusive enjoyment thereof in privateering; though, of course, the Government reserved the right to use any invention in the public service.[5]

Sage was not satisfied with the breadth of the legislation, and in 1863 wrote and distributed a pamphlet entitled, "Organization of Private Warfare," with the subtitles, "Bureau of Destructive Means and Measures," and "Bands of Destructionists and Captors." The object of the pamphlet was to stimulate Congress to create a board or bureau, which should receive, examine, and report upon all devices and methods for injuring

[5] *Statutes-at-Large*, Prov. Cong., Sess. II, Chap. I. (Richmond: R. M. Smith, Printer to Congress, 1864.)

the enemy's seapower, should coördinate the activities
of inventors, and exert general supervision over the men
and means employed in this kind of warfare. He urged
that the inventions for marine destructions be thrown
open to any and all who gave evidence of being able to
use them successfully, allowing to the inventor as royalty
a proportion of the bounty paid by the Government to
the destructor. For "these coast and river privateers,"
he advocated secret organization "under the general authority and control of the department or district commander," but "with wide discretion as to time, place, and
manner of action." He asked that they be afforded such
Government aid as transportation, use of workshops,
ordnance stores, and special details needful. In cases
when enemy's vessels were captured, not destroyed, he
proposed that the captors should be allowed all the
rights permitted under regular letters of marque as
upon the high seas.

The band could be small or large as the exigency might
require [explained Sage, picturing the operation of his
proposal]. It should be under a leader who would act more
or less under the immediate authority and protection of the
commanders of the military district where his operations are
to be. This leader would generally be the inventor, who,
with his artisans, assistants or partners, would form the
operating corps. . . . Such bands having governmental
authority for any expedition, would be protected from any
penalty for irregular warfare. Being always ready, on the
watch, and stimulated by the mingled and powerful motives
of great gain and bitter hatred to the enemy, as well as by
patriotism . . . these bands of ingenious and daring men
would not only operate all destructive contrivances, but,

324

like privateers, would make captures, and enrich themselves at the enemy's expense; "all along our shore," on our 3,000 miles of coast, and in our bays and rivers, for the enemy is pressing upon us wherever we have navigation, particularly in the Mississippi and its tributaries, tempting and provoking destruction and capture. . . . They would dash on vessels and steamboats in small boats, and capture them, or they might drench them with spirits of turpentine and other incendiary matter, and burn them. And as has been proposed, ambulating boat corps could be organized; the boats, howitzers, &c., on pontoon wagons. Such a corps could move quickly from bay to bay, or river to river, and make frequent surprises.

As an instance of the need of special legislation to secure to the inventors of warlike devices the bounties already provided by law, Sage cited the case of

a Mr. McDaniel, of Kentucky, [who] invented his ingenious contrivances, organized his bands, and was operating with a view to the reward of fifty per cent. offered by act of Congress, for destroying a war vessel by a new contrivance; when his agent obtained a commission for him, for the sole purpose of giving him the needed protection in case of capture. He destroyed the [U.S.S.] *Cairo,* in the Yazoo [River], and now the Government seems to withhold the compensation on the serious doubt whether being an officer of the Government, and under pay, he is entitled thereto.[6]

The ideas of the Louisiana planter were embodied in

[6] In a decision of April 13, 1863, the Attorney-General of the Confederate States held that McDaniel, though holding a commission in the navy, was entitled to be paid 50 per cent of the value of the *Cairo,* including her armament, and that a board of naval officers should be ordered to make the valuation.—Opinions of the Attorney-General, 1861-1865, C.S.A. (MSS. Div., New York Public Library.)

two bills introduced in the Senate at the next session[7] of Congress, in the winter of 1863-1864. One, sponsored by Edward Sparrow, of Louisiana, member of the Committee on Military Affairs, proposed to organize bodies for the capture and destruction of the enemy's property, by land or sea, and to authorize compensation for the same; and was approved by the President, on February 17. This bill went through Congress, sitting in secret session, and, as the injunction to secrecy was never removed, it was not printed among the public laws.

The other bill was introduced by Louis T. Wigfall, the junior senator from Texas, another member of the Committee on Military Affairs. It provided "for the organization of a bureau of polytechnics for the examination, experiment, and application of warlike inventions," and authorized the formation of a polytechnic corps with the grade of captain as the highest rank and with troops organized on the basis of the engineer corps. Companies and parties now irregularly organized for the application of submerged or other defenses, commonly called the torpedo corps, might be transferred to this corps. For the encouragement of the inventive talent of the personnel of the new corps, the Government would pay the usual 50 per cent bonus for destructions less whatever costs had been defrayed from the public treasury.

The bill passed the Senate and was sent to the House for concurrence, two days before the end of the session; and, of course, died there on the calendar. It was reintroduced, the following June, in the First Session of the Second Congress, by the senior Senator from Texas,

[7] Fourth Session of the First Congress.

William S. Oldham, but was voted down. During the Second Session, on December 1, 1864, Representative John B. Clark, of Missouri, introduced a somewhat similar bill "to provide for the establishment of a bureau of special and secret service." This measure got the approval of both Houses and on March 9, 1865, was sent to the President, who, however, failed to return it. The Congress adjourned *sine die* on March 18—and never was *sine die* so true an expression, for the conquest of the Confederate States was completed before the season for a third session.

In the meantime Sage had been successful in getting enacted into law the volunteer navy idea. Upon the provisions of this legislation he had collaborated with the Secretary of the Navy, Mr. Mallory, the latter yielding to him on many but not all points. The result, not wholly acceptable to the apostle of the volunteer navy but at least a start in the right direction, was a bill, "to establish a volunteer navy," introduced in the Third Session of the First Congress by Senator Albert G. Brown, of Mississippi, a member of the Committee on Naval Affairs. While the bill was pending, Sage published in the daily papers a series of supporting articles.[8] In due course and without amendment the bill went through both Houses, receiving the approval of the President, on April 18, 1863.

The act provided for the reception into the volunteer navy of any private-armed vessel, not under one hundred tons burden, which, in the judgment of the President, "shall be fit for the service." The owner of the

[8] In addition to the Richmond papers, see also the *Charleston Daily Courier.* March 13, 1863.

vessel was required to "furnish in writing to the Secretary of the Navy, the name, armament and character" thereof, and to file with him "the names of the persons to be commissioned or warranted as officers, with the evidence of their character and fitness for the service," and a descriptive list of the crew, "together with a duplicate of their shipping articles or enlistment rolls, and of the contract between owners, officers, and crew, for the division of the prize-money."

The proposed officers, if they were deemed "worthy to command," were to be commissioned by the President for the duration of the war, "unless sooner discharged." The highest line rank provided was commander; and in the staff corps, assistant surgeon, first assistant engineer, and, by amendments of February 11 and 17, 1864, assistant paymaster. The pay scale descended from commander at $25 a month to the warrant officers at $10 and the seamen at $5. Pay was only to be drawn for service actually performed at sea.

In the matter of prizes and prize goods and bounties for the destruction of public ships of the enemy, the provisions were substantially as in privateering, except that a deduction of 10 per cent in place of 5 per cent was made for the "fund for the maintenance of such persons as may be wounded, and of the widows and orphans of those slain while engaged in such service."

The uniform of the several grades of officers was prescribed in instructions promulgated on June 19, as "that of the corresponding grades in the regular Navy, with the addition of the letters V.N., plain gilt, three-quarters of an inch long on the front of the cap." The instructions also enjoined compliance with the navy regulations.

It was not long before Sage began to work for amendments. He wanted the bounty for the destruction of public ships of the enemy increased from 25 per cent to 50 per cent, and at least 10 per cent of the value of destroyed merchantmen to be allowed to the volunteers. He thought that the owners should be reimbursed to the value of the volunteer ship in case of her loss in an engagement with a man-of-war. He wanted the operations of the volunteer navy, which were confined "within the ebb and flow of the tide," to be extended to the internal waters. He urged that captured goods be admitted duty free. He thought that the Administration was inclined to stress ships at the expense of personnel. He held that the problem was to find the right men, commission them, and let them exercise their judgment and resource in getting a proper ship and armament, either at home or abroad. He preferred to go abroad; for, said he, vessels that might be equipped within the Confederacy constituted a subtraction from its slender maritime resources, whereas those acquired abroad made a valuable addition. The logic of the last point was inescapable, and it, at length, was adopted into the law.

A few weeks after the passage of the act, Sage made a written offer to the Navy Department to go abroad and purchase a suitable vessel, to load her with a valuable cargo and to run the blockade into a Confederate port, there to fit out and receive a commission. Without awaiting a proper time for reply, he addressed to the Department a second proposal, soliciting a commission as a commander and stating that he would build at Mobile a barque-rigged, propeller-lifting steamer, to be armed with four broadside guns and two pivots and to carry a crew of ninety. The promoter's nerves must have been quite jumpy by now, for he was shortly off on another tack which seemed to promise more hope of a volunteer command, namely, interesting a group of Richmond capitalists in the formation of a volunteer navy company.

The product of this turn was the incorporation by the State Legislature of the Virginia Volunteer Navy Company. Late in June advertisements appeared in the Richmond *Enquirer* giving notice of the opening of books for subscription to the capital stock of this company, at the banking house of R. H. Maury and Company. Editorial assistance in extravagant phrases, was lent to the project;[9] and, on August 5, sufficient subscriptions had been received to permit the organization of the company. That afternoon at six o'clock a meeting of the subscribers was held in the offices of the Virginia Life Insurance Company on Main Street; and a directory, consisting of Samuel J. Harrison, President, J. L. Apperson, Secretary and Treasurer, S. W. McCance, Dr. Robert J. Archer and John McDaniel was elected.[10]

Sage took the stump over the State in behalf of subscriptions, on the understanding that he was to go abroad as purchasing agent for the company and have command of the first vessel—his only qualifications for such post it would appear were his personal eagerness and several long sea voyages in his youth. Sailing ships

[9] *The Daily Richmond Enquirer*, June 24 and 27 and August 18, 1863.
[10] *Ibid.*, August 5 and 6, 1863. The organization of the company at this time must have been preliminary, for the charter of incorporation was not actually issued until October 13.

were his preference. The purchase of a steamer, of such character as the *Florida* or the *Alabama,* seemed to him like putting all the eggs in one basket. He strongly advocated a fleet of small sailing vessels, operating singly. As technical adviser to the company he sat securely until one Captain Decie appeared on the scene.

Concerning this picturesque character there is much uncertainty. He has been a source of perplexity—particularly, to writers on the yacht *America,*[11] that famous racing schooner of the eighteen-fifties, in which he came to the Confederate States in the spring of 1861, after winning the annual regatta at Plymouth in the preceding August. Decie had fitted out for a prolonged cruise in the West Indies. In the latter part of April the yacht arrived at Savannah, Georgia,[12] and lay for a long time in the river, with her owner—who received much social attention in the city—living on board under the colors of his English yacht club. The foreign correspondent of the London *Times,* in commenting on this famous racer moored in the Savannah River was moved to add: "These are the times for bold ventures, and if Uncle Sam is not very quick with his blockades there will be plenty of privateers and the like under the C.S.A.

[11] The *America* was built in New York to represent the United States in the races to be held at England's International Exposition of 1851, in the roads near Cowes Castle; and won the cup. Her owners promptly sold her to an Irish peer at a handsome profit. After ten years of vicissitudes in alien hands, the yacht, now known as the *Camilla,* became a dispatch boat in the Confederate navy, and was captured by the U.S.S. *Ottawa* in the spring of 1862 in the St. Johns River, Florida. The United States navy armed the yacht as a light cruiser and renamed her *America.* After the war the Government sold her, and she was again devoted to pleasure and racing until 1921 when the septuagenarian schooner was presented to the United States Naval Academy at Annapolis.

[12] *The Charleston Daily Courier,* April 27, 1861.

colors."[13] However, such was not then the ambition of Lord Decie, as he was known, although the *Peerage* did not carry this title. Except for the fact that Decie's flag flew over the yacht in her successful entry in the Queenstown Regatta in the summer of 1861, he disappears from the record until he turns up in Richmond in July, 1863, claiming for himself the rank of post-captain in the Royal Navy and the sentiments of a zealous Confederate.

Decie, personable, suave, almost altogether plausible, soon insinuated himself, as a naval officer of ten years' experience, into the esteem and confidence of the officers and directors of the Virginia Volunteer Navy Company. And in the middle of August an advertisement began to run in the Richmond papers that the company, "having secured services of a commander of ten years' naval experience," had determined to begin operations at once and therefore called for the prompt payment of subscriptions. The yachtsman-adventurer scoffed at Sage's ideas on sailing ships and would have nothing to do with anything but steamers—even to the point of being insulting to the original promoter. Decie's notions of money seem to have been vague, for he said that he could get in England a steamer of 350 tons, armed and equipped, for $25,000; and that he could raise $6,000,-000 in six months after he got started, but whether he intended to do so in the Confederate States or abroad does not appear.

Sage, who felt himself being frozen out, was suspicious of his rival, for he could not understand how an

---

[13] Quoted from the London *Times,* in *The Yacht* "America," by Thompson, Stephens, and Swan (Boston: Charles E. Lauriat Co., 1925).

officer might rise in ten years to the rank of post-captain in the British navy; and communicated his suspicions to the company. Upon being questioned Decie recanted slightly and said that he was an "acting post-captain." But had the Virginians thought to have looked up his name in the annual British navy lists, they would not have found Henry E. Decie under any rank whatsoever, between 1845 and 1860. But more than likely these publications were not available in Richmond.

Worked out of what he considered his rightful sphere of influence with the Virginia Company, Sage did not become sour, but continued his crusade for private-armed sea power. He wrote and printed a memorializing pamphlet addressed "To the Governor and the Legislature of the State of ———," invoking state and municipal aid in the formation of volunteer navy companies. Every important community, he urged, should be represented on the high seas by at least an armed schooner of a hundred tons or upwards. He declared that this was the way to win the war, and quoted New York papers to show how it was considered in the North that " 'the Confederate navy has become the terror of our entire mercantile marine,' " having captured " 'about 150 of our vessels, valued with the cargoes at about $10,000,-000.' "

The quotation continued:

They, the Confederate cruisers even capture and burn our vessels within sight of our commercial marts and still escape. . . . Our merchants are compelled to let their ships lie idle or resort to the disgraceful practice of putting them under the flag of a foreign power. . . . Since the breaking out of the rebellion, 585 vessels, of 166,000 tons, have been transferred to foreigners at this port alone, and most of them are now sailing under the flag of Great Britain, our great commercial rival. . . . As the same practice has prevailed at other ports, it is fair to estimate the loss of American tonnage in two years, at 300,000 tons. . . . This loss to us involves a consequent increase of the tonnage and power of our rivals.[14]

It does not seem probable that Sage did much active lobbying at state capitols. In the middle of October he was ordered to appear before a naval board at the Drewry's Bluff station, on the James River, a few miles below Richmond, for examination for appointment as a commander in the volunteer navy. Whether he received such commission is not certain; but, at any rate, he was appointed, as of October 16, a master-not-in-line-of-promotion in the regular navy, and was assigned to special duty. Armed with both State and War Department passes, he proceeded to the Trans-Mississippi Department to try to put into effect his notions of harassing the enemy with small "bands of destructionists." He was well received at General Headquarters; but, after a few months, he became discouraged by what he considered a lack of understanding and coöperation on the part of the subordinate commanders, and decided to abandon this species of desultory activity.

With the coming of spring the old lure of sea-roving again descended upon him. During the winter, in his absence from the capital, the Congress had passed his cherished amendment[15] to permit ships to be received into the volunteer navy beyond the limit of the Con-

---

[14] *New York Herald,* July 3, 1863.
[15] First Cong., Sess. IV., Chap. XXX, approved February 11, 1864.

federate States. He decided now to go abroad and get a ship of war, and began to round up his liquid resources—cotton from his Louisiana plantation. However, the selling price of cotton on the local markets was very low, and the rate of foreign exchange decidedly unfavorable to Confederate money, with, on the other hand, the fleecy staple most attractively quoted on the foreign *bourses*. He, therefore, sought to ship his cotton to Europe for sale, but was so hampered by the difficult export regulations and the blockade that he only got through an amount which netted him a scant $10,-000, whereas he needed some $60,000 or $70,000 to put through his plans. Nevertheless, he proceeded to England, *via* Havana and Paris, hoping to raise the additional capital by some other scheme. All plans ultimately failed him.

Meanwhile the Virginia Volunteer Navy Company was coming much nearer to success. In the winter of 1864, the company advertised the opening of subscription books at Richmond, Lynchburg, Petersburg, Augusta, Atlanta, Savannah, and Mobile to raise capital for the purchase of "a second steamer."[16] However, there is no other indication that a first steamer was in commission. Captain Decie does not seem to have produced results. Following the amendment permitting the outfitting of volunteer war vessels abroad, the company determined to send a purchasing agent to England to buy and send to sea a suitable steamer, and selected a Confederate naval officer for the mission. This officer, Lieutenant-for-the-War Edward C. Stiles obtained a leave-of-absence from the Navy Department, and ac-

[16] *Mobile Daily Advertiser and Register,* February 28, 1864.

cepted a commission as a commander in the volunteer navy.[17]

Arriving in Great Britain Stiles found no difficulty in securing a vessel, which, according to his report, was "one of the finest steamers of her class to be found in England, perfectly strengthened and thoroughly fitted in every respect, for immediate advance against the enemy."[18] This was the *Hawk*, barque-rigged, about 950 tons burden, 254 feet long, 28-foot beam, built of iron, with engines developing 800 horse-power. She had been completed in December, 1863, at Renfrew, on the Clyde.

While on the stocks she is said to have been examined by Commander Bulloch, C.S.N.; but she was purchased by John Sterling Begbie, agent of the Albion Trading Company (which was engaged in the blockade-running business). After the transfer of ownership, the deck was overlaid with another course of three-and-a-half-inch plank. A seven-inch deck was entirely unnecessary for any mercantile purpose, but was well adapted to withstand the recoil of guns. Interior rearrangements for increased coal bunkerage and for additional living quarters added to the suspicions of the United States spies —who infested well-nigh every shipyard in the United Kingdom. The *Hawk* sailed from the Clyde in April, 1864, for the Thames. The spies lost sight of her for several weeks, but at length they located her at Victoria Docks near London, finding to their chagrin that she was anchored off shore. The only boatman in attendance

[17] *Naval War Records, Office Memorandum, No. 8, Officers in the Confederate States Navy* (Washington: Government Printing Office, 1908), p. 132.

[18] *NWR*, II, 2, p. 671.

at the docks had been well trained and refused to take a passenger to the steamer without first rowing over to her, giving the name of the would-be visitor and the nature of his business, and, if these proved acceptable to the ship's executive, obtaining that officer's permission to bring the visitor to the ship's ladder.[19]

Commander Stiles bought her from Mr. Begbie on terms. In order to get her promptly to sea he borrowed the amount of the balance due on her, some £15,000 sterling, upon the stipulation that if sufficient funds were not presently forthcoming from Richmond, he would cause the *Hawk* to be returned to England with cotton and sold, and upon further condition that Commander Stiles himself and the ship's finance officer, Assistant Paymaster D. D. Talley, should not leave England until the debt had been settled. On June 13, Stiles transmitted to the Navy Department the descriptive data required for the enrollment of the *Hawk* in the Confederate States volunteer navy; and on the same day the *Hawk* moved down the river, and, passing Gravesend the next day, cleared for Bermuda.[20]

In the meantime some bar iron with a number of deal cases had gone on board of her. The enemy's agents were piqued because they could not find out what was in the cases. Mr. Adams, the American Minister, lodged complaint against her with the British Foreign Office; but the investigations of the commissioners of custom led Earl Russel to reply to the minister that the "officers had no difficulty in going over every part of the ship, and that in so doing they saw nothing whatever to arouse

[19] *Dip. Corres.* (U.S.), 1864, part 2, pp. 184-187 and 201-202.
[20] *NWR*, I, 27, pp. 294-295; II, 3, pp. 918, 919, 1220, and 1221.

any suspicion of the vessel; that she appeared to be a very fast merchant ship, and that the general opinion seems to have been that she was not fitted for war purposes, her iron plates being so thin and light."

Although many circumstances indicated to those at the American legation that the *Hawk* was intended to be a belligerent vessel under the Confederate flag, the discretion and care with which Stiles observed every letter of English law made it impossible to get any evidence against her. The volunteer man-of-war, unarmed, proceeded unhindered to sea, flying the English colors but apparently under the control of the remainder of her volunteer naval officers, with the executive, a Lieutenant Knox, in command. The crew was shipped only for the voyage to the Bermudas. From St. George it was intended that she should run the blockade into Wilmington to take on her armament. Unfortunately for the *Hawk*, yellow fever was raging in the islands, and Lieutenant Knox was taken ill shortly after her arrival.

The United States Consul at St. George was much impressed by the smartness of her deck and the naval uniform and discipline of her people; but, as with his compatriots in London, he could get no evidence against her to warrant the charge of a violation of Her Majesty's Foreign Enlistment Act.[21]

The Virginia Volunteer Navy Company seems to have muddled its affairs. No funds arrived in London; and early in the fall, Stiles turned in despair for help to Mason and Slidell, the Confederate Commissioners in Paris, and to Commander James D. Bulloch, the agent for the Confederate States Navy Department at

[21] *NWR,* I, 3, pp. 161-163.

A STOCK CERTIFICATE OF THE VIRGINIA VOLUNTEER
NAVY COMPANY

From an original in the possession of the United
States Naval Library and Records.

Liverpool. The Commissioners recommended to the navy agent that advances be made from the public funds to free the *Hawk* of encumbrances, but Commander Bullock declined to divert any of his moneys from their authorized purposes. At the same time, Stiles heard a rumor that Commander Robert B. Pegram, of the regular navy, was on his way out to take command of the volunteer cruiser. It seems that at last Secretary Mallory had modified his early idea that the Government should have nothing to do with a volunteer man-of-war until she was actually placed in touch with the Navy Department. Three months later, Pegram arrived in England and directed Stiles to sell the *Hawk,* which, it seems, had lately returned from Bermuda. The steamer was then put up at auction and sold to the highest bidder, about the middle of January, 1865. Stiles settled his accounts, and with his officers started homeward, *via* Havana. However, they were captured when trying to land on the Louisiana coast in May. Pegram, when he arrived in England, had intended to buy another steamer, but soon gave up the idea and followed Stiles back to America.[22]

Despite the ill fortune which characterized its affairs, the Virginia Volunteer Navy Company seems to have enjoyed a place in public estimation up to the very end, for within the fortnight preceding the evacuation of Richmond, on April 2, 1865, its stock was still being bought by investors.[23] Though the investing public all over the country did not rush into community volunteer navy companies as Sage had so earnestly exhorted them

[22] *NWR*, I, 3, p. 456; 27, pp. 194-195.
[23] See illustration (Stock Certificate).

to do, at least two such associations appear to have been formed for indulging in modified privateering.[24]

It seems that some men of Mobile armed and equipped the prize steamer *Boston*,[25] during the summer following her capture by the venturesome James Duke. According to one of Sage's letters, this little volunteer cruiser put to sea, but having no sail power and being able to carry only ten days' coal supply was forced into Havana, where she was laid up. However, the reports of the blockading squadron off Mobile indicate that in January, 1864, the *Boston,* though private-armed, was still confined to the harbor with little prospect of getting away, it being said that her crew had been conscripted by the Confederate army authorities.[26] Furthermore, the port news column, "Puerto de la Habana," in *El Siglo,* a leading daily newspaper of the Cuban capital, does not show the arrival or departure of a Confederate steamer called *Boston* during the year of 1864. This fact, however, in view of the frequency with which the names of Confederate vessels were changed, is not sufficient ground for denying the accuracy of Sage's letter.

In a letter which Sage wrote from London, on September 11, 1864, to Commander Matthew F. Maury, the eminent Confederate naval officer and scientist, who was on special research duty at the time in England, he tells of a Tennessee volunteer navy company, which sent abroad a purchasing agent and a naval officer to fit out

[24] Urging the millionaires to form volunteer navy companies, *The Charleston Daily Courier,* March 29, 1864, said South Carolina was behind other states in this patriotic matter.

[25] *NWR*, I, 20, pp. 476, 477, and 481.

[26] *Ibid.,* 21, pp. 36, 64, 65, and 106.

a sailing cruiser. The naval officer, however, got the steamer bee in his bonnet; and they put their funds in a freighter with which to run the blockade and bring out enough cotton to provide the larger amount necessary for a war steamer, with the result that the enterprise came to naught. This story was taken as the text for a discourse on the relative value of sailing and steam vessels for private-armed cruisers, under the existing conditions.

The reply of Maury, dated "Bowdon, 28th Sept. 1864," was corroborative of Sage's own views:

The efficiency of a steamer depends upon the number of coaling stations. If she have few or none of these, she is very apt to cost more than she comes to. . . . [With] people circumstanced as we are, I can not understand how there should have been any difference of opinion upon the subject. With more enemies than the flying fish, and not a single coaling station or friendly port in the wide world, an armed vessel relying upon steam in a cruise against commerce is crippled the moment she gets out upon the blue water, for she immediately begins to fall short of coal and is at her wit's end. These propositions are very clear. 1. A snug schooner or a good, fast and handy brig with one, or two guns at most, is just as good to capture merchantmen as is a line of battleship. 2. That the money which it takes to fit out, man and maintain one steamer at sea, will be enough to put and keep afloat several sailing vessels. 3. And that sailing vessels as against the steamer more than make up for their occasional lack of qualities which steam alone can give, by their numbers, by their ubiquity, by their power to keep the sea, and by the number of baskets which they furnish owners to put their eggs in.

THE CONFEDERATE PRIVATEERS

Though Maury's statement that the Confederate cruisers had not "a friendly port in the wide world" in which to coal was certainly an exaggeration—witness the long cruises of such national raiders as the *Sumter, Florida, Alabama,* and *Shenandoah,* which, sometimes with difficulty, got all the coal they needed—it, nevertheless, is a significant fact that the preponderance of the successful Confederate privateers were sailing vessels and that the volunteer cruisers, which were all steamers, failed of accomplishment.

XXVI

CONCLUSION

*I*N April, 1861, the day of privateers had passed. But this was not then apparent. The Confederates struggled manfully to place their private-armed operations on a parity with the magnificent proportions to which privateering had attained in former wars. They achieved individual successes, but the institution of privateering was obsolete and no amount of industry and valor could save it. It belonged to a vanished order of things, like the very political and social structure which the Confederate States themselves typified.

The War of Secession was a revolution, mainly on the side of the Union. The South stood for the Constitution as understood on March 4, 1789; for the conservation of the social order which existed at the birth of the States; for the preservation of the immemorial rights of the individual—which, of course, included the right to arm one's ship privately and to sail against and despoil the national enemy. The overthrow of these principles and the establishment of a new conception of Federal Government by the Republican Administration of 1861-1865 were the beginnings of a revolution, which, through a long course of interpretations and amendments to the Constitution, has transformed the United States Government from a simple republican federation into a complex bureaucratic paternalism. The swing of Time's pendulum was in the direction of radicalism, and the success of the North in the war was inevitable. Anomalously, the revolutionists fought under the guise of established government and the conservatives under the stigma of insurgency.

Another anomaly is presented in the fact that Confederate privateering—which was essentially a clinging to the traditions of the past—introduced into actual combat the first ironclad, the *Manassas,* and the first submarine, the *Hunley*. And Confederate private enterprise also brought into existence the first of the *David* class of steam torpedo-boats.

The formation of volunteer navy companies was the earliest effort to harmonize privateering with the march of civilization. Following the precedent of the Confederate States, Prussia in 1871 attempted to establish a Volunteer Navy and Russia in 1878 essayed the experiment of a Patriotic Fleet. But in each of these three steps in the modification of privateering, private control of combat sea power was progressively diminished. It disappeared altogether in the Spanish-American War, when required naval expansions were secured by taking private ships—by purchase or charter—directly into the naval establishments, and giving to them an entirely public character.

APPENDIX

PROCEDURE IN THE CONFEDERATE PRIZE COURTS

*T*HE following standing interrogatories and rules in cases of prize and capture were copied from the "Minutes of Court of Admiralty, C.S." (found by the author, April, 1926, in the attic of the Post-Office in Savannah), pages 1 to 6, inclusive:

Confederate States of America in Admiralty
In the District Court of the Confederate States of America
District of Georgia

Standing Interrogatories to be administered in behalf of the Confederate States of America, to commanders, masters, mariners, and other persons found on board any Ships or Vessels, which have been, or shall be seized or taken as prize, by any vessels of War of the Confederate States of America, or private ships or vessels which shall have Commissions or Letters of marque and reprisal, concerning such captured ships vessels or any goods, wares, and merchandize on board the same, examined as witnesses in preparatorio

Let each Witness be interrogated to every of the following questions and the answer to each be written down

1st. Where were you born, where have you usually lived, and where do you now live? And how long have you lived in that place? To what prince or state are you subject or citizen and how long have you been so?

2nd. Were you present at the time of taking and seizing the vessel or her lading concerning which you are now examined?

3rd. In what place, latitude, or port, and in what year, month, and day, were the vessel and her lading concerning

345

which you are now examined taken and seized? Upon what pretence and for what reasons were they seized and under what colors did said vessel sail? What other colors had you on board and for what reason had you such other colors? Was resistance made to the seizure and what? By what vessel were you taken, and into what port was the taken vessel carried?

4th. What is the name of the Master or Commander of the vessel taken? How long have you known him and who appointed him to the command? When and where was possession of the vessel delivered to him and by whom? Where does such Master or Commander live? Where was he born and of what Kingdom or State is he now subject or citizen?

5th. Of what tonnage is the vessel which has been taken? What was the number of mariners on board and of what country were they? When and where were they shipped and by whom?

6th. Had you, or any of the Officers or mariners belonging to the captured vessel, any, and what part, share, or interest in said vessel or her lading? Did you belong to her when she was seized? If yea In what capacity? Where was she built, how long have you known her and where and when did you first see her?

7th. What is the name of the vessel? How long has she been so called? Is she or has she been called by any other name? If so by what other name or names and when? To what ports and places did she sail during her said voyage before she was taken? Where did her last voyage begin and where was it to have been ended? What cargo had she on board at the time of her seizure? At what port was the cargo to have been delivered? At what time and from what clearing port did she sail previously to her capture? Where and at what time was the lading put aboard, which she carried at the time of her seizure? Specify the different species of the lading, and the quantities of each sort?

8th. Who were the owners of the seized vessel at the time of her seizure? How do you know they were owners? Of what nation or country are they natives? Of what country are they citizens or subjects and where do they reside?

9th. Who claimed to be the owners of the lading of the vessel? Where do they reside? Of what country or State are they subjects or citizens? Was the lading put on board at one port, and at one time or at divers ports and several times? Set forth what quantities of each sort of goods were shipped at each port?

10th. Was any charter party signed for the voyage on which the vessel was seized? If yea between whom was it made what became of it, and what were its contents?

11th. What papers, bills of lading, letters, or other writings were on board the vessel when she took her departure from the last clearing port, before her being taken as a prize and also at the time of her being so taken? Were any of them burned, torn, thrown over board, destroyed, or concealed, and when and by whom and who was then present? If any such papers are in existence produce them to the Commissioner or Commissioners if in your custody, power or control?

12th. Were there any passengers on board the said vessel? If yea who were they, when were they taken on board; to what place or places were they destined, and what was their business? Had any and which of the passengers any and what property or concern or authority directly or indirectly in or over the vessel or Lading or any part thereof at the time of capture?

13th. To what place was the vessel so seized steering when

she was pursued and taken? Was her course altered? If yea toward what other port or place and for what reason?

14th. Did the vessel seized have any guns mounted? Had she any arms or ammunition on board? If yea why? Were the arms thrown over board or destroyed? If so why? When and where were said guns, arms, and ammunition if any, put on board?

15th. What is the whole which you know or believe, according to the best of your knowledge and belief, regarding the real and true property and destination of the vessel and lading concerning which you are now examined at the time of the capture?

Form of the oath to be administered to each witness:

You shall true answers make to all such questions as shall be propounded to you on the Interrogatories and therein you shall speak the truth the whole truth and nothing but the truth So help you God!

| In the Court of the
Confederate States of America
District of Georgia | In Chambers
August 22nd AD 1861 |

It is ordered that the foregoing Fifteen Interrogatories be the standing Interrogatories in preparatory in cases of prize; and that Thomas S Wayne and Charles Grant Esquires be appointed Commissioners to take the examination of witnesses in prize cases *in preparatorio* on the standing Interrogatories now adopted by this Court and all other depositions which they are or may be empowered to require; and to discharge all other duties in relation to ships and vessels or property brought into this District as Prize and of which notice shall be given to or received by said Commissioners under and by virtue of the Rules and Orders of this Court. It is further Ordered that the Clerk issue Commissions under the authority and Seal of this Court to said Commissioners on their taking the Oath to support the Constitution of the Confederate States and to discharge the duties of their Office to the best of their skill and ability

[Signed]   EDWARD J HARDEN

In the Court of the Confederate States of America ⎫
District of Georgia   ⎬
                                                 ⎭

Rules in cases of Prize and Capture

1st. The mode of proceeding for condemnation and forfeiture shall be by Libel and Claim.

2nd. Captors shall without delay give to one of the Commissioners who have been or may be appointed, notice of the arrival of the property captured and the place where it may be found and inspected by the Commissioners.

3rd. The Commissioner upon receiving such notice shall forthwith proceed to the designated place and shall adopt all measures necessary for the safety of the property. He will examine if bulk has been broken and if so upon what occasion and cause. He will examine all chests, boxes, packages, and casks containing the property captured, ascertain if the same has been opened and whether any part has been removed. He will thereupon file with the Register his report of the property reported as captured, its present condition, the means taken for its preservation and such other matters relating to it as may be proper for the information of the Court.

4th. The Commissioner shall also secure the hatches, chests, boxes, packages or casks with seals, which shall not be opened without the Order of the Court, unless in case of absolute necessity.

5th. If the Captors shall not give information as required; upon other information one of the Commissioners shall proceed to the place where the captured property may be, and proceed in the same manner as if notice had been given by the Captors.

6th. Captors shall file or deposit with the Commissioner to whom notice of a capture has been given, all papers, charters bills of Ladings, letters, and all writings and documents found in the vessel or which refer to the captured property and which may have come into their possession And such papers shall be endorsed by the Register and the Captors shall upon oath certify that such were all the papers received or taken that the same have been produced as they were received without fraud addition subduction or enlargement and if any papers are wanting shall account for the same.

7th. The Commissioner to whom notice of a capture has been given or who has been informed of it, shall appoint an early day at which the captors shall produce three or more of the persons captured or who claim the captured property and the captain mate and supercargo if brought in must be produced; and such persons shall be examined *in preparatorio* upon the standing Interrogatories.

8th. The examination *in preparatorio* shall be only upon the standing Interrogatories unless other special Interrogatories are Ordered by the Court.

9th. The Commissioner may examine the witnesses separately and apart from each other. And if the witnesses or either of them shall refuse to answer or if the Captors refuse to give up the documents, papers, and writings relating to the captured property or refuse to produce the witnesses to be examined *in preparatorio* or in any manner delay the said examination unnecessarily the Commissioner shall certify the same to the Court that such proceedings may be thereupon had as justice may require

10th. The deposition of each witness shall be signed by him the oath appointed to the standing Interrogatories having been first administered. To the deposition the Commissioner shall put a certificate in the usual form and he shall subscribe his name to the same

11th. Upon the filing of the Libel by the Captors a monition shall be taken out and a Warrant of Arrest may be taken out also, when it is necessary.

12th. If the property captured be perishable or such as would deteriorate greatly by expense or otherwise in keeping; or by the consent of captors and claimants it may be sold or delivered to the claimant he entering into stipulation with sureties to answer the value if condemned. But no sale will be ordered except by consent unless upon the return of three or more disinterested persons, who being sworn, will certify as to the necessity for sale because of the perishable nature of the property or other reason as aforesaid, and specify particularly the property and the reason or reasons why it should be sold. And such sale if Ordered shall be made by the Marshal and the proceeds paid into the Registry.

13th. A claim may be made by any party interested and if such party be absent, by an Agent or by principal officer of the captured vessel; and must be sustained by the affidavit of such person stating the circumstances which enable the person to make the affidavit required.

14th. No Commissioner shall act as Proctor or Counsel for Captors or Claimant in any prize case

15th. In all cases of prize and capture the Libel must be filed as soon as may be practicable, after the property is brought within the Jurisdiction of the Court

16th. After the depositions in preparatorio are filed and the monition has been ordered, no further or other examination upon the standing Interrogatories shall be taken, or affidavit received without the special directions of the Court.

17th. None but the Captors can in the first instance invoke papers from one captured vessel to another; nor without the order of the Court. The invocation shall only be allowed upon the affidavit of the Captor satisfying the Court that the papers are material and necessary

18th. If the same claimants intervene for different vessels or for goods wares or merchandize captured on board different vessels, and proofs are taken in several causes which are for trial at the same time; the captors may at the hearing in Court, invoke of course in either of such causes the proof taken in any other of them; the claimant also after such invocation having liberty to avail themselves of the proofs in the cause invoked.

19th. At every stated term of the Court a statement shall be presented by the Register of all the moneys paid into Court in prize causes designating the amount in each.

20th. When property seized as prize of war, is delivered upon bail a stipulation shall be taken in double its value.

21st. A party to a prize cause may be compelled to give security for costs, to abide a decision against him; either by a stipulation with sureties or a deposite with the Register in such reasonable sums as the Register or the Court may require

22nd. A decree of contumacy may be had against any party not obeying the orders or process of the Court duly served upon him and thereupon an Attachment may be sued out against him

APPENDIX

Ordered that the foregoing Rules in Cases of Prize and Capture be adopted in the Court August 22 AD 1861.

[Signed]   EDWARD J HARDEN

NOTE: On page 7 of the Minutes there appears the oaths of Commissioners Wayne and Grant; and on pages 8 *et seq.* the minutes of the proceedings against the brig *Elsinore* (captured by the privateer schooner *Sallie*), the brigantine *Santa Clara* (captured by the privateer brig *Jefferson Davis*), and the ship *Sebasticook* (seized by the civil authorities as alien enemy property). There were other prize cases tried in this Court that do not appear in this record book, among which may be cited C.S. *vs.* U.S.S. *Water Witch*. This gunboat had been captured by a Confederate boat expedition, under Lieutenant Thomas P. Pelot, C.S.N., in Ossabaw Sound, near Savannah, Georgia, on June 3, 1864. The libel was filed late in July, and the cause appears to have been heard in August or September, 1864.

INDEX

Abaellino, prize ship, 43-44.

Abrams, A. F. W., 127n.

A. B. Thompson, prize ship, 93.

A. C. Gunnison, privateer steamer, 189, 246.

Adams, Charles Francis, United Minister to Great Britain, 208, 301, 313, 337.

Adams, J. H., South Carolina Peace Commissioner, 6.

Adams, W. R., 245.

Adelaide, U.S. transport, 113.

Admiralty Courts, Confederate States Jurisdiction, 21-22, 93; prize decisions, 40, 42n., 44, 46, 54, 69, 75, 76, 90, 92, 93-100, 121, 123, 142, 183, 190, 192, 195; citations, 97; procedure in, 345-353.

Admiralty Courts, United States, decisions in, 87-88, 128, 254, 289.

Agricola, schooner, 233.

Aiken, U.S. revenue cutter, 125.

A. J. Whitmore, privateer steamer, 201, 243.

Alabama, C.S.S., 3, 254, 272, 331, 342.

Alabama, U.S.S., 293.

Albatross, U.S.S., 69, 83.

Alcatraz, Fort, privateersmen imprisoned at, 276, 284-285.

Alexander, W. A., 170.

Alexandria, prize schooner, 224.

Allen, Captain, 264.

Allen, Ethan, 136n.

Allen, Henry, Master, *William A. Atwater,* 193.

Alliance, prize sloop, 223-224.

Alvarado, prize bark, 72-74, 75, 128.

Amanda, U.S. bark, 242-243.

America, yacht, 331-332.

Amiel, Montague, Prize Master, 85-86.

Anderson, Robert, Major, U.S.A., 5, 6, 11-13.

Anderson, U.S. bark, see *William G. Anderson.*

Andrews, George C., Acting Master, C.S.N., 200-201, 204, 206, 222.

Andrews, Robert, privateersman, 119.

Apalachicola, Fla., outfitting of privateers at, 241-242.

Apperson, J. L., 330.

Archer, Robert J., 330.

Arkansas, C.S.S., 254.

Armed merchantmen, War of Secession, 316-317; World War, 317.

Arrow, C.S.S., 47.

Arthur, Charles G., Acting Master, U.S.N., 211-212.

Atwater, prize schooner, see *William A. Atwater.*

Austin, Charles W., privateer lieutenant, 161.

Austin, Texas sloop-of-war, 63n.

Babcock, W. H., privateer surgeon, 64.

Baker, Napoleon B., privateer captain, 42.

Baker, T. Harrison, privateer captain, 49-52, 53, 56, 57, 129, 137, 143, 147.

Bald Eagle, clipper ship, 265.

Baltimore, Maryland, prizes hailing from, 91, 102-103, 181-184, 241, 247, 300; mob scene at, 305.

Bamberg, C.S. transport, 197.

Bamberg, F. M., 61n.

Bancroft, James, Jr., 51n.

Bangor, Maine, prizes hailing from, 106.

Barbiere, Joseph, 245.

Bard, James J., privateer captain, 245.

Barnstable, Mass., prizes hailing from, 103.

Barnum's Museum, Negro (Tillman) who recaptured prize schooner *S. J. Waring* displays his souvenirs at, 87.

INDEX

INDEX

INDEX

Francisco, 289; trial in Nova Scotia, 295; trial at Bermuda, 299.

Poor, C. H., Commander, U.S.N., 39, 195-197.

Pope, John, Captain, U.S.N., 161-162.

Porter, Andrew, Colonel, U.S.A., 134.

Porter, David, D., Rear Admiral, U.S.N., 164, 216, 217.

Porter, Seward, 37n.

Portland, Maine, prizes hailing from, 90, 118.

Portsmouth, U.S.S., 203.

Post Boy, C.S. army steamer, 108.

Postell, W. Ross, privateer lieutenant, 63-64, 68.

Potomac Zouaves, Regiment in Va. State Troops, 182, 185.

Potter, Major, U.S.A., hostage, 150.

Powell, Wm., 141.

Power, Thomas B., 246.

Preble, U.S. sloop-of-war, 154, 159-162.

Preston, William, Confederate Minister to Mexico, 262.

Price, Cicero, Commander, U.S.N., 47n.

Prig, Toby, privateersman, 119.

Prince Alfred, British schooner, 118.

Pringle, Robt. A., 61n.

Priscilla C. Ferguson, schooner, 127.

Priscilla, schooner, 103.

Privateering, importance of in the past, 2-3; effect of economic developments on, 3; obsolence of, 321n.

Privateering, Confederate, effect of British neutrality proclamation on, 26-29; panic caused by, in commercial classes of Union, 25-27, 29; regulations for government of, 30; early estimate of, 30-31; a burlesque episode, 31; contrasted with American during Revolution and War of 1812, 18-19, 20, 23, 31-32; Confederate commerce in relation to, 33-34, 249; difficulty in securing ships

and munitions, 236; substitutes for, 199-200, 222; on land, 213-220.

Privateering, United States, unlicensed ventures, 303-308; commissions to private-arm issued by War Department, 308-310; regular letters of marque, 311-316; letters permissive, 313; armed merchantmen, 316-317; compared with Confederate, 315-316; regulations for, 315-316.

Privateers, Republic of Texas, xii.

Privateersmen, Confederate, dress of, 64-66, 82; treated as pirates, 50, 56, 57, 84, 86, 90, 105, 126, 128, 205, 207, 226-227; trials at New York, 135-147, 228; trials at Philadelphia, 146-151; trial in England, 208-209; trial in Nova Scotia, 295; trial at Bermuda, 299; treated as traitors, 285-286; trial at San Francisco, 286-289; retaliation for mistreatment of, 133-135, 148-150, 227, 228, 252, 288.

Private Warfare, organization of, 323-327, 334.

Protector, prize schooner, 107.

Providence, R. I., prizes hailing from, 45.

Provincetown, Mass., prizes hailing from, 39.

Prussia, volunteer navy of, 344.

Purviance, Hugh Y., Captain, U.S.N., 126.

Putnam, American brig, 59-61.

Quaker City, U.S. private-armed steamer, 303-308.

Queen of the West, steamboat, 187.

Quigley, Thomas, privateersman, 147.

Raids, Cavalry, on river steamboats, 213-220.

Raleigh, N.C.S., 102.

Raleigh, C.S.S., 310.

Ramirez, Don Mateo, agent for letters of marque on west coast of Mexico, 261-262.